Becoming A
MacArtist

Vahé Guzelimian

Part of ABC Consumer Magazines, Inc.
One of the ABC Publishing Companies
Greensboro, North Carolina

Copyright 1985, COMPUTE! Publications, Inc. All rights reserved

Reproduction or translation of any part of this work beyond that permitted by Sections 107 and 108 of the United States Copyright Act without the permission of the copyright owner is unlawful.

Printed in the United States of America

10 9 8

ISBN 0-942386-80-9

The author and publisher have made every effort in the preparation of this book to insure the accuracy of the programs and information. However, the information and programs in this book are sold without warranty, either express or implied. Neither the author nor COMPUTE! Publications, Inc. will be liable for any damages caused or alleged to be caused directly, indirectly, incidentally, or consequentially by the programs or information in this book.

The opinions expressed in this book are solely those of the author and are not necessarily those of COMPUTE! Publications, Inc.

COMPUTE! Publications, Inc., Post Office Box 5406, Greensboro, NC 27403, (919) 275-9809 is part of ABC Consumer Magazines, Inc., one of the ABC Publishing Companies, and is not associated with any manufacturer of personal computers.

Animation Toolkit 1 is a registered trademark of Ann Arbor Softworks, Inc. Apple and Apple II are registered trademarks, and Imagewriter, MacDraw, Macintosh, MacPaint, and MacWrite are trademarks of Apple Computer, Inc. ClickArt Personal Graphics, ClickArt Letters, and ClickArt Publications are trademarks of T/Maker Company. CompuServe is a registered trademark of CompuServe Informational Services, Inc. Datacopy 610 is a trademark of Datacopy Corporation. da Vinci is a registered trademark of Hayden Software. Davong's Mac Disk is a trademark of Davong Systems, Inc. Dow Jones News/Retrieval Service is a registered trademark of Dow Jones and Company, Inc. Filevision is a trademark of Telos Software Products. Mac the Knife is a registered trademark of Miles Computing. MacVision is a trademark of Koala Technologies Corporation. MicronEye is a trademark of Micron Technology, Inc. Tecmar's MacDrive is a trademark of Tecmar, Inc. ReadySetGo is a trademark of Manhattan Graphics. Sharp Color Ribbon Cartridges is a trademark of Sharp Color. The Source is a service mark of Source Telecomputing Corporation.

Contents

Foreword v

Acknowledgments vii

Chapter 1. The Apple Ripens: The Computer for Everyone .. 1
The Transparent Computer 3; The Mac in Art 4; **Innovative Hardware Design 4;** A Compact Machine 4; **Under Mac's Kilt 5;** The MC68000 Chip 6; A Graphics-Only Display That Isn't 6; ROM at the Core 7; RAM for Flavor 8; The 3-1/2-Inch Disk Drive 8; **The Rest of the Mac Package 9;** The Mouse 9; The Keyboard 10; **Optional Hardware 14;** Imagewriter Printer 14; External Drives 15; Modems 300 and 1200 15; Numeric Keypad 16; Carrying Case 16; Other Products 16

Chapter 2. Software for Creating Pictures and Text 17
Using Application Programs 19; MacPaint, MacDraw, and MacWrite 20; A Note About Program Versions 20; **MacPaint—The Electronic Easel 21;** Unlimited Tools 21; Creating a Logo Design with MacPaint 22; **MacDraw—The Electronic Drafting Table 28;** A Structured Graphics Editor 28; Size, Proportion, and Rulers 28; Interactions 29; Creating a Scale Drawing with MacDraw 29; **MacWrite—The Electronic Typesetter 40;** Fonts, Styles, and Sizes 40; Creating Advertising Copy with MacWrite 40; **MacPaint or MacDraw? 45;** Complementary Programs 46; The Treatment of Forms 47; Differences in Tools 49; Organizing Objects 51; Windows and Drawing Sizes 52; Dealing with the Whole Drawing 53; Drawing to Scale 55; Changing the Size of Objects 56; Compare and Contrast 57

Chapter 3. Moving Data Between and Within Applications 59
One Limitation 61; The Clipboard 61; The Scrapbook 63; You're Ready to Start 63; Moving Data from MacPaint to MacWrite 65; Moving Data from MacDraw to MacWrite 66; Moving Data from MacDraw to MacPaint 68; Moving Data Between Documents of One Application 70; Moving Large MacPaint Drawings 70

Chapter 4. MacPaint Shortcuts, Tips, and Advanced Techniques 75
MacPaint Shortcuts 77; Getting In and Out of MacPaint 77; The Polygon 78; Clear Selection 79; Undo and Redo 79; Choose Lines and Borders 80; *FatBits* Shortcuts 80; The Shortcuts List 81; Hands for Keys and Mouse 81; **MacPaint Tips and Advanced Techniques 82;** MacPaint Work Space 82; Advanced Uses of *Grid 83;* The *Trace Edges* Feature 87; Customizing Eraser Shapes 90; Custom Repeating Shapes 90; Custom Brush Shapes 91; Working from Black 91; Text in Reverse 92; Transparency 93; Fill and Refill 96; Creating Custom Patterns 97; Creating a File of Custom Patterns 100; Clearing a MacPaint Document 103; Creating Bas-Relief 103; Shadowed Text 104; Concentric Circles 105; Shading 106; Custom Lettering 108; Creating Custom Borders and Frames 113; Creating Ornaments 119; Much More 120

Chapter 5. MacDraw Tips and Advanced Techniques 121
Using *Custom Rulers* and *Grid 123*; Draw Complete Elements 126; An Example 128; Layering—Organizing the Order of Shapes 133; *Fill, Lines,* and *Pen 139;* Taping Items Together 142; Taping Items Down 144; Perspective Drawings 145; Using Text 151; The Roll of Film 156; Masking with MacDraw to Erase, Enhance, and Repair 158; An Expert 161

Chapter 6. The Many Uses of Mac Art 163
Graphic Arts 165; Logos 166; Business Cards 167; Letterheads 170; Announcements 172; Post Cards 174; Advertising Layouts 175; Advertising Flyers 177; **Business Graphics 182;** Graphs 182; Charts 184; Maps 188; **Design Work 190;** Product Design 190; Engineering Design 195; Architectural Design 196; Interior Design 201; Landscape Design 203; **Printing and Publishing 205;** Page Layouts 205; Cover Design 207; Book and Manual Illustrations 210; **Project Development 213;** Visual Diary 213; Story Boards 214; Slides 215; Take It from Here 216

Chapter 7. Getting the Most Out of Your Imagewriter Printer 217
The Imagewriter 219; Printer Characteristics 219; Screen Size and Page Size 220; Avoiding Paper Jams 221; **Printing Printouts 221;** Printing from the Desktop 221; Printing from Applications 222; Screen Dumps 222; Window Dumps 223; *Print Catalog 223;* **Printout Quality 224;** Print Modes 224; Horizontal Streaks 225; Ribbons 226; Paper Quality 227; Matching Quality and Function 229; Laser Printers 230; Printing in Color 230; Working Directly from Disks 231; Other Printers 231

Chapter 8. Working from Originals 233
Tracing with the Mouse 235; Using Transparencies 236; The Method 236; Large Pictures 238; Using Camera Images 239; **Using Digitizer Pads 239; Using Cameras 240**

Chapter 9. Organizing Files and Disks 251
What *Is* a File? 253; The Start-up Disk 254; Ejecting Disks 255; **File Manipulation 256;** Transferring Files 256; Copying Disks 260; The "Disk Copy" Utility 261; Renaming Disks, Files, and Folders 261; Write-Protecting Disks 262; Erasing Disks and Files 263; **Disk Space Management 263;** Preparing Working Disks 263; Setting the Start-up Program 264; Removing Fonts 265; Data Disks 267; Managing Documents with One Drive 268; Managing Documents with Two Drives 270; Copying Data Disks 271; Creating Printed Disk Directories 272; Files and Disks 273

Chapter 10. A Mac Gallery 275
Jim Alley 277; Daniel Pinkwater 282; Robert Fichter 285; Paul Rutkovsky 291; Richard Bloch 295; Bill Jonas 299; Your Gallery? 300

Appendix A. Products for the Macintosh 301
Appendix B. Cairo Font 305
Appendix C. Fallingwater Font 307
Index 309

Foreword

In the short time that the Macintosh has been available, the term *revolutionary* seems to have become a standard adjective. With good reason. The Macintosh, unlike many other computers, is a tool that can be used almost immediately by anyone. There's no need to learn a new language, no jargon to mystify or confuse. The Macintosh works much as we do, so becoming comfortable with it is easy.

Perhaps that's why so many people who had never used a computer before bought a Macintosh. Thousands of the machines, in offices, studios, and even homes, have made work more productive, made writing or designing or illustrating simpler and faster.

The Macintosh is especially effective as a graphics device. It's a visual machine—you use pictures and symbols to operate it—and that characteristic extends into the kind of work it's good at. *Becoming a MacArtist* shows you how you can use your computer this way. With MacDraw, MacPaint, and MacWrite, you'll quickly be able to design letterheads and logos, produce camera-ready advertisements and flyers, or enhance business reports and presentations.

Even though the Macintosh is easy to use, and its application programs are easy to learn, you'll still profit greatly from using this book. Step by step, this guide takes you through MacDraw, MacPaint, and MacWrite, showing you their capabilities and pointing out their weaknesses. But *Becoming a MacArtist* doesn't stop with the basics. It goes much further, detailing shortcuts and advanced features that are often undocumented. You'll see how to use the three programs together, to lend even more flexibility to your designs and creations.

Do you want to learn how to use shadowing or how to design custom lettering? Do you want to see how you can draw multipoint perspectives? *Becoming a MacArtist* shows you. With its hundreds of illustrations, all created on the Macintosh with MacDraw, MacPaint, or MacWrite, this book shows you exactly what to do. There are also ideas and demonstrations of what others have done with the Macintosh. After seeing what *can* be done with your computer, you'll be eager to try out your own ideas. Your creativity is vital, and this book understands that.

With chapters that show how to best use your printer, how to duplicate originals and modify them on the screen, and how to organize your files and disks efficiently, *Becoming a MacArtist* contains everything you need to start drawing, writing, sketching, painting, and printing. If you already have a Macintosh, this book will quickly have you working even more productively. And if you're still trying to decide whether to buy the computer, this book will show you what's possible.

Becoming a MacArtist is a unique book. Comprehensive, yet clearly written, it's indispensable to anyone who has a Macintosh. With your computer and what you learn here, you'll tap your creativity in ways you never thought possible.

Acknowledgments

This book is not the product of one person's labors alone. A number of Macintosh users made generous contributions of their time and Macintosh creations. Bill Jonas of Artworks, Inc. was particularly helpful. He has not only mastered MacPaint, he is a magician with it. It was always a pleasure to receive disks full of Robert Fichter's fantastic creations, several of which appear in *MacArtist*. I also want to thank Jim Alley, Richard Bloch, Paul Rutkovsky, Bob Lee, Michael Beaucage, and John Kohlenberger for their contributions.

Bill Atkinson and Mark Cutter were very responsive to my inquiries about their brilliant software for the Mac—MacPaint and MacDraw. They were kind enough to read parts of the manuscript and make useful recommendations.

A book is molded and shaped by good editors. I want to thank Linnea Dayton for her editorial assistance and advice throughout the preparation of the manuscript. Gregg Keizer of COMPUTE! Books was committed to the project and made its execution smooth and efficient.

Finally, I want to thank my wife, Linda, for her love and patient support during a period of intensive and rewarding activity.

V.G.

Dedication

To the memory of my parents.

Chapter 1
The Apple Ripens:
The Computer for Everyone

Chapter 1

The Apple Ripens:
The Computer for Everyone

Why use a computer for producing graphics when pen and ink have been adequate for hundreds of years? After all, it's a simple matter to sketch, erase, and resketch the old-fashioned way. *How can a computer enhance the process I use to produce visual material? Why should I learn how to use a computer just to be able to draw on a screen rather than on paper?* This sort of resistance to using a cold, rational machine to participate in the warm, intuitive medium of art is understandable, but no longer valid. The controversy isn't new. Some artists and critics still maintain that photographs cannot be art because they're produced by a machine—machines just cannot produce art, they believe. But just as art and technology can be combined to produce photographs that *are* art, so art and microcomputers can be wed. The computer is just another tool, like a camera or a T square, that can make some aspects of creating visual art easier, faster, and even more fun.

The design of the Macintosh computer's hardware and software makes it fast and easy for graphics applications. This chapter introduces you to the hardware that makes up the Macintosh system.

As you explore the features of the Macintosh and the powerful applications software available for it, keep in mind that the computer was designed to be almost foolproof. It's hard to damage either the computer or the disks. Learn by trying whatever comes to mind. Feel free to experiment. If you get stuck, take a look at the user's manual that came with your computer. Once you use some of the Macintosh's features a few times, you'll probably be able to put the manual away.

The Transparent Computer

By injecting the concept of easy use into the Macintosh's design and into the applications software that would be created for it, Apple has produced the transparent computer. You don't have to cajole the Macintosh into performing by learning an arcane language of codes and abbreviations. With the Macintosh, Apple has achieved the humanized personal computer—a computer for ordinary users, not computer experts. Using the Mac is as easy as manipulating pens and sheets of paper on your desk.

This flexible and familiar working environment makes the Macintosh easy for you to work quickly and efficiently. As you

Chapter 1

get more experienced with the mouse, menus, windows, and other Mac features, you'll stop thinking of the computer as something to be conquered. The Macintosh will become transparent, its technical apparatus receding into the background, freeing you to concentrate on the work you want to do, whether you're preparing technical illustrations, project plans, layouts, or just doodles.

The Mac in Art

The Macintosh's graphics prowess will bring to homes, schools, and businesses a portable print shop, a portable art room, even a portable darkroom and photography studio. All this without ink-stained fingers, X-Acto knife cuts, smelly chemicals, or expensive cameras. Additional programs developed for the Mac help make it a wonderful tool for graphic artists, technical illustrators, writers, architects, and art directors, to name just a few.

Innovative Hardware Design

Just when dissatisfied owners were pushing their computers closer and closer to the computer closet (from which few machines return), the Macintosh arrived. Its claim may have seemed arrogant, but it smiled all the way to the best-seller lists. And even when it frowned at you for putting the wrong disk in the drive, or when it displayed a bomb with fuse lit, telling you there'd been a system error, the Macintosh was still arresting.

When you unpack your Macintosh, it's already a complete computer system. The built-in monochrome monitor and disk drive are part of the package. All you do is plug the computer in. If you want to add a printer, a modem, or a second disk drive, just plug it into the appropriate port, or socket, at the back of the case.

A Compact Machine

By using the latest technology, the designers at Apple have been able to trim the Macintosh to a small 10 × 10 × 13 inch case. The 3-1/2-inch microfloppy disk drive and the 9-inch screen are two reasons why the Macintosh is so compact. The screen, though smaller than most stand-alone monitors, is quite adequate for the computer's advanced graphics features.

Chapter 1

Figure 1-1. The Macintosh System

Apple Computer's Macintosh is shown here with mouse and detachable keyboard. Peripheral devices and accessories include a numeric keypad, an external disk drive, the Imagewriter printer, a modem, and the Macintosh carrying case.

The Mac's small size and its all-in-one case eliminate the need for a special computer desk. The Mac hardly takes up more desk space than a pad of paper. Since it's detachable, the keyboard can be placed either on your desk or in your lap. Other than the computer itself (assuming you're using no peripherals), the only additional space you need is for the mouse. It needs a smooth surface, about 8 × 10 inches, on your desk for proper movement.

The Macintosh weighs only about 20 pounds. That light weight (lighter than most "portable" computers), along with its small size, makes it easy to move from office to home or even to school. With an optional padded carrying case, you can even fly with it.

Under Mac's Kilt

Let's first take a look at the elements which make up your Macintosh's impressive circuitry.

5

Chapter 1

The MC68000 Chip

Mac's brain is a Motorola MC68000 microprocessor chip. This state-of-the-art chip gives the Macintosh its characteristic speed and ability to carry out complex tasks. The MC68000 chip can process and move more information faster than most other personal computers' microprocessors.

Because the Mac can process information more than eight times faster than computers like the Apple II, it can have terrific graphics capabilities. It's easy for the Macintosh to quickly display and edit the shapes and forms you draw with programs such as MacPaint.

A Graphics-Only Display That Isn't

The Macintosh displays its output on a 9-inch, black-and-white, high-resolution video screen. If you've worked with other computers, you'll be immediately struck by the clarity and crispness of the computer's display. It looks so good because the Mac's screen has more tiny picture elements, or pixels, than any other personal computer. Mac's video output is made up of 175,104 pixels, 512 pixels wide by 342 pixels high. By comparison, an Apple II's display is made up of only 53,376 pixels (278 × 192). The resolution, or sharpness, of pictures made up of dots (such as newspaper photographs, for example), increases as the number of dots per inch increases. Macintosh's display, then, is more than three times as sharp as the display of many other popular computers.

The shape of Mac's pixels also contributes to the clarity of its display. The pixels are square rather than round. Round pixels, like those used on most TV sets, are adequate for the resolution expected from television broadcasts, but square pixels provide a better image. There's no empty space around a square pixel as there is with a round one, so solid images and horizontal and vertical lines appear sharper. However, diagonal lines still appear stepped, not completely smooth, as Figure 1-2 illustrates. The thousands of pixels in Mac's display make up for this somewhat.

Another of Mac's unique capabilities is that it can display both graphics and text on the screen at the same time. Typically, combining graphics and text is difficult for a computer. But the Macintosh, always in its graphics mode, has the ability to display both at once. Since the Mac isn't restricted to fixed, built-in characters, it can display a variety of styles and sizes of letters. At any one time, the Mac screen can display words in boldface and

Chapter 1

italics, in 12-point and 36-point sizes, in gothic and serif typefaces. More impressively, that text can appear on the same screen as high-resolution pictures. This powerful and innovative feature of the Macintosh makes it a particularly useful tool for art, design, and illustration.

But perhaps you were disappointed with the lack of a color display on the Macintosh. Why *doesn't* the Mac use color? Its designers gave up color in favor of monochrome because the latter provides better picture clarity. A crisp picture, with more pixels making up the image, was more important than color. And providing a color display with the necessary resolution would have made the Mac much more expensive. However, the ability to handle color is built into the Macintosh. Future products will enable the computer to send color information to printers and to color monitors.

Figure 1-2. Square Versus Round Pixels

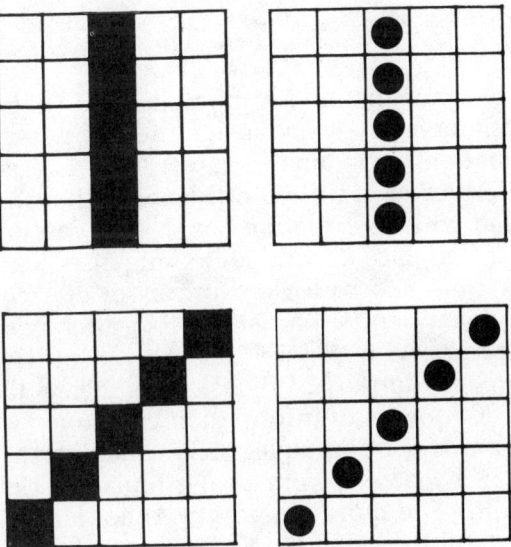

ROM at the Core

A large number of built-in routines have been placed in the Macintosh by Apple's designers. These routines, or short programs, give the Mac its unique personality and way of interacting with

Chapter 1

its users. All the built-in routines are permanently stored in the Macintosh on ROM (Read Only Memory) chips. When you turn off the power, these routines aren't forgotten. Highly efficient programming techniques have squeezed over 500 of these routines into the Mac. Macintosh's native programs, elegantly written, make it an easy computer to use.

The built-in routines also make it easy for programmers to design applications software for the Macintosh. That's because programmers writing for the Macintosh can use these routines in their own programs, rather than writing them from scratch. It's like having a complete programmer's tool kit at your fingertips.

Since each programmer has the same tool kit, all programs written for the computer will have a characteristic look and design. And that will make them easier for you to use. Once you know how commands are given for one Mac program—by using icons, windows, and pull-down menus, for example—you know how to do it for all programs. You don't have to memorize hundreds of command codes or search through a dozen manuals, one for each program.

RAM for Flavor

ROM is the permanent memory of a computer. RAM (Random Access Memory) is the memory space inside the computer that can store new information (programs, data you type in, and so on), but only until the power is turned off. RAM is like a chalkboard—it can be filled with information, and when you no longer need it, you can replace it with something else. RAM gives a computer the power to be a word processor one hour, a financial manager the next, and an artist's helper after that.

The Macintosh comes with either 128K or 512K of RAM space (1 K, or *kilobyte*, contains 1024 bytes). This means that over 128,000 or 512,000 pieces of information can be temporarily stored in Mac's RAM area. (If you have a 128K Macintosh, you can upgrade it to 512K by having your dealer replace a circuit board under Mac's kilt.) The more memory a computer has, the larger and more powerful the tasks it will be able to perform.

The 3-1/2-Inch Disk Drive

Apple has made the Macintosh even more distinctive by using a Sony 3-1/2-inch microfloppy disk drive. At present, 5-1/4-inch floppy disk drives are standard for personal computers. The

Chapter 1

Mac's success and the convenience of the compact 3-1/2-inch format may help make it the new standard.

One advantage of 3-1/2-inch disk drives and diskettes is their small size. And microfloppy disks can store twice as much information on one side of a diskette as standard 5-1/4-inch disks. The microfloppy's design makes it even more attractive. As you can tell by looking at one of your Macintosh diskettes, it's permanently mounted inside a protective hard plastic case. The opening that allows the drive to access the disk is covered by a sliding metal shield.

The 3-1/2-inch microfloppy is kept dust-free and safe from sticky fingers by its sliding shutter. You don't even have to keep track of paper dust jackets, as when you use 5-1/4-inch floppies. Parents can feel comfortable letting their children handle the 3-1/2-inch diskettes. You can even mail them without heavy cardboard insulation. They fit perfectly into business-size envelopes. Of course, don't mistreat your disks. They're not foolproof. Keep them away from electromagnetic sources, such as stereo speakers, telephones, and television sets, and store them in a dust-free environment as much as possible.

The Rest of the Mac Package

The mouse and keyboard are input devices that complete the Mac package.

The Mouse

The mouse is the device that makes the computer and its programs so easy to use. With it, you can make program and file selections without using the keyboard, roll down menus, and even have a conversation with the computer about certain options. It takes time to learn *mouse dexterity*, but most people find it very easy to use after only a little practice.

The first time you use the mouse, you may find it hard to make movements with your entire arm. You're used to moving just your hand and wrist to manipulate objects like pens, pencils, and paint brushes. But within a short time you'll find it easy to draw freehand with the mouse. Just relax your wrist and shoulders, hold the mouse gently, and move it lightly.

Make sure that the surface your mouse rolls on is clean. About every two weeks, you'll probably have to clean the mouse—just follow the instructions in the Macintosh manual.

Chapter 1

If your desk surface is too rough for mouse travel, paint a few coats of polyurethane on an 8 × 10 inch piece of wood, sanding between coats with fine sandpaper. A polyurethane surface causes very little sticking as the mouse moves on it. Such a surface also deposits the least amount of dirt on the ball and feet of the mouse.

The mouse button allows you to make selections from menus, select additional items, and move various objects around the screen. You can click to select and execute single or multiple items or tasks. Don't apply too much pressure on the mouse as you press its button—this could wear out the rollers. Your mouse is a friendly, but fragile device. Be gentle with it and it will work for you without fail.

The Keyboard

The Macintosh's other standard input device—the keyboard—looks much like a typewriter keyboard. It doesn't have a forest of extra keys, like many other computer keyboards, because the mouse eliminates the need for most of them. Since you move around on the screen and make your option selections with the mouse and its button, there's no need for keys devoted exclusively to controlling the cursor or for sending commands. The Mac keyboard is mainly used for old-fashioned keyboard functions, such as text and numeric data entry.

If you have lightning-fast, touch-typing fingers, the Mac's keyboard memory is there to help. When you press keys faster than it can display characters on the screen, the computer remembers which were pressed and in what order, and the screen display will catch up with you.

Alphabetic and numeric keys. The Mac character keys—alphabetic, numeric, punctuation, and symbol—are laid out like a typewriter's. You won't have to adjust to the Mac's keyboard if you're at all familiar with a typewriter. Figure 1-3 shows the characters which appear on the screen when you press each key.

Mac's special keys. The Macintosh keyboard has only 58 keys. Several special keys provide multiple uses for many of these. As on a typewriter's keyboard, the Shift key (either the one on the right or the one on the left) is pressed along with another key to give uppercase letters and the punctuation and symbol characters marked on the top halves of the keys. The characters you'll see when you press the Shift key and another key are illustrated by Figure 1-4. The Macintosh also uses the Caps Lock key,

Chapter 1

the Option key, and the Command key to modify the functions of various keys. You can use the Key Caps option from the Apple menu to refresh your memory of the key combinations.

Figure 1-3. Unshifted Characters

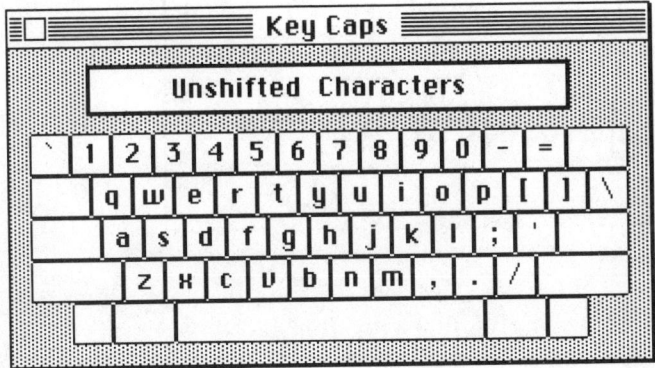

Figure 1-4. Shifted Characters

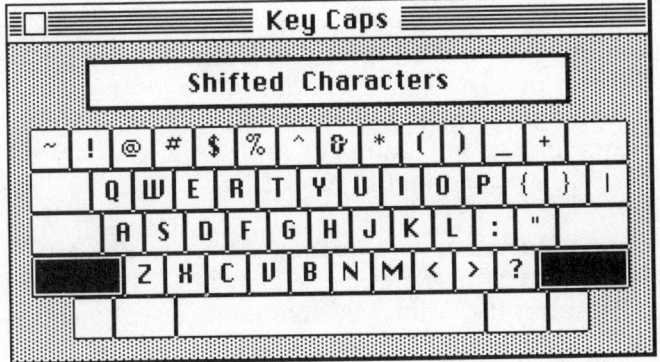

The **Caps Lock** key acts like the Shift key to give you all the uppercase characters, but with one important difference. Using the Caps Lock key doesn't affect the numeric and punctuation keys. This makes it easier to type in uppercase without getting unexpected symbols. Figure 1-5 shows the effect of the Caps Lock key.

Chapter 1

Figure 1-5. Caps Lock Characters

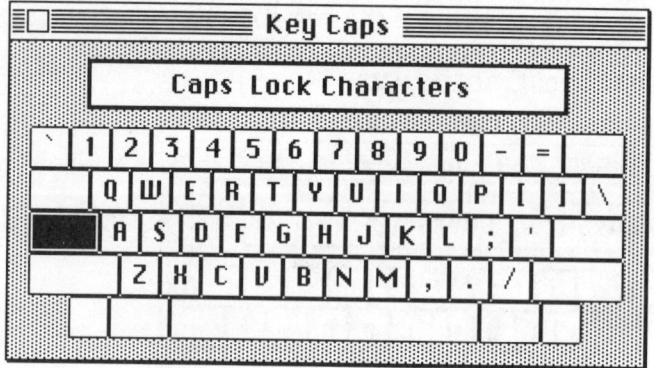

The **Option** keys give many of the Mac's keys a third capability. Figure 1-6 shows all the special characters you can get by holding down an Option key while pressing another key. You'll find some of the special characters very useful. They include foreign language notations, scientific and mathematical symbols, the copyright symbol, the trademark symbol, and the cent symbol. To have the same flexibility with a typewriter, you would have to maintain a store of several typewriter elements, one for each set of features. For the first time, I've been able to put the accent over the *e* in my first name without having to go through several extra steps replacing typing elements. With the Mac, I just type *Vah* and then press the Option key and the E key at the same time, followed by a normal E. Now I have *Vahé*, looking the way it should!

The **Shift** and **Option** keys, if pressed at the same time, allow you to access a few more special characters when a third key is typed. These Shift-Option key characters are shown in Figure 1-7.

(Note that all the figures illustrate the special characters as outlined by the Key Caps option from the Apple menu. When you're using MacWrite, however, you may receive different characters, depending on the font you previously selected.)

12

Chapter 1

Figure 1-6 Option Key Characters

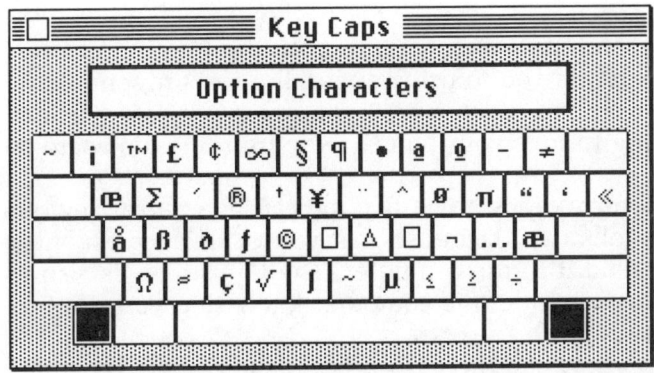

Figure 1-7. Shift-Option Key Characters

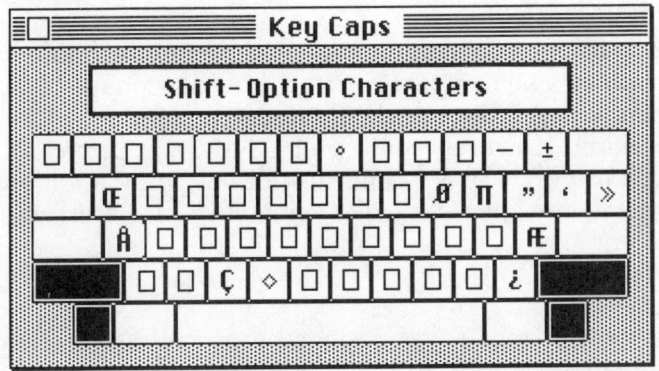

The **Command** key (⌘) also modifies the function of some of the keys, but it doesn't give you different characters. In most cases, the Command key does what its name suggests: it sends commands. For instance, the Command key can be used to stretch the figures you draw with the MacPaint program. It can also be used with other keys to send different types of commands. For example, whenever you want to print a copy of the entire screen (assuming you have a printer suitably connected), you can press Command-Shift-4. The actual uses of the Command key differ

13

Chapter 1

from one application program to another. You may have to consult a program's manual to learn how to use Command key combinations.

You can send mouse commands with the Command key combinations while you're using an application program like MacWrite. If you're a touch-typist, you can enter data quickly without having to take your hands away from the keyboard to use the mouse.

Mac's **Return** key is much like the carriage return key of a typewriter. It tells the Macintosh that you've finished an entry and want to send it to the computer. The Return key is also used in word processors to let the computer know that you want to start a new paragraph.

The **Enter** key, like the Return key, usually ends the entry of a command and sends it to the computer. However, some software packages may define other functions for this key. See the program's manual to see if Enter has been given a special duty.

Optional Hardware

The Macintosh brings you state-of-the-art hardware technology and software art in one compact package. You don't have to buy additional hardware (cards, boards, monitors, or disk drive) to get your Mac working. However, you'll probably want a printer. You may also want to purchase a second disk drive. These additions are not necessary, but they can make using your Macintosh much more convenient and more fun to use.

Imagewriter Printer

Apple's Imagewriter printer was designed especially for the Macintosh. It's a high-speed, dot-matrix printer that can print both text and graphics just as they appear on the screen. Other manufacturers' printers will work with the Mac only with a special printer interface which enables them to understand Macintosh's printer output.

As noted earlier, the Macintosh's video display is made up of thousands of square dots. Although dot-matrix printers with square pins are sometimes used in the computer industry, Mac's designers chose to use the round pin standard, probably to keep costs down. Any loss of image quality that results from this is made up for by the high resolution. The Imagewriter printer provides more resolution, or dots per inch, than even the screen display.

Chapter 1

What you see is what you get with the Macintosh and a connected Imagewriter. You don't have to guess what the printer is going to do with the text or graphics you've painstakingly created. If it can be displayed on the screen, the Imagewriter can print it. This is one of the Mac's most powerful features, especially for those who want to mix graphics and text.

The Imagewriter doesn't limit you to printouts the size of the video screen. The Mac's screen image represents only a portion of a printed page. You can design a page using up to four Macintosh screens. You can get a printout of just what's on the screen (screen dump), or you can choose to print out an entire 8-1/2-by-11-inch page.

Chapter 7 provides a detailed discussion of the Imagewriter printer and how to get the best results with it. You'll see how to choose paper, printer mode, and ribbon darkness for specific applications such as camera-ready art and photocopies.

External Drives

Someday you may want to add a second disk drive to your Macintosh system. A second drive makes it easier to use applications and to copy disks. You won't have to swap disks in and out of the drive. A large percentage of Mac owners will probably acquire a second drive, if for no other reason than convenience.

Another drive will give you double-sided drive capability, allowing the Macintosh to record information on both sides of a disk. With a double-sided disk drive, a diskette's storage capacity will double to 800K—400K on each side.

Hard disk drives are also available for the Macintosh. They can store from 10 to 80 times as much data as a 3-1/2-inch diskette. Hard drives can move information many times faster than regular disk drives. The only disadvantage of hard disk drives is their expense. Most cost in the neighborhood of $2,000. If you'll be using your Macintosh for serious business applications where speed and efficiency are important factors, you may want to investigate this option.

Modems 300 and 1200

With a modem, you can use your telephone to contact (call up) other computers and access services such as The Source, CompuServe, and Dow Jones News/Retrieval Service. Telecomputing is certainly part of the future of computers. It puts you in touch with an entire world of information from your home, office, or school.

Chapter 1

One way I've used telecomputing is to transmit the chapters of this book over telephone lines directly to the publisher. Some publishers can typeset directly from these transmitted files without having to manually retype manuscripts.

Apple has modems available with either 300 or 1200 baud rate (the rate at which data is transmitted).

Numeric Keypad

If you plan to use your computer for business applications, you may want to purchase the optional 15-key numeric keypad to make number entry easier and quicker. The keys are positioned in the same way as on most standard cash registers and adding machines.

Carrying Case

The Mac, since it's so small and relatively light, is certainly portable. Apple, as well as a host of other companies, offers optional carrying cases for your computer. Many of them are light, zippered bags that hold the computer, the keyboard, and the mouse.

Other Products

Hundreds of other hardware products are available for the Macintosh. For a list of products of particular interest to visual and graphic arts applications, refer to the Appendix.

Chapter 2
Software for Creating Pictures and Text

Chapter 2

Software for Creating Pictures and Text

The first time you used the Macintosh, you had a smile on your face. The computer seemed to respond to you on a human level. It asked you to feed it a disk. It smiled. Sometimes it frowned. And once it digested a program on the disk, the Macintosh became a drawing tool, a word processor, or even a game.

Sophisticated applications software puts the computer's power in your hands without the normal lengthy initiation period. Even chores like writing letters are fun when you can include pictures and a variety of text styles. Applications such as MacPaint, MacDraw, and MacWrite make it a joy to work with the Macintosh.

MacPaint, MacDraw, and MacWrite give you the capabilities you need to create almost any visual design—from doodles to magazine page layouts. MacPaint is your electronic easel; it lets you draw in a free and easy way. MacWrite is your electronic typesetter; it helps you create and edit text in different type styles. And MacDraw is your electronic drafting table; with it you can create technical drawings, charts, maps, even product illustrations. If the Macintosh had been around in the fifteenth century, Leonardo da Vinci would probably have used it!

Using Application Programs

This chapter will introduce you to using three programs: You'll see how to create a logo with MacPaint, a product design with MacDraw, and some text with MacWrite. Before you start, however, you should be familiar with the basic operations of your computer. If you're working with the Macintosh for the first time, read the manuals and instructional materials that came with the computer. If you're already familiar with some of these programs, try the examples included here anyway; they'll help you become familiar with the tutorial style used throughout the book—this will prepare you for the more complex visual examples presented in later chapters.

After you've created the three samples in this chapter, go on to Chapter 3. There you'll learn how to exchange information among the three application programs—MacPaint, MacDraw, and MacWrite. In fact, you'll combine the three examples you produced in this chapter into a one-page advertising flier.

Chapter 2

MacPaint, MacDraw, and MacWrite

MacPaint, MacDraw, and MacWrite give you many powerful features. Most of the visual display work needed by designers and small businesses can be created with just these programs.

When the Macintosh was first released, MacPaint and MacWrite were bundled with the computer. Now, however, you'll have to pay for them. Both programs come on one microfloppy diskette; the price of the disk is $195. To get the most flexibility in creating *all* types of visual material, you should also purchase MacDraw. It should be available by the time you read this. MacDraw complements MacPaint's features. What can't be done with one is often a feature of the other.

Figure 2-1. Application Icons

MacPaint   MacWrite   MacDraw

MacPaint can help you create detailed pictures of all sorts. With MacPaint you can draw various shapes, fill them with patterns, and even zoom in on parts of your picture to change the smallest details.

MacDraw lets you design and produce mechanical illustrations, technical drawings, flow charts, and floor plans. It's a graphic designer's dream come true. With MacDraw you can create carefully sized and scaled illustrations from 8 × 10 inches to 4 × 8 feet.

MacWrite gives you the ability to write and edit text in a variety of fonts, styles, and sizes. It provides many of the essential features of a word processor, including search and replace, page numbering, headers and footers, and justification, to name just a few.

The most important feature of the Macintosh is that whatever appears on the screen can be represented almost exactly by the printer. There are no unfortunate surprises in printing with the Mac—only predictable results completely under your control.

A Note About Program Versions

After a program is released, newer versions of it are sometimes made available. These later versions usually correct problems and sometimes make improvements. Your Apple dealer is the best

Chapter 2

source of information concerning updates for your software. Keep in touch with your dealer and inquire about updates. Most of the time, updates are made available either at no cost or for a minimal charge.

In preparing this book, every effort has been made to use the most recent versions of the software. If you find a reference to features that are not available in your application program or that operate differently when you use it, contact your local Apple dealer.

MacPaint—The Electronic Easel

MacPaint is one of the most powerful and versatile drawing programs available for microcomputers. It takes advantage of the Macintosh's sophisticated hardware to give you a quick, easy-to-use set of illustrating tools. Novice and professional artists alike will find it invaluable. MacPaint's large selection of drawing tools and palettes makes it simple to create all sorts of pictures. With it, you'll be able to produce beautiful and evocative visual creations.

Unlimited Tools

When you use MacPaint, you're not limited to the set of tools and patterns that it offers. There are thousands of ways to combine the tool selections to give your drawings a wide range of characteristics. For example, when you double-click on the paint brush icon, you're given a choice of 32 brush shapes. Combined with the 38 patterns provided in the palette at the bottom of the MacPaint window, you suddenly have 1216 possible brush effects. Just these 38 patterns give you more "rub-on" patterns than some graphic arts shops have. But with MacPaint you aren't limited to 38 patterns—you can edit any of the patterns to make your own designs.

If MacPaint's tools don't do what you want, you can choose to zoom in to your picture and change its details pixel by pixel until you have just the effect you want. Since one MacPaint window includes over 100,000 pixels, and because there are about four windows in one MacPaint picture page, you have control over each of the 400,000+ pixels that compose a picture on the Macintosh.

Using MacPaint is like having an infinite supply of rub-on letters, pictures, and patterns. By changing size, style, and pattern, you can create thousands of combinations.

Chapter 2

Creating a Logo Design with MacPaint

Let's create a picture with MacPaint to discover some of its features and how to use them. Even if you already know how to use MacPaint, try this example. It may offer techniques you haven't used or methods you're unfamiliar with.

When you've finished, the logo will look like this:

Figure 2-2. The Finished Logo

Here are the steps you need to complete to create this design

Insert MacPaint disk. Turn your Macintosh on, then insert the MacPaint disk. Click twice on the disk icon to open it if it's not already opened.

Open MacPaint. Open your electronic easel by double-clicking the MacPaint application icon. The rectangle filled with the grid pattern is the first element you'll draw.

Create a filled rectangle. Click the small, square grid pattern at the bottom of the MacPaint window. The pattern should be reproduced in the larger box at the left end of that double line of pattern choices.

Chapter 2

Figure 2-3. Choosing a Pattern

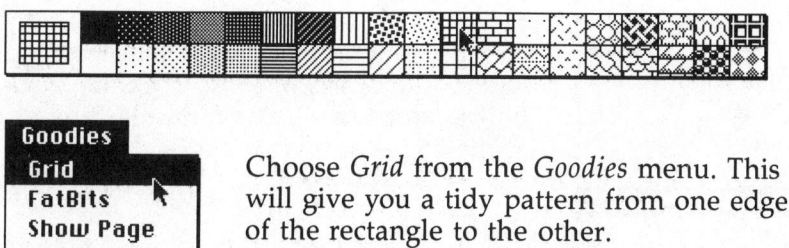

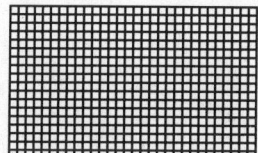

Choose *Grid* from the *Goodies* menu. This will give you a tidy pattern from one edge of the rectangle to the other.

Click on the filled rectangle tool from the left side of the MacPaint window.

Now position the mouse's arrow near the center of your work space and drag the mouse diagonally to create a rectangle filled with the small grid pattern.

Figure 2-4. The Filled Rectangle

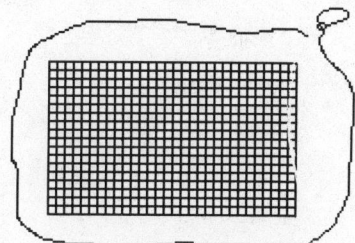

Invert the rectangle. To make a negative image of the patterned rectangle, first select the rectangle with the lasso. (The lasso is the tool at the top left of the two columns of MacPaint tools on the far left of the screen.)

Figure 2-5. Lasso the Rectangle

23

Chapter 2

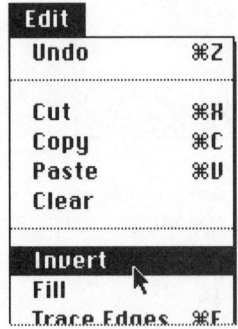

Choose *Invert* from the *Edit* menu to make the negative image. As soon as you do this, the rectangle in your work space should change, so that it looks like that shown in Figure 2-6. Make sure you click the mouse button again to eliminate the flashing effect at the edges of the rectangle.

Figure 2-6. Inverted Rectangle

Outline the inverted rectangle. Now you'll enclose the inverted rectangle with an outline. Make sure that the thinnest solid line is chosen from the line and border thickness selection box.

Choose the hollow rectangle tool. Carefully move the pointer to the top left corner of your filled rectangle and drag the pointer to the opposite corner to outline the rectangle.

Figure 2-7. Outlined Rectangle

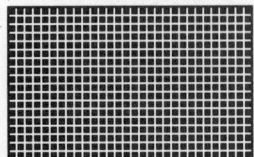

Chapter 2

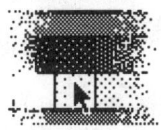 **Create the circle.** To create the circle, first click the next thicker line from the line thickness box. This will give your circle a wider outline. Then choose an open dot pattern for the filled circle.

Select the filled oval tool from the toolbox on the far left. Hold down the Shift key as you drag the mouse to create the circle. The Shift key restricts the shape so that only perfect circles can be drawn.

Figure 2-8. The Filled Circle

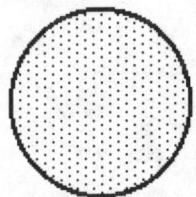

Move the circle. Choose *Grid* again from the *Goodies* menu to disable (turn off) the feature. Lasso the circle and drag it to a position on the center of the rectangle. Click the mouse button when the lasso icon is anywhere outside the combined circle-rectangle form to unselect the circle. Its edges will stop flashing.

Figure 2-9. Circle on Rectangle

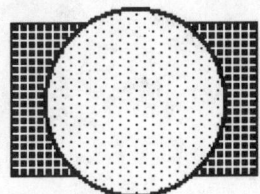

Duplicate the circle-rectangle. Now you're ready to make the drop shadow, the shadow cast by the form you've just made. Make sure you have enough blank space to duplicate the circle-rectangle form within the MacPaint window. If you don't, select the hand icon and move your picture over to one side.

25

Chapter 2

Now you'll make a copy of this shape. First, select the form with the lasso. To create and move a copy of it, hold down the Option key while you drag the shape to an empty spot.

Fill the copy. One of the shapes (the copy) should still be shimmering—that's because it's selected by the lasso. The two designs will look something like Figure 2-10.

Figure 2-10. Duplicate Shapes

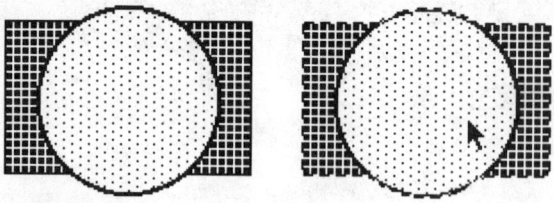

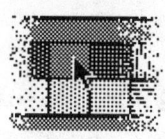 Now choose the 50 percent gray pattern.

Choose *Fill* from the *Edit* menu to fill the shape which has shimmering edges. This fills the entire shape with the 50 percent gray pattern. The result is illustrated by Figure 2-11.

Figure 2-11. Fill with Gray

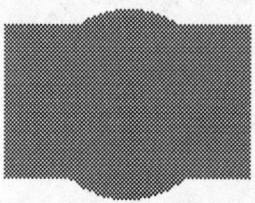

Move the form. Now select the circle-rectangle shape with the lasso and drag it so that it's partially covering the gray shape. Look at Figure 2-12 for the approximate positions of each shape.

Chapter 2

Figure 2-12. The Drop Shadow

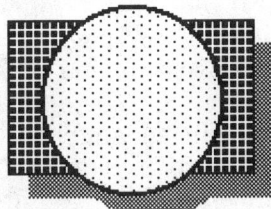

Type the text. The font used for this logo's letters is 12-point Chicago. Choose *Chicago* from the *Fonts* menu and 12 from the *FontSize* menu. Now choose both *Bold* and *Shadow* from the *Style* menu. Since you want to center your text, you must also choose *Align Middle* from the *Style* menu.

Working outside the circle-rectangle shape, type M & W and press Return. Now type DESIGNS. The lettering is automatically centered for you.

Move the text. Select the lettering with the lasso and move it into position inside the circle. The logo is complete.

Figure 2-13. Inserting Text Completes the Logo

Save your logo. Save this logo on your MacPaint working disk. Choose *Save As* from the *File* menu and name the document logo. You'll use this same design in Chapter 3 to create the advertising flyer.

27

Chapter 2

MacDraw—The Electronic Drafting Table

After working with MacPaint for awhile, you've probably found that it takes a long time to create certain types of drawings. If you used MacPaint to design a scale drawing, for instance, you'd have to hold rulers up to the screen or put little pieces of tape on it to get the sizes of your elements just right. And since it's rare that the screen size of an object corresponds exactly to the size of the object when printed out (unless your Macintosh's video output has been carefully adjusted by a service technician), you can't expect *precise* results. MacDraw solves these problems.

A Structured Graphics Editor

MacDraw is a structured graphics editor. That means it allows you to create and edit distinct forms such as rectangles, circles, and polygons. Unlike MacPaint, though, MacDraw remembers each shape you draw. This gives you the freedom to edit any shape, even if it's lying atop or beneath another, without disturbing other shapes around it. The last section of this chapter describes the differences between MacPaint and MacDraw in more detail. For now, just think of MacPaint as an artist's tool for creating freehand drawings and MacDraw as a picture object editor.

MacDraw isn't intended to be a freehand drawing tool. With it, you'll be making geometric objects, or elements, from which you'll build your pictures. This makes MacDraw very easy to use if you're not very experienced at drawing. But since it is intended to be a designer's tool, it's also packed with advanced features—*Custom Rulers, Drawing Size, Show Size, Bring to Front/Back* and *Group/Ungroup*, among others. You'll need to practice with these features before you can use them successfully in your visual designs. Chapter 5 will show you some special things you can do with MacDraw.

MacDraw's features also make it an excellent tool for many visual arts applications. You can use it for product design, architectural renderings, layouts, organizational charts, flow charts, and maps, as well as general mechanical and technical illustrations.

Size, Proportion, and Rulers

MacDraw's features make it especially easy to design scale drawings. You can define rulers and scale to either the metric or the British measuring system. It allows you to "tape" items in position on your "drafting table," leaving other items free to be

Chapter 2

moved. You can even tape certain objects together to make a larger form that can then be taped down or moved from place to place. By simulating the drafting table, MacDraw lets you design and edit your drawing elements without having to redraw them each time you make a change. Just as a word processor lets you make changes in words simply and easily, MacDraw allows you to modify and restructure pictures. In effect, it's a "picture processor."

Interactions

It's possible to take items from MacDraw and paste them into MacPaint for additional modification. You can reverse the process, and paste MacPaint drawings into MacDraw. This way you get the best of both worlds—you can use one program's specialized features to do the basic drawing and the other's special features to put on the finishing touches. You can also paste MacDraw picture elements into your MacWrite documents to illustrate letters and articles. This ability to share information between applications gives you a flexibility unheard of before the Macintosh.

Creating a Scale Drawing with MacDraw

By following along with this example, you can learn a lot about MacDraw's features. It looks simple, but these instructions (which create a scale drawing of a dresser) use techniques and methods you'll quickly find invaluable.

The finished screen, when you've gone through all the steps, should look like Figure 2-14.

Figure 2-14. The Finished Dresser Screen

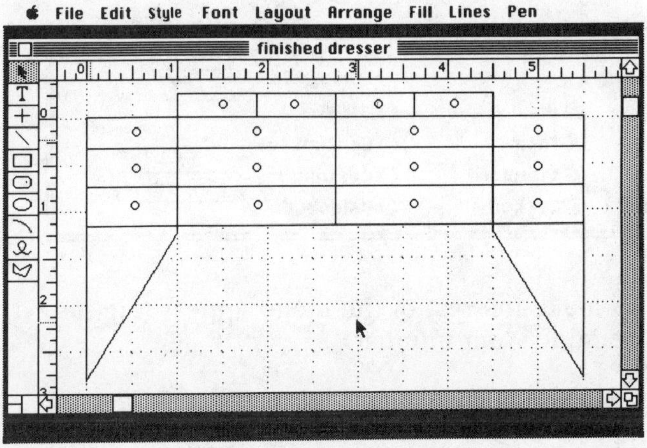

Chapter 2

Before you start creating a drawing with MacDraw, you should consider two things: what's the easiest way to create the drawing using MacDraw's features and what scale should be used? The dresser is bilaterally symmetrical—the left and right sides are mirror images of each other. This means you have to draw only one half of the dresser, duplicate it, and flip the duplicate to get the second half.

Take your computer and MacDraw through these steps.

Insert MacDraw disk. Turn your Macintosh on, then insert the MacDraw disk. Click twice on the disk icon to open it if it's not already opened.

Open MacDraw. Double-click the MacDraw application icon to open your electronic drafting table.

Customize your rulers. Consider the dresser's dimensions. Since its length is 5-1/2 feet, let 1 inch on the drawing equal 1 foot in actual dimensions. Each inch should be divided into 12 units, so that 1/12 inch in the drawing is equal to 1 inch on the dresser. To customize your scale, choose *Show Rulers* from the *Layout* menu.

Horizontal and vertical rulers appear on the top and left edges of the screen. Each major (numbered) increment is 1 inch. Each inch is subdivided into 8 minor units. To change the number of minor units in 1 major unit, you have to customize the rulers. Select *Custom Rulers* from the *Layout* menu.

Figure 2-15. *Custom Rulers* Dialog Box

```
Custom Rulers:
    Ruler:       ● On           ○ Off            [  OK  ]
                 ● Inch         ○ Centimeter
                 ● Standard     ○ Custom         [ Cancel ]
    Zero Point:  ● Locked       ○ Unlocked
```

Click *Custom* to make the rest of the menu appear (Figure 2-16). Select 12 as the minor unit number.

30

Chapter 2

Figure 2-16. The Complete *Custom Rulers* Dialog Box

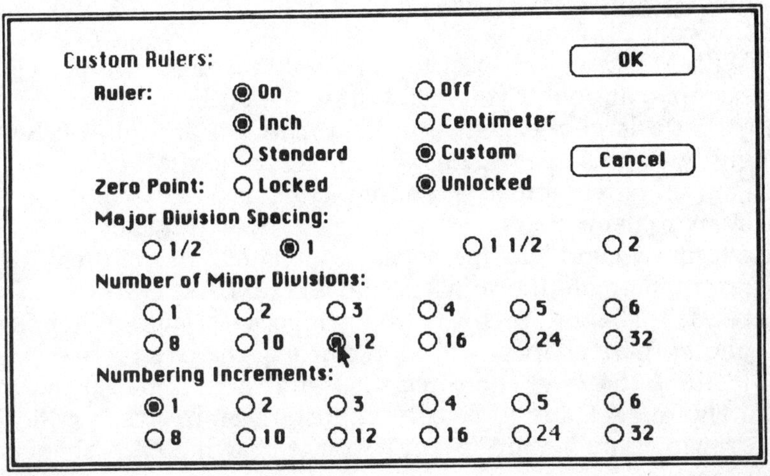

```
Custom Rulers:                              ┌─────────┐
    Ruler:     ● On          ○ Off          │   OK    │
               ● Inch        ○ Centimeter   └─────────┘
               ○ Standard    ● Custom       ┌─────────┐
    Zero Point: ○ Locked     ● Unlocked     │ Cancel  │
    Major Division Spacing:                 └─────────┘
        ○ 1/2        ● 1          ○ 1 1/2      ○ 2
    Number of Minor Divisions:
        ○ 1      ○ 2      ○ 3      ○ 4      ○ 5      ○ 6
        ○ 8      ○ 10     ● 12     ○ 16     ○ 24     ○ 32
    Numbering Increments:
        ● 1      ○ 2      ○ 3      ○ 4      ○ 5      ○ 6
        ○ 8      ○ 10     ○ 12     ○ 16     ○ 24     ○ 32
```

The *Major Division Spacing* (inches) and the *Numbering Increments* should be left at 1. Select and click *OK* to exit the dialog box. Notice that each inch is now divided into 4 units, each of which is subdivided into 3 smaller units. One inch now consists of 12 minor units.

Set the zero point. The zero point of both rulers is in the top left corner, behind the rulers. You'll want to have the zero point inside your window where you can see it. First, click anywhere on one of the rulers and drag to move the zero point as shown below.

Figure 2-17. Setting the Zero Point

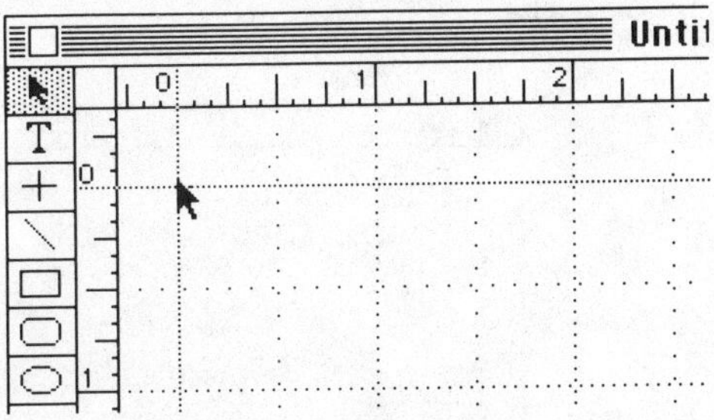

31

Chapter 2

MacDraw lets you change the zero point at any time while you're creating a picture. This makes it easy to size shapes in different parts of your drawing.

With MacDraw, it's best to draw individual picture objects. For example, although you could draw the outline of a set of drawers as a large rectangle and then mark off each drawer with straight lines, this goes against the philosophy of MacDraw. MacPaint may remember an entire picture as a series of dots, but MacDraw remembers objects rather than dots. It makes more sense to draw complete and separate elements. In the dresser example, you'll create the drawers, the legs, and the drawer pulls as independent shapes. This way you can go back later and change any one of these shapes without disturbing the others.

It's time to draw. The three small drawers on the far left (refer to Figure 2-14) are to be 5 × 12 inches. Since size is critical to this drawing, you'll want to know you're drawing each element to its proper size.

Show Size. Choose *Show Size* from the *Layout* menu; now when you draw a shape, its dimensions (in decimal fractions of an inch) will be shown on the screen.

Draw a rectangle. Select the rectangle tool from the column at the far left of the screen and draw a rectangle 5/12 inch high by 1 inch long (0.42 × 1.00 inch). This is the first drawer.

The rectangle is white outlined in black, with eight "handles" around it. The handles tell you that the form is the current selection for editing. You can also drag these handles to change the shape of the rectangle.

Duplicate the rectangle. The two drawers below this first one are to be the same size, so you'll use MacDraw's *Duplicate* feature to create them quickly. Press Command-D (or choose *Duplicate* from the *Edit* menu) to make a second rectangle identical to the first.

Figure 2-18. The First Two Drawers

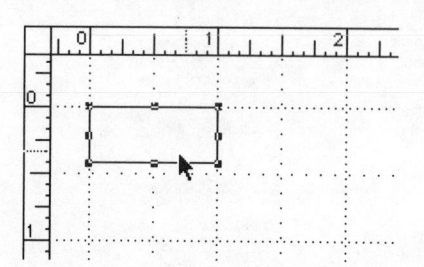

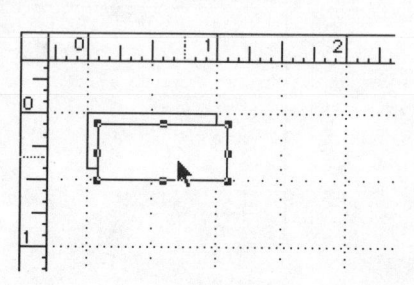

Chapter 2

Position the second rectangle. Drag the second rectangle into its position, directly below the first. When the top of the second drawer is exactly aligned with the bottom of the first, the line common to both becomes dotted.

Duplicate again. Now press Command-D again to duplicate this second drawer. MacDraw is smart; it puts another duplicated form in the right place—you don't have to move it into position. If you make a mistake, check that the unwanted form is selected (has handles around it) and press Backspace to delete it. (Or, if you haven't done anything else since the error, you can choose *Undo* from the *Edit* menu. It works just like *Undo* in MacPaint, returning you to the previous condition of the drawing.)

Figure 2-19. Duplicate Again

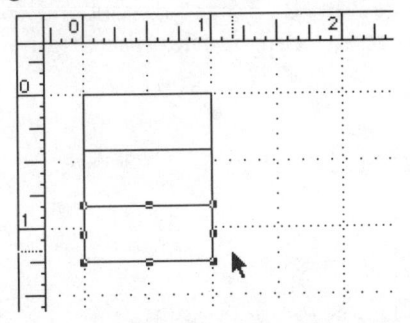

Draw three large rectangles. Now you'll draw the larger drawers which appear in the middle of the dresser. Choose the rectangle tool again to create one that is 5/12 × 1-3/4 (0.42 × 1.75) inches. This represents a drawer 5 × 21 inches. Duplicate it and put the copy below the first. Duplicate again to add the third drawer automatically.

Figure 2-20. Three Large Drawers

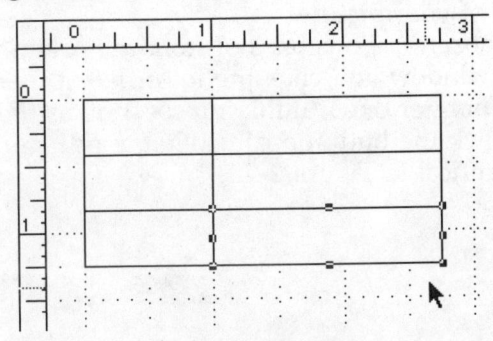

Chapter 2

Draw a small rectangle. The smallest drawers, those right above the large drawers you just created, are next. Their dimensions are 1/4 × 7/8 (0.25 × 0.87) inches. Select the rectangle tool once more. Try to draw a rectangle with these dimensions. It can't be done! You can't get increments of 8 because you divided each inch into 12 units. The 7/8-inch dimension can't be obtained with your custom rulers set at a minor increment of 12 units. For now, just leave this drawer in its proper position.

Adjust your ruler. To solve this problem, you have to customize your rulers again so that they show increments in factors of 8. Choose *Custom Rulers* from the *Layout* menu and select 16 for the number of minor increments. Click OK.

Stretch the rectangle. Now drag the middle handle of the small rectangle to stretch it out until it's 7/8-inch wide.

Duplicate and position the rectangle. To get the second top drawer, duplicate the first and place the copy beside the original.

Figure 2-21. Completed Drawers

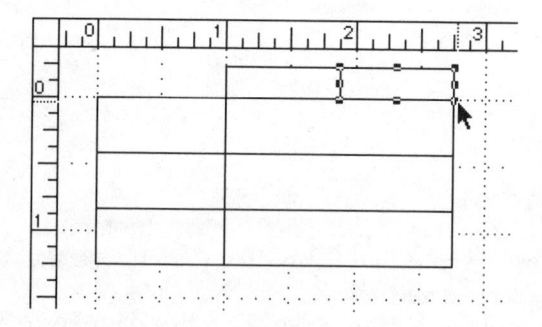

Readjust your rulers. The leg is easy to draw. First, set your custom rulers back to 12 minor divisions. Move the down scroll arrow (at the bottom right corner of the window) so that you have more space at the bottom of your picture.

Draw a polygon. Choose the polygon tool from the column at the far left of the window and click the lower left corner of the drawers. Move the pointer down until you see 1.50 as the vertical dimension, then click the button again. What appears on the screen should look identical to Figure 2-22.

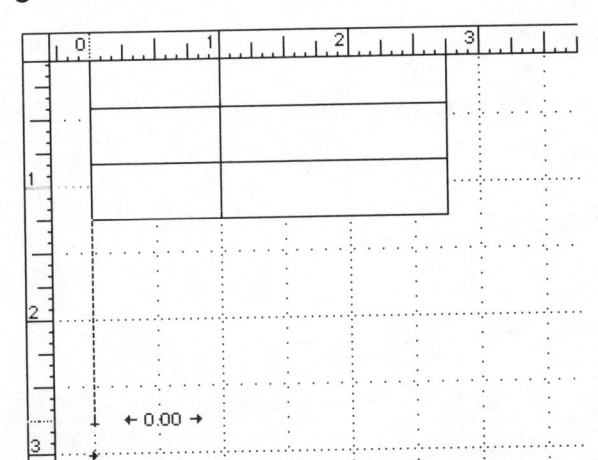

Figure 2-22. Drawing the Leg

Move the pointer at an angle to just below the right edge of the lower left drawer. When you see the dimensions 1.00 on the horizontal axis and 1.42 on the vertical, click again. Move up until you touch the intersection of the two drawers and click. The shape is now complete; you could click twice to stop drawing your polygon here, but it's better not to. Remember, with MacDraw it's best to draw complete, closed objects whenever possible. Continue to the left and click on the point where you started drawing the polygon. (You know you're drawing right on top of another line when the line underneath appears white.) The polygon mode terminates, and you see the handles around the leg. (Some of them are not actually on the polygon, but off to the side or below it.) Scroll the drawing back down by clicking once on the up scroll arrow at the top right corner of the window. Your drawing so far looks like Figure 2-23.

Customize your rulers. To complete one half of the chest of drawers, you must put on the drawer pulls. Since each one has to be positioned exactly in the center of its drawer, customize your rulers one more time so that the minor increments are as fine as possible—32 minor units per inch. Although the rulers will show only 16 units per inch, you'll be able to operate at 32. This will let you drag objects in one-pixel steps.

Chapter 2

Figure 2-23. A Finished Leg

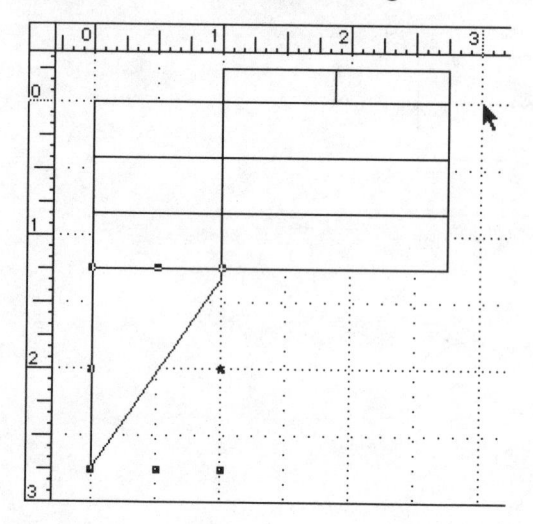

Draw a circle. Select the oval drawing tool and hold down Shift so that you'll draw a perfect circle instead of an oval (this feature is identical to the one in MacPaint). In an area outside the dresser drawers, drag the mouse until you get a circle 0.09 inches in diameter.

Position the circle. Now move this circle to its position in the middle of the top leftmost drawer.

Duplicate the circle twice. Duplicate the circle (with Command-D or the *Duplicate* function of the *Edit* menu) and position the copy on the drawer below. Press Command-D again to automatically create a third pull in the right place below the second. Figure 2-24 illustrates the progress you've made on the drawing.

Position more copies of the circle. Duplicate the third drawer pull and move it into position on one of the smallest drawers at the top. Duplicate the drawer pull and put the copy on the matching drawer. Duplicate this one, and place it in position on the first large drawer. Duplicate again and put the copy on the drawer below. Duplicate one more time to automatically place the third one in its position.

Chapter 2

Figure 2-24. Handles in a Row

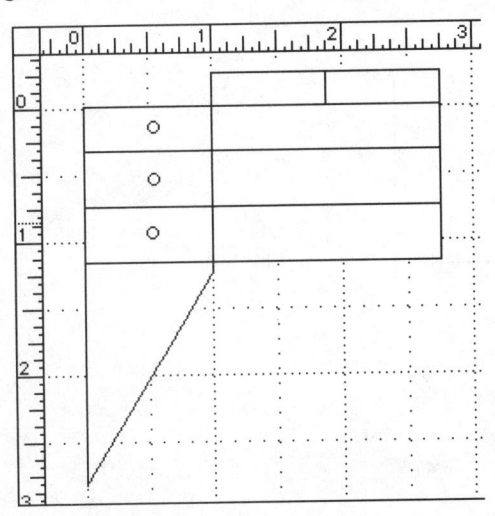

Group the elements. You now have half of the dresser. Before you go on, however, you should group all its elements into one complete form. Make sure the pointer arrow tool is selected and click to get the pointing finger. Drag the finger from a point at the upper left, outside the drawing, diagonally to the lower right, outside the drawing, enclosing the half dresser within the selection rectangle, and let go the mouse button. The rectangle selects all the elements that make up the half dresser—that's why you see all the handles. (You could also have done this by choosing *Select All* from the *Edit* menu.) Choose *Group* from the *Arrange* menu. Now only eight handles appear around the drawing.

37

Chapter 2

Figure 2-25. The Grouped Dresser

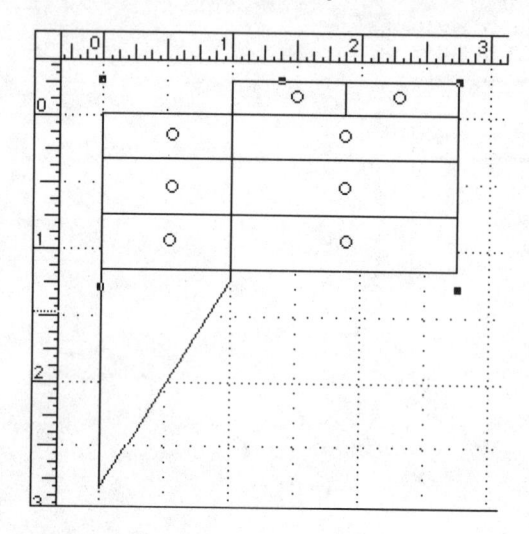

Duplicate and flip it. Duplicate this selected form. Choose *Flip Horizontal* from the *Arrange* menu. You now have two halves of the drawers, one flipped laterally.

38

Chapter 2

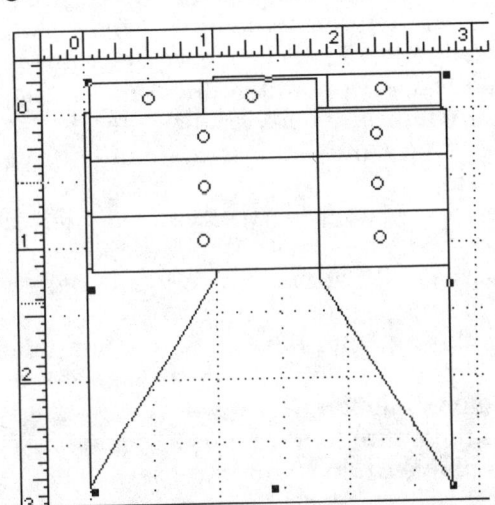

Figure 2-26. Flipped Dresser

    Position it. Move the copy into position and you've finished. Check what you see on the screen with Figure 2-14. The two should be identical—if they're not, read through the steps again to see if you can find something you forgot to do.
    Save it. Before you go any farther, remember to save this design on your MacDraw working disk. Choose *Save As* from the *File* menu and name this document "Dresser."

39

Chapter 2

MacWrite—The Electronic Typesetter

More than likely, you've already written something using MacWrite, perhaps a personal letter. Its recipient was probably impressed with the outlined text, script, and gothic fonts. Perhaps you even included a picture within the body of the letter. It was fun and easy learning to use MacWrite—in less than an hour you were writing and editing text.

Like other word processors, MacWrite saves you from tedious retyping. For instance, if you write a letter to a friend and save it on disk, the next time you write to that person, you can open the letter document, erase the old text, and type in the new. The return address, greeting, and closing don't have to be retyped unless you want to change them. This can save you a great deal of time. Word processors are even more valuable when you're rewriting. Instead of having to retype the entire letter, report, document, story, or even novel, all you have to do is enter the revisions. Your printer does all the rest. After using a word processor, most writers refuse to go back to a typewriter.

But MacWrite is more than a word processor. With it, you can design your own letterhead, even adding a logo with MacPaint. Once you've created the letterhead and logo, and saved it to disk, all you need to do is open the letterhead document and type in your letter.

MacWrite can also be used as a typesetter. You can design text for announcements, advertising flyers, and newsletters, using all of MacWrite's features to enliven the basic copy.

Fonts, Styles, and Sizes

One of MacWrite's strengths is its ability to display on the screen exactly what you'll see on paper. You can choose from a variety of fonts, font sizes, and font styles. Whenever you change the character of the font or its style, the screen will display your text accordingly. If you choose an outlined, 12-point, New York font, you'll see it on the screen exactly as it will appear on paper. There are no unexpected surprises with MacWrite.

You can even change the formatting of your text and see the results immediately. You can choose to justify both left and right margins and then change the margin width.

Creating Advertising Copy with MacWrite

An example can probably best show MacWrite's capabilities. If you read through the step-by-step instructions below and use

Chapter 2

your Macintosh to follow along, you'll see how to prepare the copy for a one-page advertising flyer. (Chapter 3 will illustrate how you can complete the flyer by combining the copy with the logo and dresser you've already designed in this chapter.)

When you're through with the copy, it will look like this.

Figure 2-27. Finished Copy

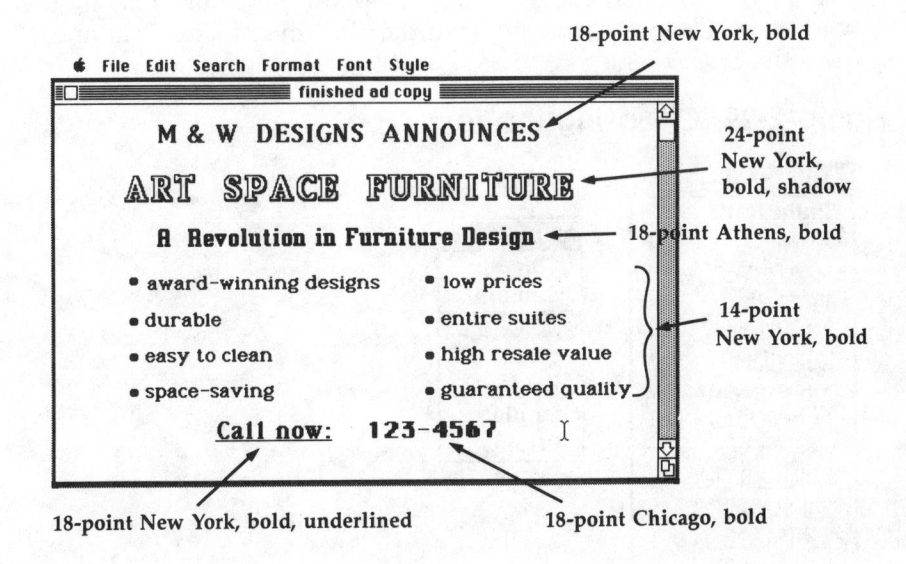

```
                                    18-point New York, bold
 ⌘  File  Edit  Search  Format  Font  Style
▄▄▄▄▄▄▄▄▄▄▄▄▄▄ finished ad copy ▄▄▄▄▄▄▄▄▄▄▄▄▄▄
        M & W DESIGNS ANNOUNCES           24-point
                                          New York,
        ART SPACE FURNITURE               bold, shadow

          A Revolution in Furniture Design    ← 18-point Athens, bold

       • award-winning designs   • low prices
       • durable                 • entire suites       14-point
       • easy to clean           • high resale value   New York, bold
       • space-saving            • guaranteed quality

              Call now:   123-4567

  18-point New York, bold, underlined       18-point Chicago, bold
```

Insert MacWrite disk. Turn your Macintosh on and insert the MacWrite disk. After a few moments, the disk's window will grow to fill most of the screen.

Open MacWrite. Double-click the MacWrite icon to open the word processor.

Set your format. The ruler is your formatting tool. With it, you'll set margins, tabs, line spacing, centering, and justification. Since you want centered text and 1-1/2 line spacing, click the center icon and the 1-1/2 spacing icon. Those icons are the ones highlighted in Figure 2-28—the center icon on the right, the spacing icon on the left. The left and right margins are to be set at 1 inch and 7 inches, respectively, so drag the Left Margin and Paragraph Indentation markers to the 1-inch mark.

Chapter 2

Figure 2-28. The Adjusted Ruler

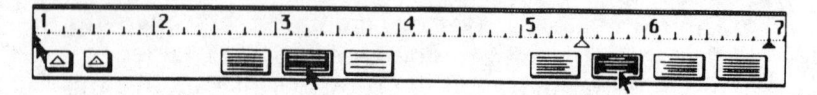

    Choose font type, size, and style. The first line you'll type is *M & W DESIGNS ANNOUNCES* in 18-point New York font in a bold style. Choose *New York* from the *Font* menu, and *Bold* and *18* from the *Style* menu.

Figure 2-29. Choosing the Text

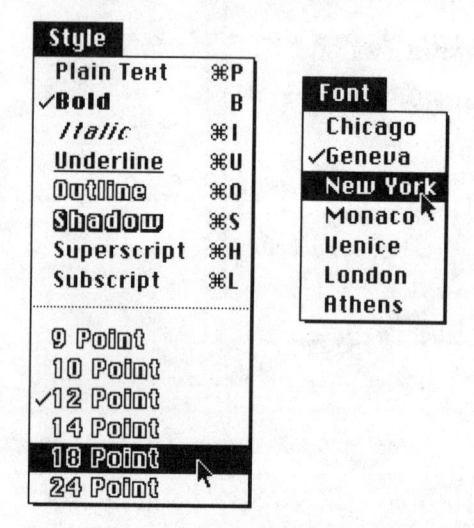

    Type the first line of text. Type the first line and press Return. The insertion point moves to the next line at the center.

    Type two more lines of text. Go ahead and type in the next two lines. The first is *ART SPACE FURNITURE*, which should be 24-point bold, with shadow, using New York font. Type *A Revolution in Furniture Design* in 18-point Athens bold. The three lines will appear as in Figure 2-30.

    If you make a mistake, it's easy to make corrections. Just press the Backspace key to delete the last letter you typed. To delete a word, double-click the word to select it (it becomes highlighted) and press Backspace. To erase a larger portion of text, Shift-click to highlight everything from the insertion point to your current position and press Backspace.

Figure 2-30. Copy So Far

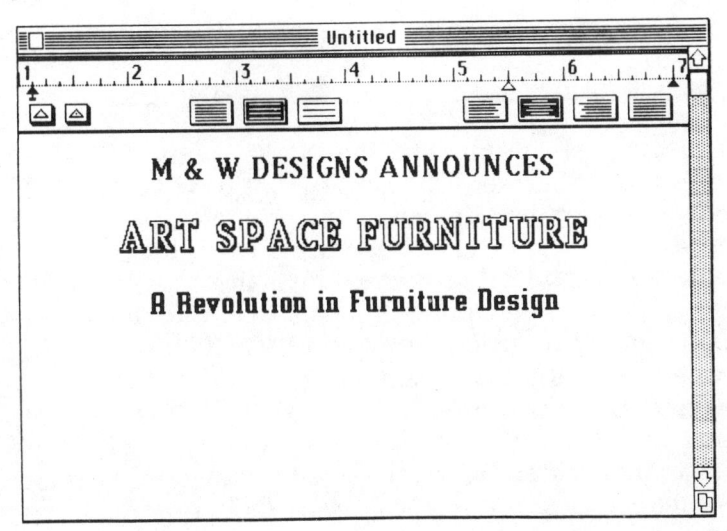

```
M & W DESIGNS ANNOUNCES

ART SPACE FURNITURE

A Revolution in Furniture Design
```

Insert a second ruler. Now you're ready for the two columns of listed features. You have to change the formatting for this text, so choose *Insert Ruler* from the *Format* menu. A second ruler appears at the insertion point.

Change the format. You want tabs for the two columns of text to be set at 1-3/4 inches and 4-3/4 inches. Drag a tab marker (shown as an empty triangle shape) from the well of tab markers at the left side of the screen to the 1-3/4-inch position. Then move the existing tab marker on the right to the 4-3/4-inch position. Select left justification (the leftmost icon from the group of four at the right part of the ruler), because centering is no longer required.

Chapter 2

Figure 2-31. The Second Ruler

Text in the first column. Use the Tab key to move the insertion point to the tab marker. Choose 14-point New York in bold. Press Option-8 to get the large dot. Now press the space bar once and type *award-winning designs*, but don't press Return.

Text in the second column. Press the Tab key again to get to the second column, press Option-8, then space, and enter *low prices*. (Don't enter the period, however.) Press Return.

Complete the columns of text. Continue until you've typed in all the features of the dresser. Refer to Figure 2-27 for the required copy.

Insert another ruler. Now you have to change the formatting again to center the next line. Choose *Insert Ruler* from the *Format* menu and click the center icon.

Figure 2-32. The Third Ruler

Type the last line. Type *Call now:* in 18-point New York, bold and underlined. Select 18-point Chicago bold, insert two spaces, and enter *123-4567*. If you entered the spaces before you chose the new type style and font, the spaces would have been underlined.

Hide rulers. To see the text without the rulers, choose *Hide Rulers* from the *Format* menu. Though this erases the rulers, their effect is maintained.

Chapter 2

Figure 2-33. The Finished Advertising Copy

```
 File   Edit   Search   Format   Font   Style
```

M & W DESIGNS ANNOUNCES

ART SPACE FURNITURE

A Revolution in Furniture Design

- award-winning designs
- durable
- easy to clean
- space-saving
- low prices
- entire suites
- high resale value
- guaranteed quality

Call now: 123-4567

Save it. Before you go any further, save this document on your MacWrite working disk. Choose *Save As* from the *File* menu and name the document "Ad Copy."

Now you've completed the three elements for the advertising flyer that you'll put together in the next chapter.

MacPaint or MacDraw?

Together, MacPaint and MacDraw form one of the most powerful sets of visual arts and graphics tools available for microcomputers. These two programs have set a new standard for quality in software development.

But to use these tools effectively, you must understand the differences between them. This section will help you decide which program is best suited for your own graphics applications.

Chapter 2

Complementary Programs

MacDraw and MacPaint complement each other—what one program lacks, the other often includes. As you get comfortable with these two programs, you'll probably use both of them to create one finished drawing. MacDraw allows you to prepare the first stage of your drawing, and MacPaint lets you add such details as shading. Study some of the MacPaint and MacDraw menus to better understand the differences between the two programs.

Figure 2-34. MacPaint and MacDraw Menus

Goodies
- Grid
- FatBits
- Show Page
- Edit Pattern
- Brush Shape
- Brush Mirrors
- Introduction
- Short Cuts

Edit
- Undo ⌘Z
- Cut ⌘X
- Copy ⌘C
- Paste ⌘V
- Clear
- Invert
- Fill
- Trace Edges ⌘E
- Flip Horizontal
- Flip Vertical
- Rotate

MacPaint

Edit
- Undo ⌘Z
- Cut ⌘X
- Copy ⌘C
- Paste ⌘V
- Clear
- Duplicate ⌘D
- Select All ⌘A
- Reshape ⌘R
- Smooth
- Unsmooth
- Round Corners...

Layout
- Show Rulers
- Custom Rulers...
- ✓Normal Size
- Reduce To Fit
- Reduce
- Enlarge
- Turn Grid Off
- Hide Ruler Lines
- Show Size
- Hide Page Breaks
- Drawing Size...

Arrange
- Bring to Front
- Send to Back
- Paste in Front
- Paste in Back
- Rotate Left
- Rotate Right
- Flip Horizontal
- Flip Vertical
- Group ⌘G
- Ungroup
- Lock
- Unlock
- Align to Grid
- Align Objects...

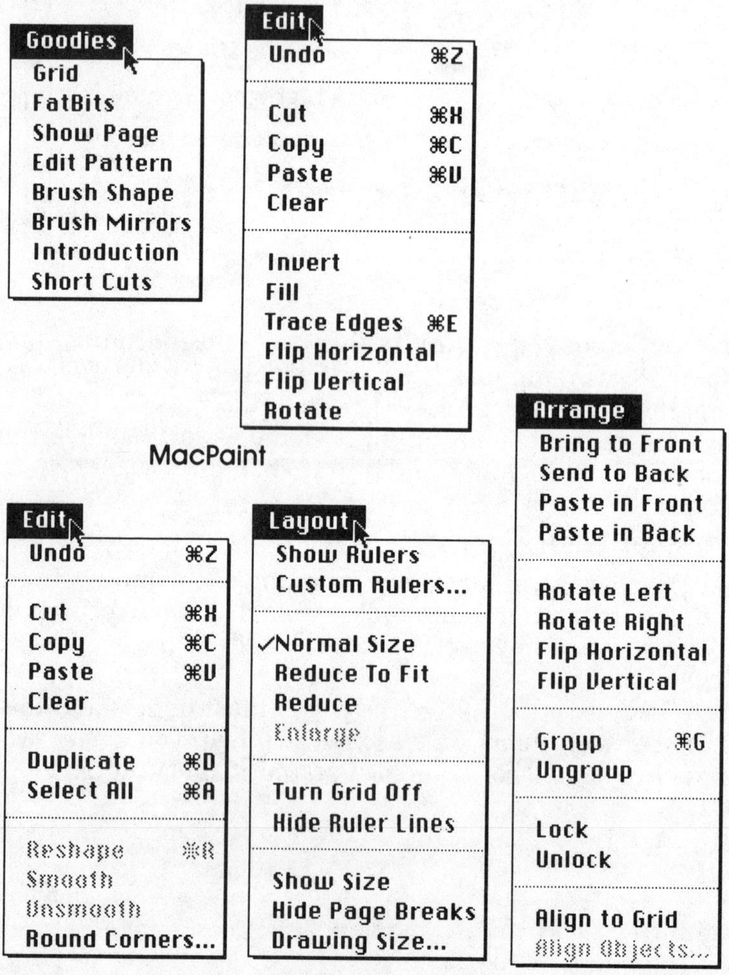

MacDraw

Chapter 2

The Treatment of Forms

Once you understand how MacPaint and MacDraw differ in the way they remember forms, their advantages and disadvantages will become clearer. If you know the strengths and weaknesses of the programs, you'll be better able to decide when to use each one.

MacPaint remembers forms as a bunch of pixels, or dots. It doesn't keep track of a circle as a round shape—it just remembers the entire page as a group of pixels, each being either on (set to black) or off (set to white). The fact that some of the pixels describe a circle has no significance to MacPaint. Though it gives you the tools to draw geometric shapes, such as circles and rectangles, once it has drawn a shape, MacPaint loses the memory of the shape in a forest of dots. The circle is no longer remembered as a distinct, independent object.

If you want to move, erase, copy, or stretch your circle, you must first tell MacPaint to set the circle apart from all the other shapes on the page. You do this by using either the dotted rectangle (called the *marquee* from now on) or the lasso to separate the shape from the rest of the pixels. Sometimes this can be difficult, even impossible.

What if there's a filled rectangle with a filled circle sitting on top of it? To move the circle off the rectangle with MacPaint, you have to wrap the lasso tightly around the circle freehand, without any tools to guide your wandering hand. Then when you move the circle away from the rectangle, the rectangle has a hole in it—its integrity as a rectangular shape is destroyed. The whole process isn't very efficient.

Figure 2-35. Separating Forms with MacPaint

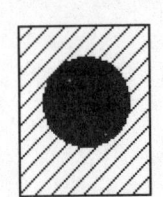

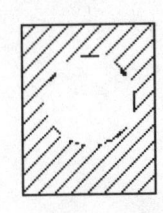

Unlike MacPaint, MacDraw keeps track of the shapes you draw as distinct and independent objects. MacDraw is an object-oriented graphics editor. When you finish drawing a circle, you'll see eight small black squares, or handles, around it. They tell you that the object is currently selected. If you draw a filled rectangle

47

Chapter 2

and then draw a circle on top of it, you can select either the circle *or* the rectangle by simply clicking on it. The handles reappear and you can drag them to stretch or shrink your selected shape. You can move a selected shape to a new position by dragging it, without dragging one of its handles. If you move the circle off the rectangle, for instance, the rectangle remains intact.

Figure 2-36. Separating Forms with MacDraw

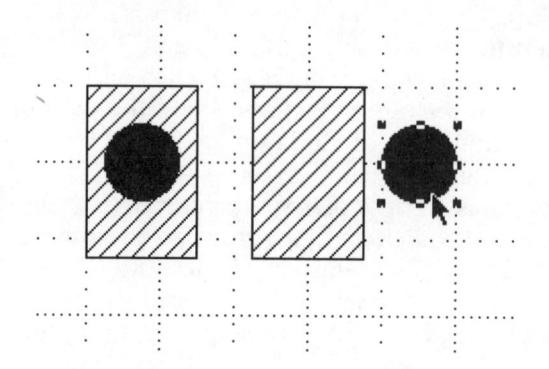

With MacDraw, you can make the circle disappear behind the rectangle by selecting the circle (clicking on it) and choosing *Send to Back* from the *Arrange* menu.

Figure 2-37. The Circle Behind

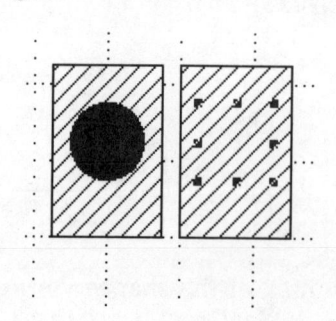

Since the handles remain in the rectangle, you know that the circle is still there, even though you can't see it. If you click on

Chapter 2

the rectangle and move it away, the circle will reappear. Thus, MacDraw gives you the freedom to create and reorganize many overlapping forms.

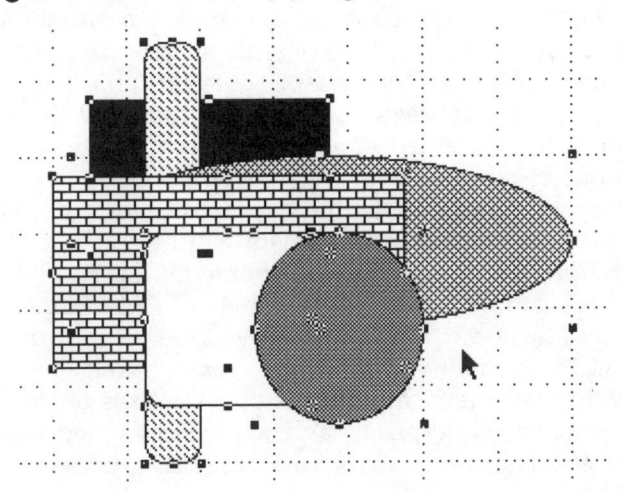

Figure 2-38. Overlapping Forms

MacDraw always keeps track of every object you draw. You can modify the position of an object not only on the two-dimensional drawing surface, but also in the third dimension, manipulating its place within a stack of other forms.

An analogy might help you to understand these differences better. While using MacPaint is like finger painting, using MacDraw is like working with templates. With MacPaint you have the freedom to paint or draw any design you want. With MacDraw you have the tools to create individual shapes like circles and rectangles, which you can put together to form larger constructions.

Differences in Tools

With MacPaint you can draw freehand drawings. You have direct control over each pixel in an 8 × 10 inch picture frame. Since it isn't trying to keep track of each form you draw, MacPaint gives you the freedom to create shapes of any sort, from individual dots to complex patterns, anywhere on the page.

Tools such as *FatBits* and the eraser help you control the details of your drawings. MacPaint can let you do this because the

49

Chapter 2

entire page is *bitmapped,* or remembered as a matrix of pixels. On the other hand, MacDraw lets you draw geometric shapes that can be moved, copied, stretched, or shrunk at any time after they're created. But you can't erase part of a MacDraw shape once it's been placed. (Except immediately after creating it by using *Undo* from the *Edit* menu.) Why not? Because MacDraw can remember forms only as distinct and complete geometric shapes. You can change the size and proportion of a shape, but you can't tell MacDraw to forget part of it. Features such as *FatBits* and the eraser are absent from MacDraw—they contradict the logic of MacDraw as an object-oriented drawing program.

There are other MacPaint tools that counter the logic of MacDraw. Since it's object-oriented, MacDraw can't give you the liberty of creating groups of dots outside geometric forms. The spray-can tool, for example, which is available with MacPaint, cannot be used by MacDraw. MacPaint lets you create your own patterns, but MacDraw limits you to 36 patterns, without giving you the freedom to alter them. MacPaint's pencil makes black lines when you start on white pixels, and white lines when you start on black pixels. This won't work with MacDraw, because it can't be told to forget part of a form.

MacDraw does provide *some* drawing freedom. If you want to draw freehand forms, use the freehand tool. True to form, MacDraw even remembers the shape you created with this tool. Each time you stop a freehand drawing, eight handles appear around your shape.

Figure 2-39. A Freehand Shape

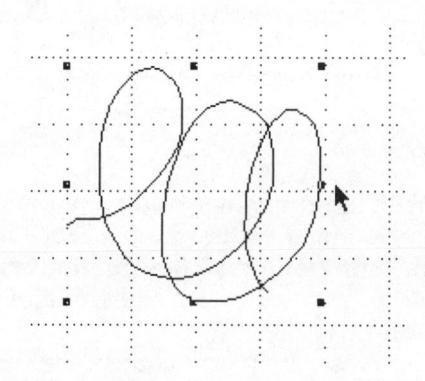

Chapter 2

You can select your freehand shape at any time to move, stretch, or shrink it. Erasing part of a freehand drawing, though, is not a feature of MacDraw.

MacDraw provides an arc-drawing feature not found in MacPaint. It helps you draw portions of circles and ellipses. You can even choose *Reshape Arc* from the *Edit* menu to make a selected arc longer until eventually the entire circle is drawn.

Figure 2-40. Altering the Shape of an Arc

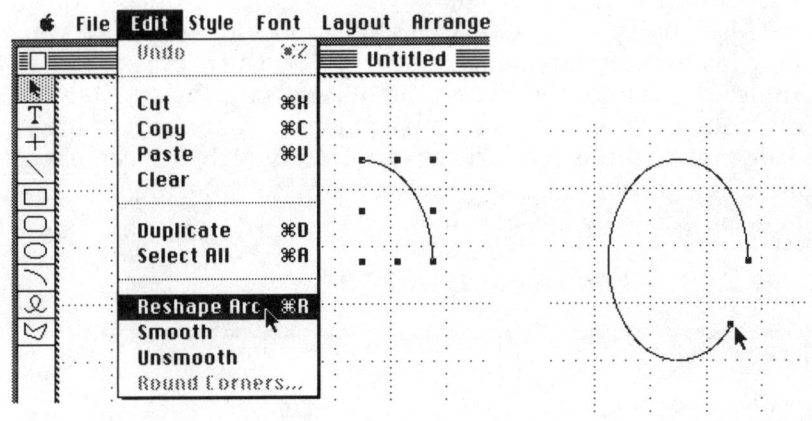

If you want to create thumbnail sketches, logos, or pictures that include nongeometric shapes, use MacPaint. If it's important to be able to create forms that can be moved independently of each other—to create floor plans, mechanical drawings, or flow charts—use MacDraw.

Organizing Objects

Group and *Ungroup* are two options in MacDraw's *Arrange* menu that make it easy for you to override the program's belief that all shapes are independent. Select two or more forms by Shift-clicking or by dragging a selection rectangle to surround them. Choose *Group* to make these elements act as one form. Using *Group* is like taping several pieces of a drawing together to make one larger drawing. It allows you to move the combined forms together from place to place.

(In contrast, all items that make up a MacPaint drawing are always grouped until you separate one element with the lasso or marquee.)

51

Chapter 2

If you want to create overlapping forms precisely arranged, or if you want to be able to move your forms after creating them, use MacDraw.

Like MacPaint's *Grid* feature, MacDraw's *Align to Grid* option from the *Arrange* menu helps you align your objects to the smallest unit of your ruler. When this feature is turned on, objects move in jerky increments equal to the smallest unit of your scale. MacPaint's *Grid* option is more limited than MacDraw's *Align to Grid*. MacPaint's *Grid* cannot be customized—it always aligns objects to an invisible grid made up of 8 × 8 pixel units.

MacDraw provides another alignment tool as well. If you want to align the top edges of several MacDraw objects, for example, you can first surround the objects with the selection rectangle and then choose the *Align Objects* option from the *Arrange* menu. You'll see a dialog box from which you can choose one of six ways of aligning the shapes. You can choose to align their top edges by clicking *Tops*.

Figure 2-41. *Align Objects* **Dialog Box**

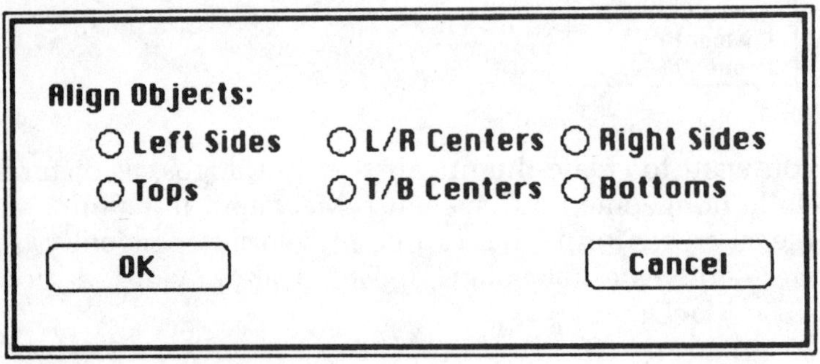

```
┌─────────────────────────────────────────────┐
│  Align Objects:                             │
│     ○ Left Sides    ○ L/R Centers  ○ Right Sides │
│     ○ Tops          ○ T/B Centers  ○ Bottoms     │
│   ┌──────────┐                  ┌──────────┐  │
│   │    OK    │                  │  Cancel  │  │
│   └──────────┘                  └──────────┘  │
└─────────────────────────────────────────────┘
```

Windows and Drawing Sizes

Since MacDraw has to remember only shapes and their orientations, it requires much less memory space to store pictures than MacPaint does. Bitmapped pictures use up a lot of memory, because whether an area of the page has drawings in it or not, all the page's dots still have to be stored. A drawing of a one-inch circle, stored on disk as a MacPaint document, takes up about 452 bytes of memory space. In contrast, a MacDraw document containing the same one-inch circle takes up about 28 bytes of memory space—1/18 the memory used by MacPaint!

Chapter 2

This accounts for two differences in what these programs can do.

- You can have up to four MacDraw documents open at one time as overlapping windows on the screen. This lets you cut and paste among as many as four illustrations without having to close one window before opening a second. MacPaint can afford to show you only one window at a time.
- MacDraw's efficient handling of disk space lets you work on as many as sixty 8 × 10 inch pages. You can thus create drawings ranging in size from 8 × 10 inches to 4 × 8 feet. You can use *Drawing Size* from the *Layout* menu to choose the size you want.

Figure 2-42. *Drawing Size* **Dialog Box**

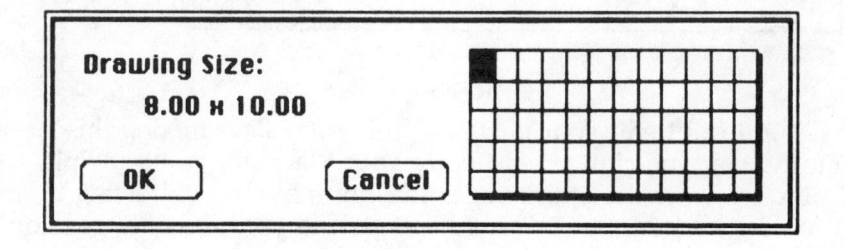

```
Drawing Size:
   8.00 H 10.00
   [ OK ]      [ Cancel ]
```

A large drawing made with MacDraw is printed out as several 8 × 10 inch sheets that you can tape together.

Dealing with the Whole Drawing

MacPaint and MacDraw handle the relationship between the screen window size and the total picture size in different ways. MacPaint's window is only part of an 8 × 10 inch page. This full page contains a little more space than four MacPaint windows. To view other parts of a MacPaint page, select the hand tool and drag the page. It's like moving a piece of paper on your desk while looking at it through a small window. If you want to see the entire page, double-click the hand icon, or choose *Show Page* from the *Goodies* menu. This way you can see the whole page as it will look when it's printed.

Chapter 2

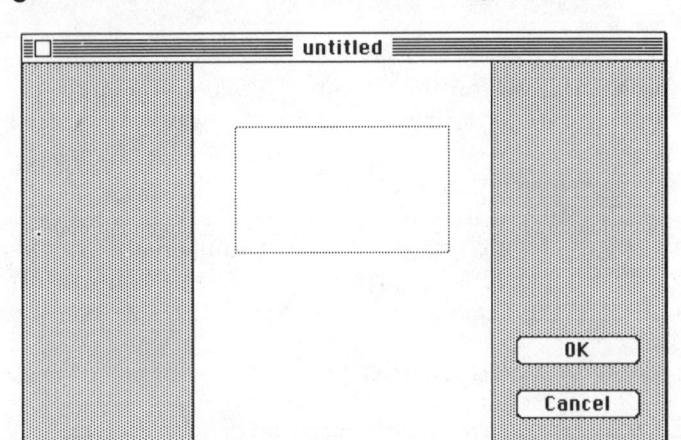

Figure 2-43. MacPaint's *Show Page* Screen

You can't edit your picture in this *Show Page* mode. This means that you can never modify your MacPaint picture while you're viewing the entire page. You can move your drawing in *Show Page* mode, but be careful—if part of your drawing goes off the edge of the desk and you click *OK*, you'll lose that part of it. It's like sliding a piece of paper around on your desk; but when something falls off the MacPaint desk, it falls into a black hole and is lost forever unless you click *Cancel*.

MacDraw's screen window is only a little larger than MacPaint's. To see more of the complete MacDraw page, use the scroll bars to move your drawing either horizontally or vertically. To view your entire drawing, choose *Reduce to Fit* from the *Layout* menu. This reduces the entire drawing, allowing you to see the whole picture, whether it's 8 × 10 inches, 4 × 10 feet, or some intermediate size.

One of MacDraw's most attractive features is that it allows you to modify your drawing in the reduced mode. When you're in this mode, you can do everything you can in normal mode. You can click on individual objects, move them, and even change their shape by dragging handles. You can add new forms by using the standard tools. You can, for example, draw a circle spanning four 8 × 10 inch sheets. This feature is particularly stunning.

The *Reduce* option in the *Layout* menu shrinks your picture by 50 percent. You can repeatedly use this feature to reduce a draw-

Chapter 2

ing by 50 percent each time it's called, to make the entire drawing visible within the window, for instance. Conversely, *Enlarge* lets you expand your reduced picture in 50 percent enlargements until it's back to normal size. (It's not possible to blow up a normal-size drawing with MacDraw.)

If large drawings are important for your projects, use MacDraw.

Figure 2-44. MacDraw's *Reduce to Fit* **Screen**

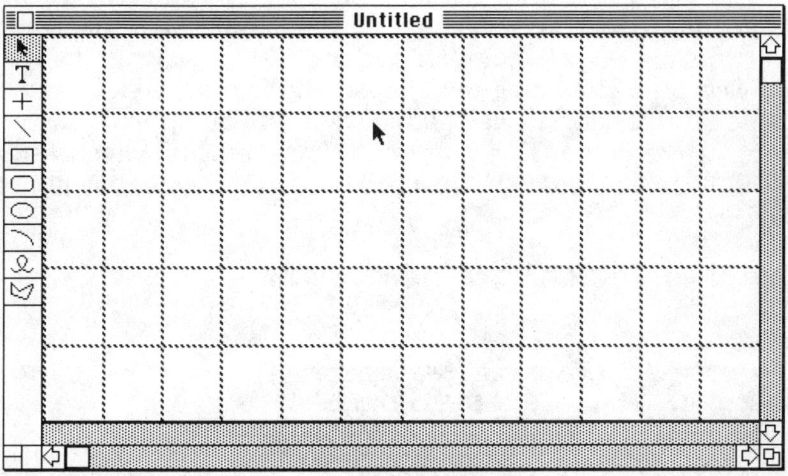

Drawing to Scale

As you saw when you created the dresser, MacDraw lets you draw to scale. The *Custom Rulers* option from the *Layout* menu helps customize the divisions of the rulers you see on the screen. If size relationships are important for your illustrations, use MacDraw. Architects, interior designers, technical illustrators, and product designers will all be delighted when they use MacDraw for scale drawings.

To make it easy for you to neatly organize the drawing's elements, MacDraw provides a screen grid of vertical and horizontal dotted lines. When you print your drawing, the grid lines will not appear on paper. This grid is marked out in major and minor units that you can customize with the *Custom Rulers* dialog box.

MacDraw makes it even easier to draw forms to precise dimensions. When you choose *Show Size* from the *Layout* menu,

Chapter 2

MacDraw indicates the dimensions of the shapes as you draw; the dimension numbers change as you change the size of the object. Even after you've drawn a shape, *Show Size* will tell you its dimensions when you click on it. And when you stretch or shrink a shape, its changing dimensions are displayed as you drag a handle. This makes it very easy to draw shapes to specific dimensions.

Changing the Size of Objects

Since MacDraw remembers the basic shapes, it can help you alter them after they're drawn. Dragging the handles of a shape alters it. If you want to make a filled rectangle twice as long, first turn on *Show Size*. Then drag the middle handle on one side of the shape. The rectangle's new dimensions will be displayed as you elongate the figure. This way, you'll know exactly when to stop to get the size you want. The pattern inside the rectangle will not be affected.

Figure 2-45. Stretching with MacDraw

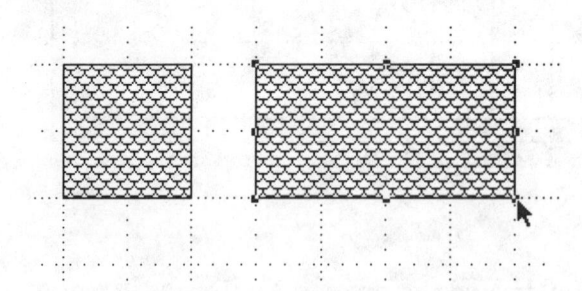

MacPaint also lets you change the size of any form you select with the marquee. You can stretch or shrink the form horizontally or vertically by dragging the shape with the Command key held down. To stretch or shrink without changing the proportions of the selected form, hold down Shift *and* the Command key. Unfortunately, MacPaint also changes the character of the lines and patterns as it stretches or shrinks the shapes.

Chapter 2

Figure 2-46. Stretching with MacPaint

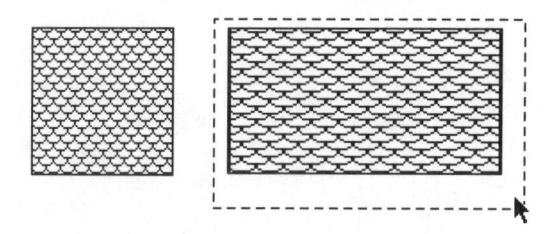

In Chapter 4 you'll learn a technique for stretching pattern-filled shapes with MacPaint without altering the structure of the pattern.

The *Edit* menu of MacDraw allows you to select *Reshape Arc, Reshape Polygon, Smooth, Unsmooth,* and *Round Corners* for even more control over the shapes of drawn forms.

Compare and Contrast

MacPaint gives you more control over each detail of your picture than MacDraw does. With MacPaint you can create complex, free-hand forms and you can decide exactly what each will look like. The thousands of pixels which make up a MacPaint drawing allow you to do this. MacDraw, however, draws picture elements that you can fit together to make even larger shapes. But MacDraw has limitations—you don't have the ability to manipulate the drawing's individual pixels.

Each MacPaint drawing can be up to 8 × 10 inches. MacDraw offers you picture sizes up to 4 × 8 feet.

MacDraw gives you very sophisticated tools for creating and organizing a variety of shapes. You can't control your MacDraw picture on a dot-by-dot basis, but if this is important, you can transfer a MacDraw picture to MacPaint for enhancements. MacDraw has the tools you need to create involved geometric shapes—designs, floor plans, technical illustrations, and mechanical illustrations—which need to be drawn to scale.

MacPaint has the tools which artists, cartoonists, and doodlers need. It can even be used to enhance designs prepared with MacDraw. Both kinds of drawing tools are necessary to give you maximum flexibility in developing visual material.

The next chapter will show you just how flexible MacPaint and MacDraw can be when they're used together.

Chapter 3
Moving Data Between and Within Applications

Chapter 3

Moving Data Between and Within Applications

A unique feature of MacPaint, MacDraw, and MacWrite is that they can share information. This is one of the Macintosh's most powerful capabilities. You can take a technical drawing from MacDraw, touch it up in MacPaint, and then paste it into a MacWrite document. Or you can produce text with MacWrite and paste it into MacPaint or MacDraw documents. This lets you use the unique attributes of more than one program as you're creating a picture.

You may also want to move information between documents of the same application. This is a simple procedure, requiring fewer steps than the transfer of information between applications.

The Clipboard and Scrapbook give you this ability to transfer data between application programs. *Copy, Cut,* and *Paste,* from the *Edit* menu, are the tools you'll use. In this chapter, step-by-step instructions will show you how to:

- Transfer a picture from MacPaint to MacWrite
- Transfer a picture from MacDraw to MacWrite
- Transfer a picture from MacDraw to MacPaint
- Transfer a large MacPaint drawing from one MacPaint document to another

No Limitations

At press time, Apple announced that MacDraw will have the ability to accept drawings created with MacPaint. This is a change from previous versions of the program, which did not allow such sharing. Now, however, MacDraw has been enhanced so that it can take bit-mapped images from MacPaint, and alter them with any of its tools. This is a major modification.

It *is* possible to move data from MacWrite to MacDraw using the Clipboard. It's unlikely, however, that you'll ever do this because MacDraw has an advanced text editor built into it. Chapter 5 will show you how to use MacDraw to create text for a variety of purposes.

The Clipboard

The Clipboard provides a temporary storage space within the Macintosh's RAM. It can hold only one piece of information at a time. Any time you *Cut* or *Copy* a selected item, it goes into the

Chapter 3

Clipboard. When you do this, whatever was in the Clipboard from an earlier *Cut* or *Copy* is lost. If you want to remove a selected picture element from a document without losing the item presently in the Clipboard, choose *Clear* from the *Edit* menu, or press Backspace.

Remember, both *Clear* and Backspace delete a selected item without placing it in the Clipboard. If you decide you want these elements back, and assuming you haven't done anything else, you can recover them by choosing *Undo* from the *Edit* menu.

The Clipboard can also be used to transfer data between programs. If you quit a program after placing an item in the Clipboard with *Cut* or *Copy*, the item remains in the Clipboard even after a second application is opened. *You lose the Clipboard item only if you turn the computer off, since it isn't stored on disk.* After opening the second application, you can choose the *Paste* command from the *Edit* menu to take the item in the Clipboard and place it into a document generated by the second application.

Viewing the Clipboard. You can view the contents of the Clipboard at any time by choosing the *Show Clipboard* command from the *File* menu (*MacPaint* does not have this feature).

Figure 3-1. Show Clipboard

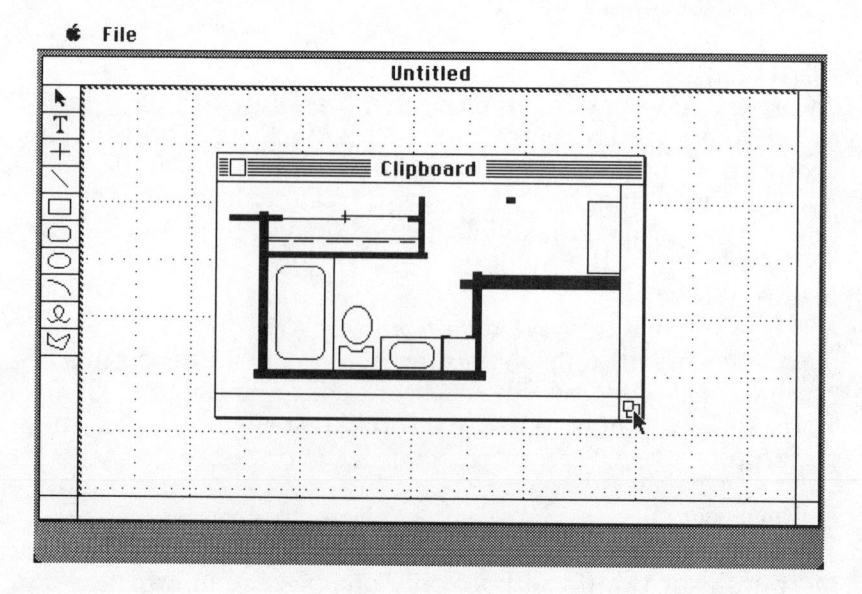

Chapter 3

The lasso and marquee. If you use the lasso tool to select the picture before you copy it to the Clipboard, the pasted picture will appear with the lasso still around it. You can now move it to the desired position. If you use the marquee tool to select the picture, it will be pasted with a marquee around it. A pasted item always appears in the middle of the application window surrounded by the same tool with which it was originally selected.

The Scrapbook

What if you want to move several items to a second application? What if you want to use *Copy* or *Cut* without losing the item in the Clipboard? What if you want to retain what's in the Clipboard so you can paste it into your drawings tomorrow or next week? The answer to all these questions is to use the Scrapbook.

The Clipboard versus the Scrapbook. There are two major differences between the Scrapbook and the Clipboard. First, Scrapbook items are stored on disk, not in RAM. That makes the Scrapbook a permanent storage place. Whatever is pasted into the Scrapbook remains there until it's cut. Second, the Scrapbook can hold more than one item. You can store all the items that you frequently use in the Scrapbook and paste them into documents when necessary. Each application program disk has its own Scrapbook. This means that if you have separate working disks for MacPaint, MacDraw, and MacWrite, you can have a unique Scrapbook for each.

The lasso and marquee. To paste an item into the Scrapbook, it must first be put into the Clipboard by a *Cut* or *Copy*. The lasso and marquee have the same effect on items pasted into the Scrapbook as they do when using the Clipboard. If the lasso was used to select the picture, the picture in the Scrapbook is remembered as chosen by the lasso. When this item is copied from the Scrapbook and pasted into a MacPaint document, it appears in the middle of the window with a lasso around it. If the marquee was used to select a picture that went into the Scrapbook, the marquee shows when the picture is cut and then pasted into a document. Of course, you can remove the lasso or marquee simply by pressing the mouse button when the pointer is outside the tool's boundaries.

You're Ready to Start

In this chapter, you'll combine the logo, dresser design, and advertising copy you created in Chapter 2 to form an advertising

63

Chapter 3

flyer as a MacWrite document. Follow the step-by-step instructions. The process may seem somewhat complicated at first, but the Mac makes it easy. After you complete the advertising flyer, you'll transfer a picture from MacDraw to MacPaint so that you can use the latter's features to complete it. When finished, your flyer will look like this:

Figure 3-2. The Finished Flyer

M & W DESIGNS ANNOUNCES

ART SPACE FURNITURE

A Revolution in Furniture Design

- award-winning designs
- durable
- easy to clean
- space-saving
- low prices
- entire suites
- high resale value
- guaranteed quality

Call now: 123-4567

64

Moving Data from MacPaint to MacWrite

Follow these steps to transfer the logo you drew in Chapter 2 to the advertising copy you created with MacWrite. If you don't have an external drive, you'll have to perform several disk swaps to carry out these operations.

Open the logo document. Insert your MacPaint working disk—it contains the logo you prepared in Chapter 2. Open the disk window if it isn't already open and click twice on the logo document icon. The logo should now be on the screen.

Copy the logo into the Clipboard. Select the logo with the lasso. Choose *Copy* from the *Edit* menu to put the logo in the Clipboard. You can't see the Clipboard, but the logo is there.

Open the ad copy document. To exit MacPaint and return to the desktop, choose *Quit* from the *File* menu. After the disk window appears, again choose the *File* menu, this time selecting the *Eject* option. The MacPaint disk will pop out of the drive. Insert your MacWrite working disk. If the disk's window isn't open, double-click the disk icon. Double-click the MacWrite document icon that contains the ad copy you created in Chapter 2. After a couple of disk swaps, the ad copy displays on the screen.

Paste the logo into the ad copy. Make sure that the insertion line is at the top left part of the ad copy document. (You can move it to this location from wherever it was last by placing the pointer at the top left of the window and clicking once.) The logo now in the Clipboard is to be pasted above this line of text. Choose *Paste* from the *Edit* menu to insert the logo. As if by magic, the logo appears and the text moves down.

Center the logo. But the logo is on the left side of the document. How can you center it? It's easy. Click on the logo to select it. You'll see handles at the lower edge of the logo. These handles let you know that the logo is selected. Drag the right or left edge of the logo (not one of the handles) to the right until it's centered. Click outside the logo to unselect it. Now your ad copy document has the logo centered at the top.

Save. Choose *Save* from the *File* menu to record the changes you made to the MacWrite document.

Chapter 3

Figure 3-3. Centering the Logo in MacWrite

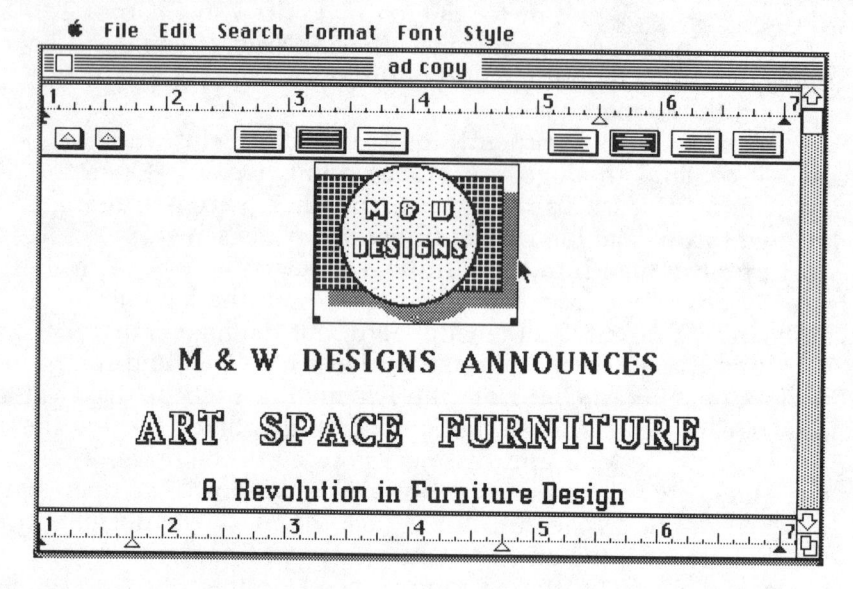

Moving Data from MacDraw to MacWrite

The steps described below will help you transfer the dresser you drew in Chapter 2 into the MacWrite advertising copy document which now contains the logo.

Open the dresser document. Quit the current application, eject the disk, and reset the Macintosh by turning it off, then back on. Insert your MacDraw working disk and open its window. The dresser design you created in Chapter 2 should be on this disk. Click twice on the dresser document's icon. When the dresser appears on the screen, you're ready to put it into the Clipboard.

Copy the dresser into the Clipboard. Choose *Select All* from the *Edit* menu. Handles will appear on the dresser drawing to indicate it's selected. Choose *Copy* from the *Edit* menu to put the dresser into the Clipboard. To confirm that the dresser is there, choose *Show Clipboard* from the *File* menu. When the Clipboard appears, you can move it from place to place by dragging the title bar. You can also use the size box at the lower right side of the Clipboard to modify its size to show more or less of the drawing. Click on the Clipboard's close box at the top left to put it away.

Chapter 3

Open the ad copy document. Now that the dresser is in the Clipboard, you're ready to paste it into the ad copy. Choose *Quit* from the *File* menu to return to the desktop. Eject the MacDraw disk and insert your MacWrite disk. Click twice on the advertising copy document. After a few disk swaps, the ad will appear on the screen, complete with both text and the logo you earlier inserted.

Paste the dresser into the ad copy. If necessary, scroll down by clicking the down scroll arrow until you see the words *A Revolution in Furniture Design*. Click to place the insertion point at the beginning of the next line. Choose *Paste* from the *Edit* menu to insert the dresser into the text. Again, computer magic makes the dresser appear at the left margin of the document.

Center the dresser. You can center the dresser just as you did the logo. Click on the dresser to select it and drag it to the right until it's centered.

Figure 3-4. Centering the Dresser in MacWrite

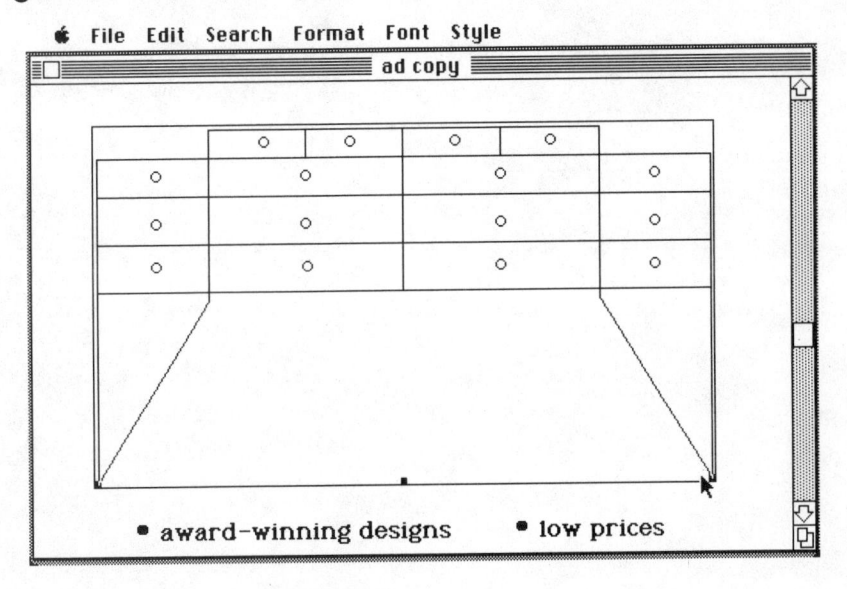

Save it. Choose *Save* from the *File* menu to record the completed advertising flyer.

Print it. Print the flyer, using *Print* from the *File* menu so that you have a hard copy of it.

67

Chapter 3

Moving Data from MacDraw to MacPaint

On some occasions, you may want to draw something to scale in MacDraw and then enhance it with MacPaint. Since MacDraw doesn't offer tools for adding shading to create a sense of volume, for example, you could transfer your MacDraw illustration to MacPaint and then add shading with the spray-can tool. Try this example.

Copy from MacDraw. Choose a drawing from an open MacDraw document with the marquee.

Figure 3-5. Select from MacDraw

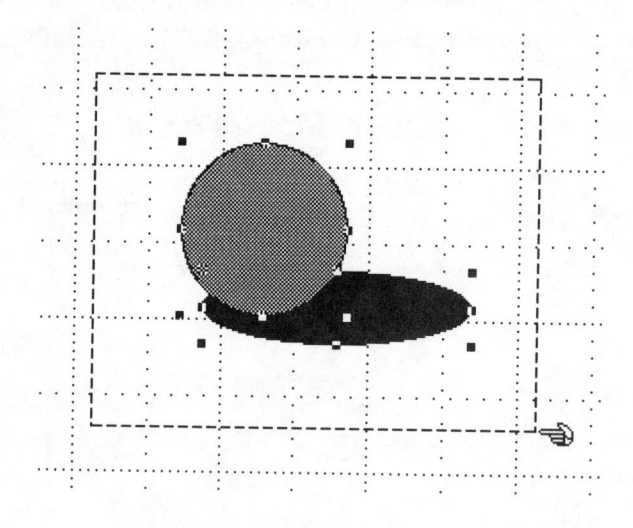

Chapter 3

Choose *Copy* from the *Edit* menu to put your selection into the Clipboard.

Figure 3-6. Copying into the Clipboard

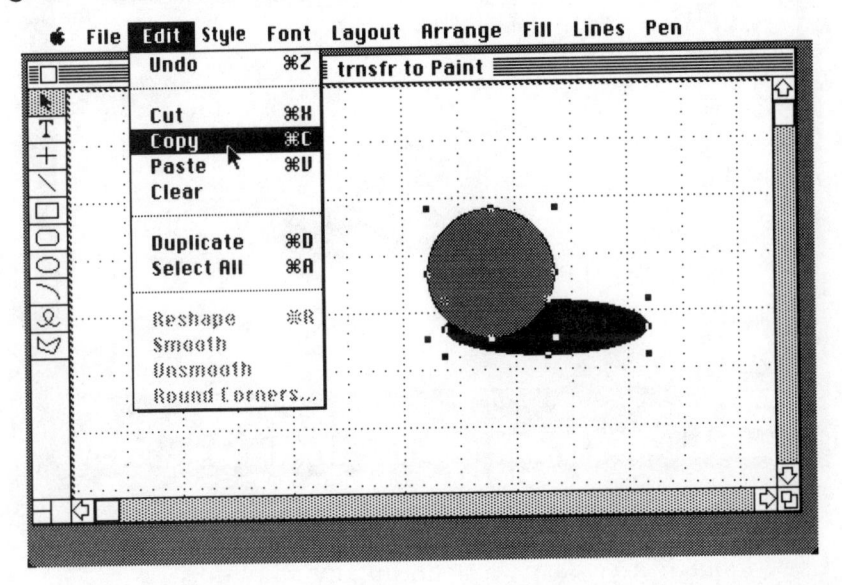

Open a MacPaint document. Choose *Quit* from the *File* menu to return to the desktop. Eject the MacDraw disk and insert MacPaint. Open the MacPaint window.

Paste it. Choose *Paste* from the *Edit* menu to insert the item from the Clipboard into your MacPaint document.

Touch it up. Click the spray-can icon and do the shading. See if you can get a similar effect to that shown in Figure 3-7.

Chapter 3

Figure 3-7. Enhancing with MacPaint

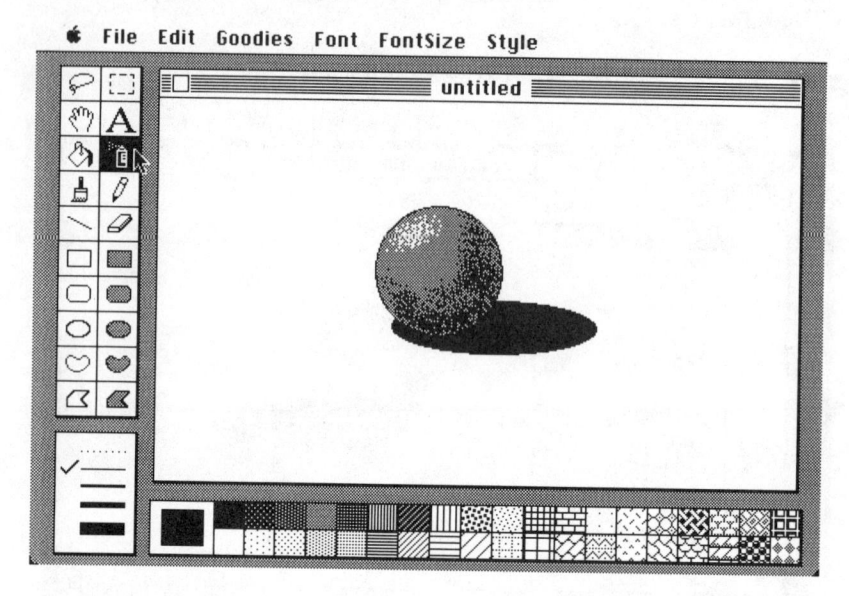

Use *FatBits*, if necessary, to clean up any stray dots.

Save it. Choose *Save As* from the *File* menu to name and record the changes as a MacPaint document.

Moving Data Between Documents of One Application

You can also use the Clipboard to transfer data between documents generated by a single application. A portion of a picture from one MacPaint document can be moved to another MacPaint document via the Clipboard. Copy the selected picture into the Clipboard and put away the first document. Open the second document and paste the Clipboard picture where you want it. This procedure can help you combine several visual or verbal documents into a larger one.

Moving Large MacPaint Drawings

To move a MacPaint picture that's larger than the size of the window, you can use the Scrapbook to temporarily store segments of the picture, and then paste these into a second document. Use *Cut* instead of *Copy* to put selected sections into the Clipboard before pasting them into the Scrapbook. This makes it easier to see what

Chapter 3

sections have already been moved. Try these steps with one of your own large drawings.

Open the document. Click twice on the document icon which contains a drawing larger than a MacPaint window.

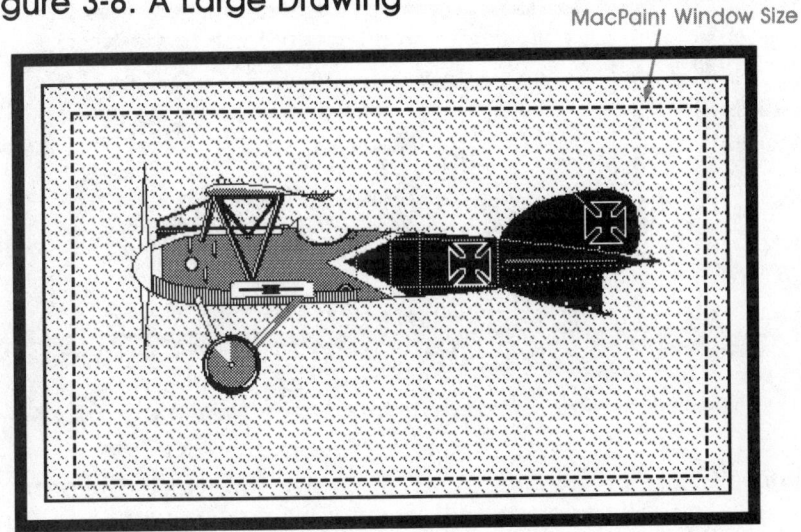

Figure 3-8. A Large Drawing

MacPaint Window Size

Cut one part. Use the hand tool to move your drawing so that the top left part is visible in the window. Double-click the marquee to select the entire window.

71

Chapter 3

Figure 3-9. The Window Selected

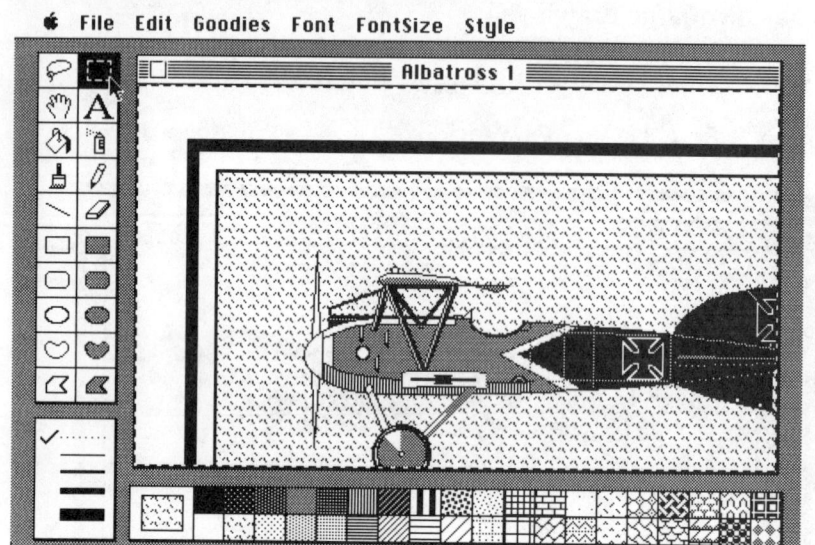

Choose *Cut* from the *Edit* menu to remove the selected item from the drawing. The window will become blank. The window's contents are now in the Clipboard. If you view the entire drawing by double-clicking the hand icon to enter *Show Page* mode, you'll see a rectangular piece missing from your drawing, just as is the case with the picture in Figure 3-10.

Figure 3-10. *Show Page* **with Window Cut**

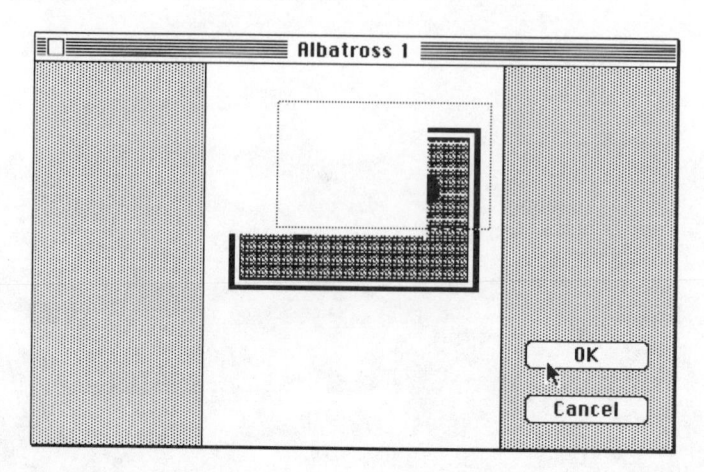

Chapter 3

Paste into the Scrapbook. Choose Scrapbook from the Apple menu, then *Paste* from the *Edit* menu to put the first part of the large picture into the Scrapbook.

Cut a second part. Use the hand tool to get another part of the large drawing into view in the window. Use the lasso to select it.

Figure 3-11. Lasso Remaining Part

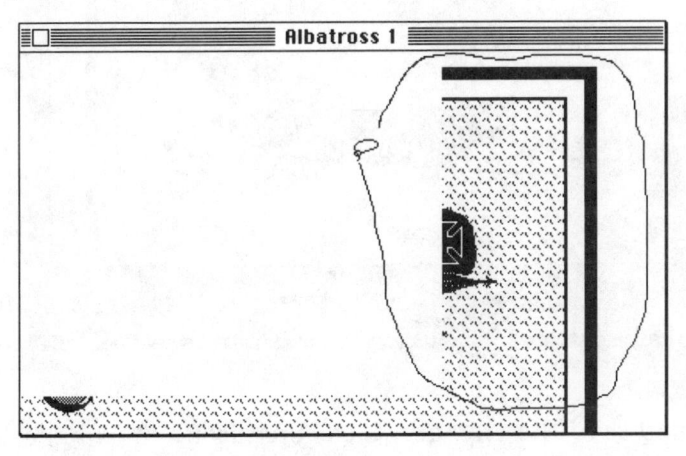

Choose *Cut* from the *Edit* menu.

Paste into the Scrapbook. Paste this second segment of the large drawing into the Scrapbook.

Put the rest into the Scrapbook. Use the lasso to cut the rest of the segments of the large drawing into the Scrapbook. When you're finished, close the document without saving the changes.

Paste into the second document. Open the second document. View the Scrapbook and use the scroll bar to locate the first segment of the large drawing. Cut it from the Scrapbook, put away the Scrapbook, and paste the segment into the document. Now paste the other segments of the large drawing into your document, dragging them carefully into place.

Chapter 3

Figure 3-12. Move the Second Piece into Position

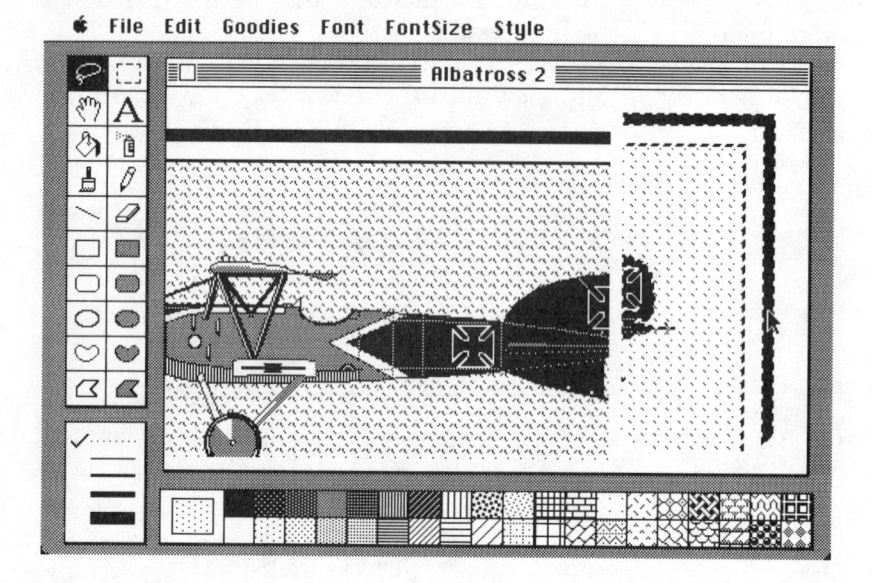

Close and save the changes. Close the second drawing, saving the changes.

With practice, you'll quickly master the process of transferring data from one document to another. Experiment, try out various tranfers—the experience will help you use the powerful features of MacPaint, MacDraw, and MacWrite for the creation of your visual designs.

Chapter 4

MacPaint Shortcuts, Tips, and Advanced Techniques

Chapter 4

MacPaint Shortcuts, Tips, and Advanced Techniques

Think of MacPaint as a picture processor—a tool that can help you develop graphics quickly and easily. Using MacPaint, you can afford to be daring with your visual experiments. If you're not happy with something you draw, you can either undo it or go back to an earlier version on disk. This flexibility lets you try things just to see what an idea looks like. You can experiment as much as you want, testing variations of a visual idea, undoing those you don't like with the touch of a key.

MacPaint puts a wide variety of features at your fingertips. Sometimes these features can give you ideas that will shape your visual creations. What will happen if I stretch this? What if I trace the edges of that? You'll discover things about MacPaint as you experiment. The best way to learn about MacPaint is through a process of intensive, creative play.

However, MacPaint has many complex, interacting features, several of which are not described in the program's manual. To take full advantage of MacPaint's powers, you must learn its hidden capabilities. Is there a shortcut for creating this detail or that complex form? Can I make this shape transparent? This chapter will help you explore the ins and outs of the electronic easel. Among other things, you'll learn how to make forms transparent or opaque, how to create hundreds of custom patterns, how to customize the size of the eraser, and how to create variously spaced multiple copies. With a little practice, the techniques described here will help you set your visual imagination free.

MacPaint Shortcuts

Getting In and Out of MacPaint

You can have the MacPaint window automatically open when you insert MacPaint as the start-up disk. Just set MacPaint as the start-up application on your working disk. (If you don't know how to do this, refer to Chapter 9.) When you insert the disk, the MacPaint window will open immediately, bypassing the desktop.

There's also a fast way of getting out of MacPaint. To leave MacPaint and open another application (such as MacDraw or MacWrite), you usually choose *Quit* from the *File* menu to return to the desktop, and then *Eject*. As a shortcut, choose *Quit* to get out of MacPaint while holding down the Command key. This

Chapter 4

closes the MacPaint window, ejects the disk(s) in the drive(s), and resets the computer. Now you're ready to start another application. When you reset the Macintosh this way, any item in the Clipboard will be lost, so don't try to use this method for transferring information between applications.

The Polygon

MacPaint's hollow polygon tool helps you create any shape made up of straight lines. With it, you can make shapes ranging from simple triangles to complex, many-sided geometric forms.

Open polygons. Choose the polygon tool and click when the mouse pointer is positioned where you want to start the shape. Stretch out a line and click each time you want to turn a corner. The polygon will stop when you click to close the figure. To create an open form, click twice to stop the feature before closing the shape.

Figure 4-1. Open Polygon

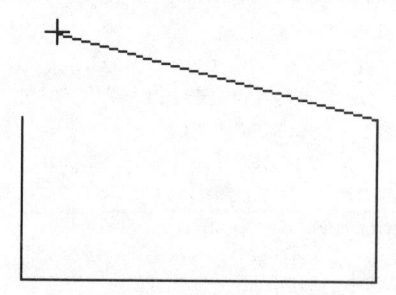

Automatically filled polygons. To create polygons filled with the current pattern, choose the filled polygon tool. Click to start the polygon and click each time you want to turn a corner. When you have only one line left to close the polygon, double-click to automatically close and fill it.

Chapter 4

Figure 4-2. Filled Polygon

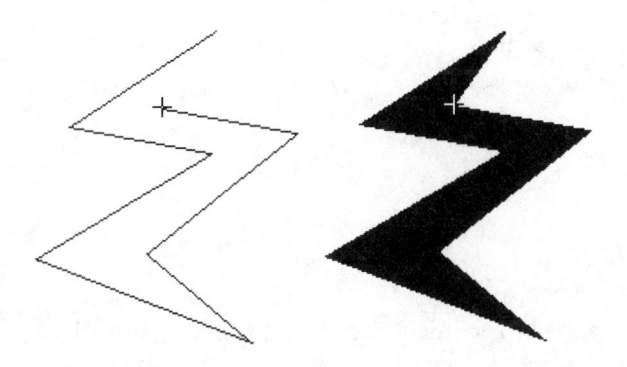

Clear Selection

You can clear part of your picture by first selecting it with the marquee or the lasso and then choosing *Clear* from the *Edit* menu to delete it. A faster way to do this is to press Backspace after making your selection. Remember, the only way to recover material deleted with *Clear* or Backspace is by choosing *Undo* from the *Edit* menu before you click somewhere else. A cleared selection does not go into the Clipboard, so it cannot be recovered by pasting it in at a later time.

A safer way to remove parts of your drawing is to select first and then choose *Cut* from the *Edit* menu. This puts the item into the Clipboard. Whatever was in the Clipboard is replaced (remember that the Clipboard can hold only one item at a time). You can retrieve the last item cut by using *Paste* from the *Edit* menu.

Undo and Redo

If you make a mistake while working on a MacPaint document, you can put it back the way it was by choosing *Undo* from the *Edit* menu, or by pressing Command-Z. An easier way to undo is to press the Tilde key (the key at the far left on the top row).

But what if you decide that what you undid wasn't so bad after all. Press the Tilde again to redo it (this is like undoing the previous undo). You can have fun with this feature by creating animation on the screen. Draw one form and then add something to it. Now you can press Tilde over and over again to simulate simple animation.

Chapter 4

Figure 4-3. Simple Animation with *Undo*

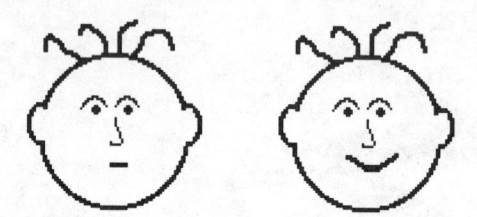

Choose Lines and Borders

To get the current pattern for lines and borders instead of black, hold down the Option key while creating a line or a shape. For example, if you want to create a rectangle thickly outlined with the current pattern, select the thick line and press Option while creating the form.

Figure 4-4. Pattern for Rectangle

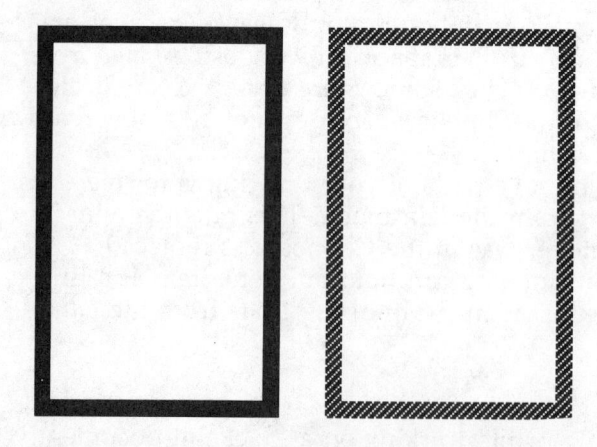

FatBits Shortcuts

FatBits lets you control each pixel which makes up your MacPaint picture—it's like working on your drawing while looking at it through a microscope. You can use all the drawing tools while in *FatBits*—lines, open and filled rectangles, circles, and polygons. You can even select parts of your drawing with the marquee and the lasso. The pencil, however, is the most useful tool for *FatBits*.

Chapter 4

If you click with the pencil on a white pixel, it turns black; if you click on a black pixel, it becomes white.

Getting in and out of *FatBits*. There's an easy way of getting into *FatBits* at precisely the part of the picture you want to edit. Move the pencil to the desired area and Command-click. Now you're in *FatBits*, ready to work on that part of your picture. To go back to your normal-sized drawing, click with any selected tool in the small window showing at the upper left, or Command-click anywhere in the *FatBits* window when the pencil is selected.

Moving around in *FatBits*. There's a shortcut for moving to a different part of your picture while in *FatBits*. With the pencil tool selected, press the Option key to get the hand tool. This is faster than pulling down a menu. Also, since you don't have to move the mouse, you keep your place. Now you can drag a different part of your picture to the *FatBits* screen. Use this method, and your speed in the *FatBits* mode will be considerably faster than before.

The Shortcuts List

A list of some of MacPaint's shortcuts is displayed on the screen when you choose *Short Cuts* from the *Goodies* menu.

Hands for Keys and Mouse

Here's a list of keys that are important for drawing with MacPaint:

Key(s)	Function
Tilde	Undo and redo the last change
Shift	Constrain lines to give right angles and lines at 45 degrees only
Option	Hand tool while in *FatBits*
	Patterned lines and borders
	Copy selected form
Command	Enter or leave *FatBits*
	Stretch selected form
Option/Command	Multiple copies of selected form

It's best to keep your left hand (or your right, if you're left-handed) poised over the left side of the keyboard. This puts the Shift, Option, Command, and Tilde keys within reach and gives you fast access to these features. You don't have to pull down menus for every operation.

81

Chapter 4

MacPaint Tips and Advanced Techniques

MacPaint puts an incredible array of tools in your hands. There are some hard-to-find capabilities that will give you even more flexibility than those described in the MacPaint manual. This section demonstrates some almost magical things you can do with MacPaint. Open the MacPaint window and try these techniques.

MacPaint Work Space

When you create pictures with MacPaint, you'll be creating forms to be duplicated, stretched, shrunken, or moved on top of other forms. You can make it much easier to organize the forms you alter and move by maintaining a work space within each picture document.

Each MacPaint document is 8 × 10 inches. This is a bit larger than the area of four MacPaint windows.

Figure 4-5. The MacPaint Page

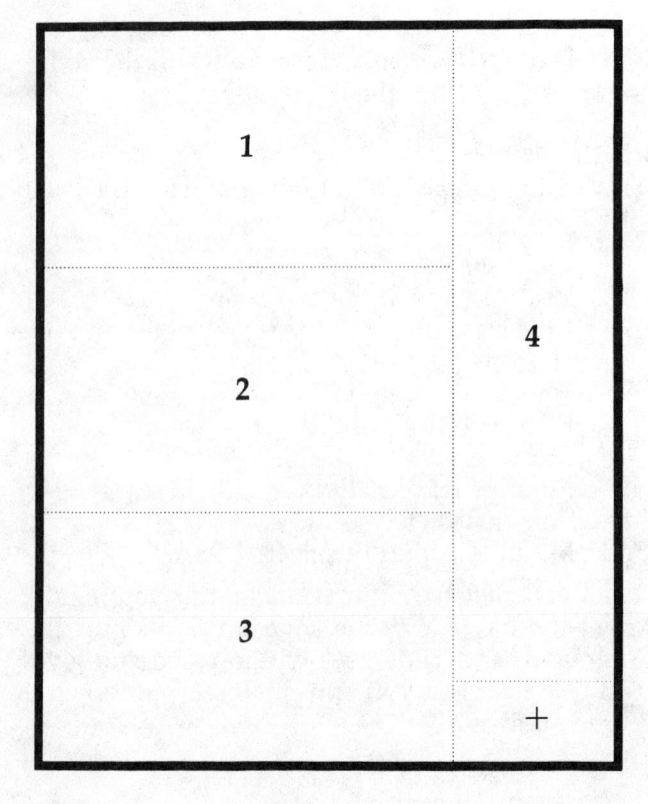

Chapter 4

Reserve some space at the bottom or at the right side of each window for your working space. Use this area to create small parts of your pictures, then move copies of them to the main picture. If something happens to the picture element you move, you'll still have a copy of it in your work space.

Advanced Uses of *Grid*

The *Grid* feature in the *Goodies* menu can be very helpful as you develop pictures. It's easy to forget to use this feature's capabilities. The MacPaint manual, for example, spends very little time on its use.

Grid **for lining up.** When you choose *Grid*, moving the mouse moves the pointer in eight-bit steps. In effect, this gives you an invisible grid on the screen.

Figure 4-6. MacPaint's Invisible Grid

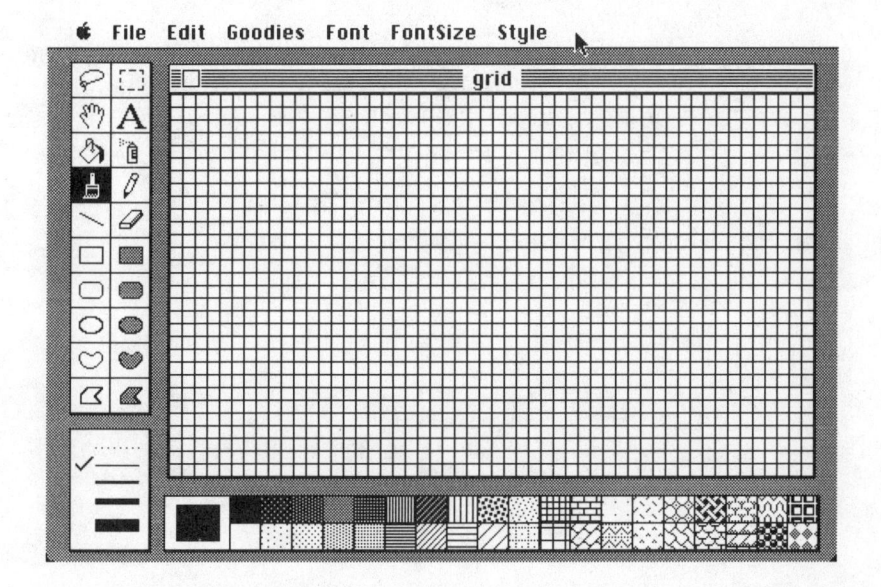

This means that you'll be able to move shapes to precise locations on the screen quickly and easily.

Let's try an example. Make sure *Grid* is off. Draw one large rectangle and then several satellite rectangles which use segments of the original's outline as common borders. Place one rectangle at a corner of the original rectangle. The drawing should look

83

Chapter 4

something like Figure 4-7. Notice how difficult it was to place the borders and corners exactly?

Now erase what's in the window by double-clicking the eraser tool. Turn *Grid* on and redraw the rectangles. See how much easier it is to place the shapes?

Figure 4-7. Rectangles

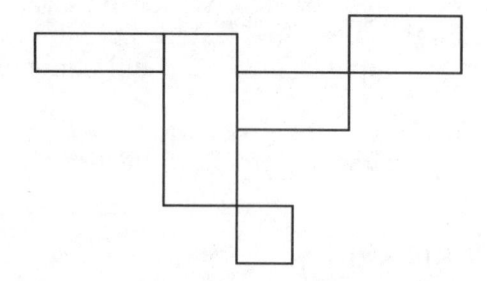

Grid also makes it easy for you to move shapes into position within a picture. With the *Grid* feature on, draw two rectangles—one large and one small, outside the first. Now lasso and move the small rectangle so that one corner touches a corner of the large rectangle.

Figure 4-8. Moving Shapes

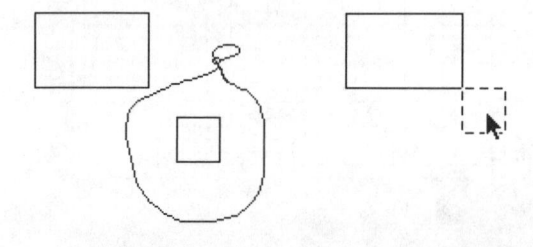

Try this without the *Grid* on, and you'll see how hard it is to get the rectangles to match up exactly. You can check to see how close you came by accessing *FatBits*. Look closely at the junction of the two rectangles. With *Grid* on, the corners will match perfectly.

***Grid* for even patterns.** You've probably noticed that forms filled with patterns sometimes look ragged at the edges. This happens when the outline of the form interrupts the pattern before

Chapter 4

it's completed. With *Grid* on, however, any shape you draw will be laid out in eight-pixel increments. Since patterns repeat in units of eight pixels, any pattern will fit exactly within the shape's perimeter. This gives you uniform edges. In Figure 4-9, the shape on the left was created with *Grid* off, while the rectangle on the right was made when *Grid* was on. See the difference?

Figure 4-9. Filled Shapes

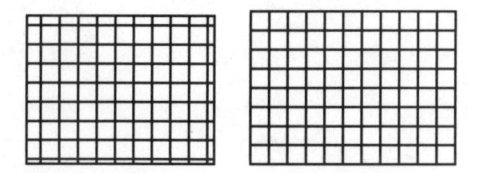

***Grid* for matching patterns.** *Grid* is most useful when you're manipulating patterned forms. With *Grid* on, you can move one patterned form on top of another (which has the same pattern) so that no seams show. Leave *Grid* off, lasso, and move one patterned shape so that it overlaps another.

Figure 4-10. Overlapping Patterns—*Grid* Off

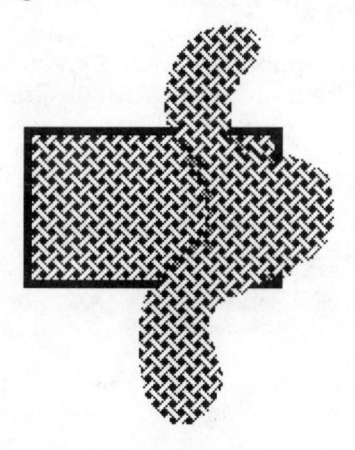

Press the Tilde key (upper left on the top row) to undo. Turn *Grid* on and try again.

85

Chapter 4

Figure 4-11. Overlapping Patterns—*Grid* On

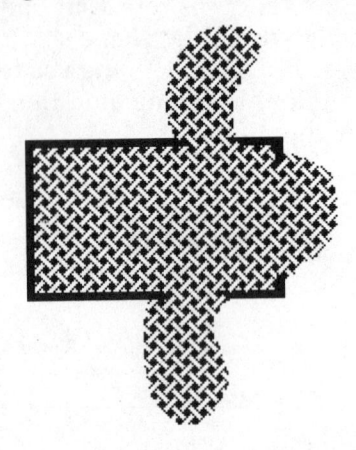

Which was easier and faster?

Grid for elongating or shortening patterned forms. Suppose you've drawn a pattern-filled shape and later decide to make it longer. With *Grid* off, select one side of the shape with the marquee. Move the mouse so the pointer appears on the area inside the marquee and press Shift-Option-Command while dragging to stretch it out. (The Shift key constrains the action so that you move only in restricted directions, and Option-Command creates multiple copies of whatever is inside the marquee.) Without *Grid*, the pattern is distorted as it's stretched.

Figure 4-12. Elongating with *Grid* Off

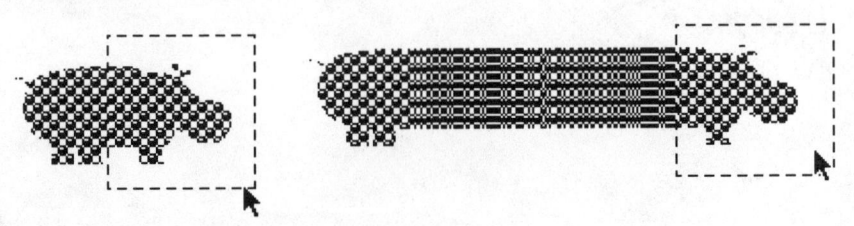

With *Grid* on, multiple copies of the pattern area are made in eight-pixel jumps, the same number that forms one pattern unit. Now the pattern is maintained as you elongate patterned forms. Undo the distorted stretch you just made, turn *Grid* on, and elongate with the mouse and Shift-Option-Command key combination. The hippo shape will appear as in Figure 4-13.

Chapter 4

Figure 4-13. Elongating with *Grid* On

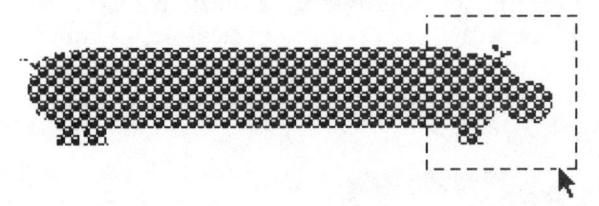

You can use the same technique to shorten your patterned forms. Leaving *Grid* on, select one part of your shape with the marquee and press Shift-Option-Command as you drag the marquee toward the interior of the shape. The pattern is not distorted.

Figure 4-14. Shortening with *Grid* On

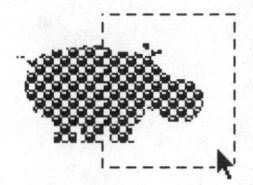

The *Trace Edges* Feature

The *Trace Edges* option in the *Edit* menu puts an outline around the contours of the part of your picture selected by the marquee.

Creating op-art effects. Select an area of a picture, perhaps one like Figure 4-15, with the marquee.

Figure 4-15. Select a Form

87

Chapter 4

Press Command-E several times to repeat tracing over and over. You can continue until the perimeter of the marquee is reached. These outlined forms look like the optical art of the sixties.

Figure 4-16. Tracing Edges

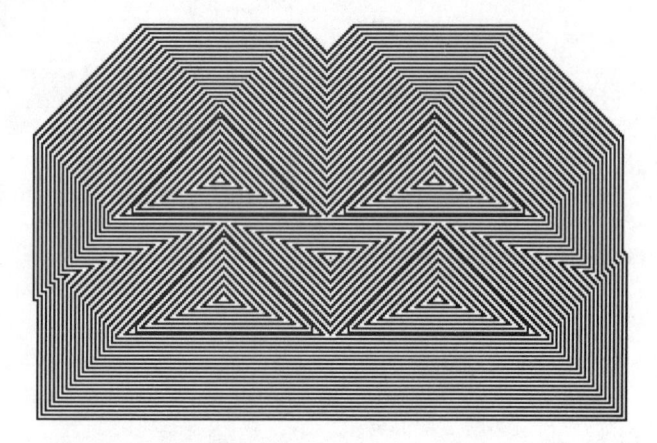

Try using the *Trace Edges* command with the Shift key to create shadowed outlines.

Figure 4-17. Shift with *Trace Edges*

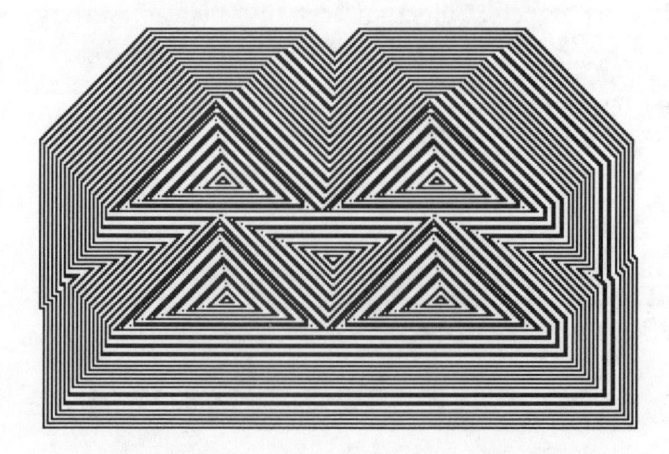

Chapter 4

Creating fancy borders. It's easy to create fancy borders with the *Trace Edges* command. Just draw the border shape, select it with the marquee, and press Command-E until you get the desired effect. (Remember, you can produce patterned borders by holding down the Option key as you create hollow shapes.)

Figure 4-18. Fancy Borders

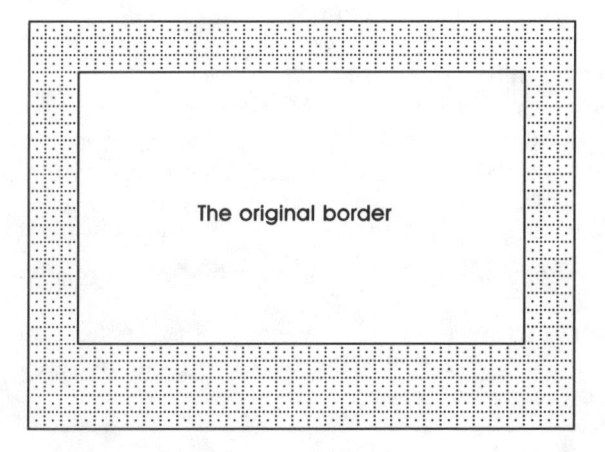

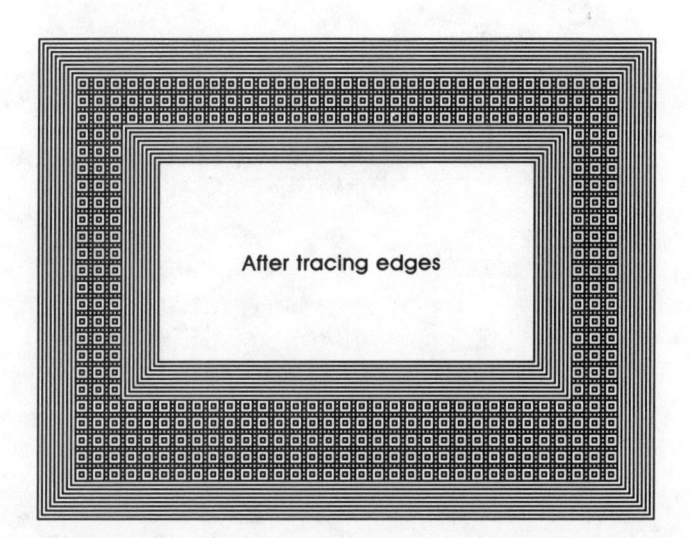

89

Chapter 4

Customizing Eraser Shapes

Have you ever wanted a small eraser so you could get into narrow spaces to clean up fine details? MacPaint provides only one eraser shape—a 16 × 16 pixel square—but you can erase with something smaller if you use a white paint brush. Double-click the paint brush and choose the shape you want. Now select white as the pattern, and paint whatever you want to erase with white. Painting with white gives you 32 new eraser shapes.

Custom Repeating Shapes

How would you create dotted lines with MacPaint? It's easy if you keep in mind how the lasso and multiple-copy features can interact. First, use the pencil to create one dot. Lasso the dot. Move the lasso to the dot until it turns into the pointer arrow. With the second thickness line selected, make multiple copies of the dot by holding down Option-Command while dragging the mouse.

To space the dots farther apart, select one of the thicker lines. The dot doesn't change; only the spacing between dots changes. The thicker the line, the more distance between dots.

Figure 4-19. Dotted Lines

Try making repeating copies of other forms. Choose the Cairo font in 18-point size and press the 1 key to get the palm tree. Lasso it and choose the thickest line. Now press Option-Command and drag the palm tree. *Voilà!* Dotted palms. You can repeat copies of any shape you want.

Chapter 4

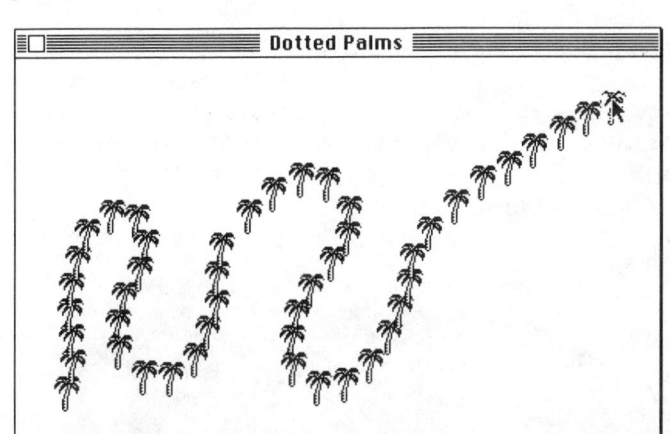

Figure 4-20. Dotted Palms

Custom Brush Shapes

If you get tired of the 32 brush shapes MacPaint provides, you can create your own. Make a filled shape (not an outlined figure) for your brush. Turn *Grid* on and lasso the shape. To paint, just press Option-Command while dragging it.

Figure 4-21. Painting with Custom Brush

Working from Black

You can get some interesting effects by working from black instead of white. White on a black background can create dramatic illustrations.

To make the MacPaint window completely black, double-click the marquee tool to select the whole window. Make sure

91

Chapter 4

that black is the selected pattern at the bottom of the MacPaint screen and choose *Fill* from the *Edit* menu. Now use the pencil to draw in white on black. Try other tools, such as the spray can and the paint brush, after changing the pattern to white. Experiment with various patterns for even more bizarre results.

MacPaint can even make a negative of an existing drawing. Select the entire drawing with the marquee and choose *Invert* from the *Edit* menu. Dramatic, isn't it?

Figure 4-22. Invert

Text in Reverse

When you draw or paint in white on black, you'll want text to be white on black, too. It's simple. Type the text in a large, boldface style outside the black area. Use the marquee to select the text.

Figure 4-23. Select Text

92

Chapter 4

Choose *Invert* from the *Edit* menu. The text is now a negative image of the original.

Figure 4-24. Invert Text

Drag it onto the black area. That's it.

Figure 4-25. Move Text to a Black Form

Transparency

Graphic artists often use opaque and transparent forms. An opaque form obscures those underneath it. A transparent form combines with those under it to create a new shape. MacPaint gives you the power to create both opaque and transparent forms.

Transparency by leaking. If you select a form with the lasso and move it on top of another, any closed shapes within that lasso will be opaque. The closed shapes will obscure the part(s) of

93

Chapter 4

the picture beneath them. Take a look at Figure 4-26—it shows a picture of a Macintosh partially obscuring a drawing of a face.

Figure 4-26. Opacity

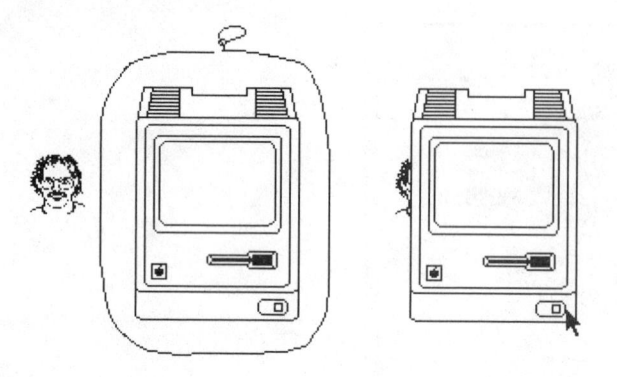

To make the closed shape transparent so that you can see the picture underneath, use *FatBits* to punch holes in the perimeter of the closed space. There should be an opening from the white space *inside* the shapes to the white space *outside*. This is like letting the outside leak into your shapes. Now when you use the lasso and move the shape atop another, the other picture will show through.

Figure 4-27. Transparency

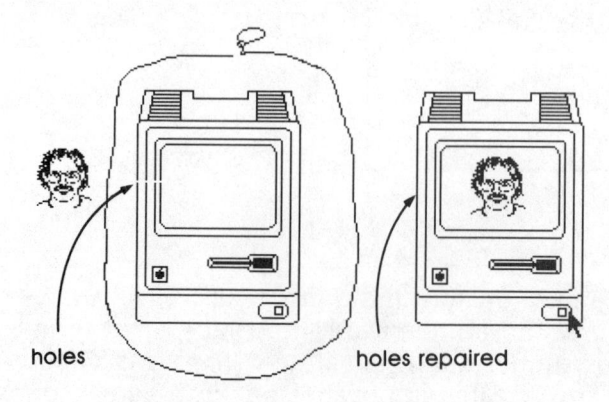

holes   holes repaired

After the second form has been moved to its position atop the first, use *FatBits* to repair the holes.

Chapter 4

Transparent painting. Sometimes you'll want to put one pattern against an existing one without any overlap. If you're not really careful when you paint one pattern against another, the second may cover part of the first, creating a ragged border. To make it easier to paint against forms, hold down Command while painting. This makes the second pattern transparent. If the original pattern is dark, it probably won't be altered. And sometimes the two will combine to produce a third pattern.

The drawing on the left of Figure 4-28 was made without pressing the Command key. Note that the second pattern has obscured part of the one beneath it. On the right, however, the second pattern has become transparent, for the Command key was used.

Figure 4-28. Transparent Painting

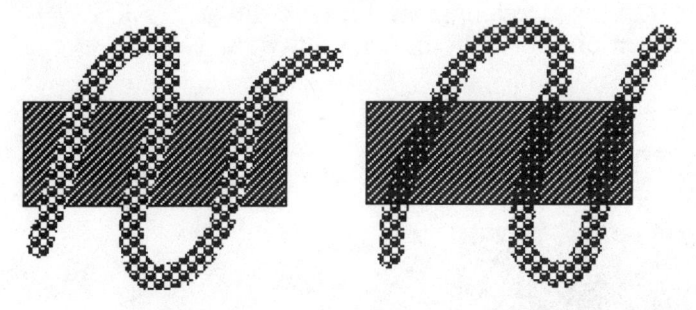

You can also hold down the Command key as you use the spray can to create transparent spray paint. This combines the applied pattern with the pattern beneath it.

Creating shadows. One terrific application of transparency is the depiction of shadows falling on patterned surfaces. Choose a dot pattern for the shadow and paint with the Command key held down. This combines the dot pattern with the pattern of the surface underneath to give a true shadow effect.

95

Chapter 4

Figure 4-29. Creating Shadows

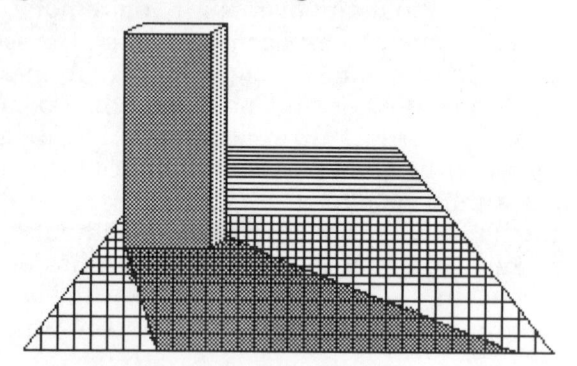

Transparent forms. It's easy to combine patterns. First, create a filled form, such as a rectangle, and then create a second one with a different pattern on top while holding down the Command key.

Figure 4-30. Combined Filled Forms

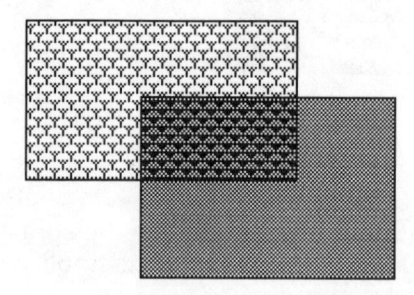

This ability to combine patterns will help you design your own custom shadings. It's discussed later in this chapter.

Fill and Refill

You've probably noticed that sometimes you can't fill a shape with the paint can if the shape already has a pattern in it. Completely white or black shapes can be filled with a new pattern, but forms that include closed spaces can't be filled entirely with something new. The new pattern stays within the enclosed space it's poured into.

Chapter 4

Figure 4-31. Filling Closed Patterns

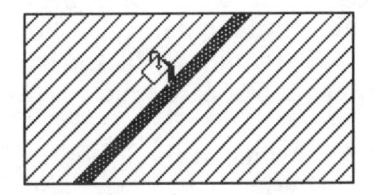

A pattern with an open design *can* be filled, however. The new pattern is a combination of the old and the one used to fill it.

Figure 4-32. Refilling

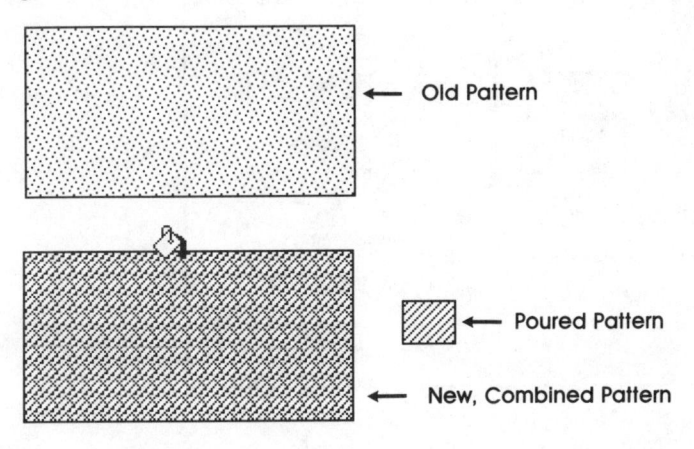

← Old Pattern

← Poured Pattern

← New, Combined Pattern

To entirely and reliably replace one pattern with another, you must use the *Fill* option from the *Edit* menu. Use the marquee or lasso to select the section of the drawing you want refilled and then choose *Fill*. This fills the selected space with an opaque pattern.

Creating Custom Patterns

MacPaint lets you create custom patterns by editing the existing patterns at the bottom of the screen. Double-click on a pattern to get the pattern edit box and edit by clicking on pixels until you have what you want.

Picking up patterns. You can even create custom patterns without having to design them by hand. Double-click a pattern to

Chapter 4

enter pattern edit mode. Now click the button when the arrow is on any part of your picture. The pattern in an 8 × 8 pixel area under the pointer is picked up and put into the pattern edit box. The location of the middle of the arrow determines which pattern is picked up. If you click *OK*, this pattern replaces the old one in the palette.

You'll get surprising results when you click at the intersection of shapes and patterns. Click in various locations until you get a pattern you like. Then click *OK* to store it. Figure 4-33 shows a custom pattern you could create.

Figure 4-33. Picking Up Patterns

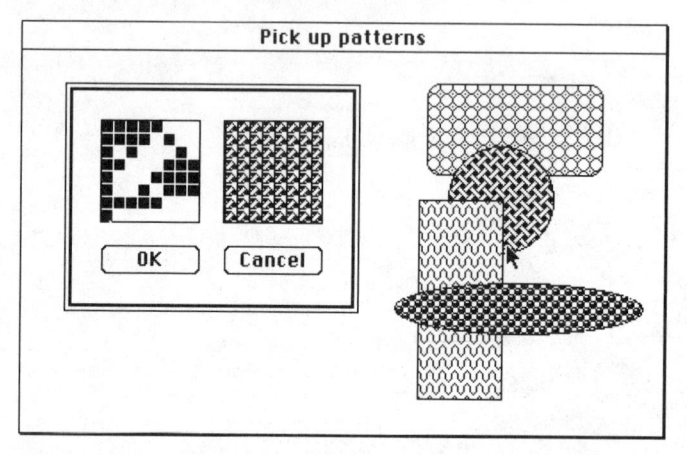

Picking up combined patterns. You'll get even more interesting shadings if you create some combined patterns. Hold down Command while creating overlapping patterned forms. Double-click a pattern in the palette and pick up some of these new patterns, just as you did above.

98

Chapter 4

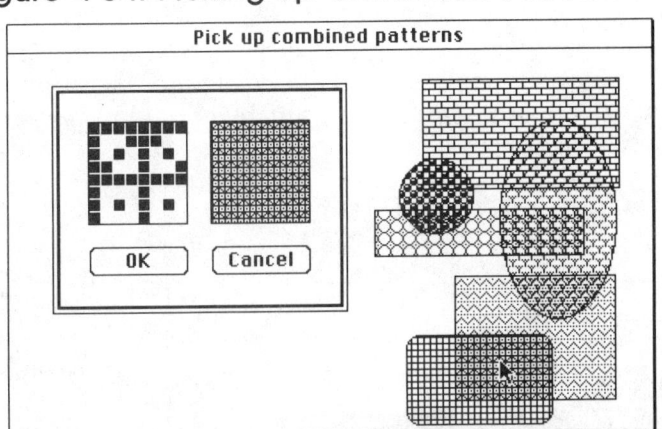

Figure 4-34. Picking Up Combined Patterns

Picking up random patterns. Go one step further by using the spray can with a white pattern to eliminate some details of the combined patterns. Select a pattern and spray over others while holding down the Command key to combine them. This will give you random textures to pick up. Double-click a pattern and click on different parts of your random textures. It's fascinating to watch the Macintosh pick up patterns this way. You can create literally hundreds.

Figure 4-35. Picking Up Random Patterns

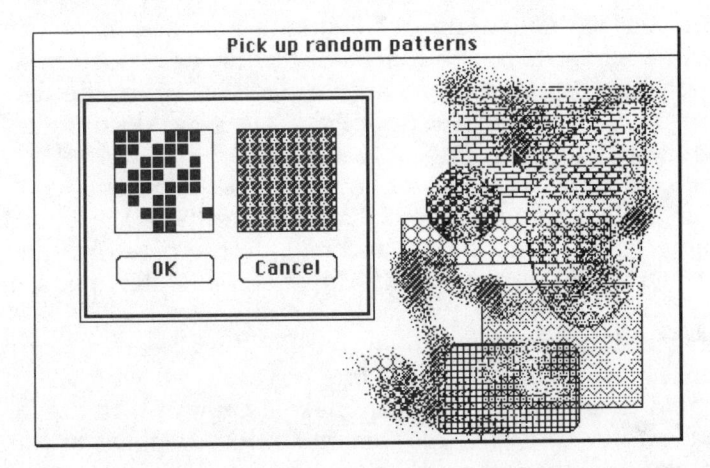

Chapter 4

You can create even more patterns by stretching existing ones. Lay down several rectangles of dot patterns with *Grid* on. Use the marquee to select them, and stretch them with the Command key. Then you can pick up parts to create more custom patterns. This can give you patterns you probably wouldn't have thought of designing yourself.

Figure 4-36. Picking Up Stretched Patterns

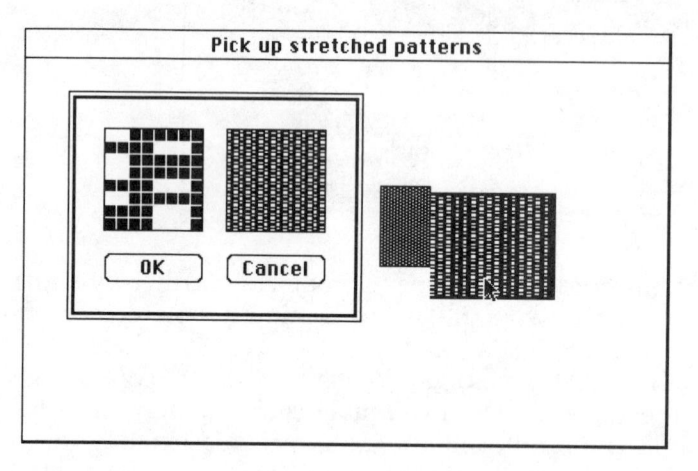

Creating a File of Custom Patterns

Using the techniques you've just seen, you can pick up custom patterns until the pattern palette is filled with new designs. However, each time you start a new MacPaint document or load in an existing one, your custom patterns are replaced by either the default patterns or the patterns set up for the MacPaint document that was opened.

But you can create swatches of your favorite patterns and save them as a MacPaint document. Later, you can load in your swatches, enter edit pattern mode, and pick up the patterns you want. Then you can erase the swatch document and start painting a document using the new patterns.

To start building your pattern swatch file, first create a matrix of empty boxes. With *Grid* on, draw one box, select it with the lasso, and hold down Shift-Option to make a copy of it to the right. (The Shift key constricts movement so that dragging to the right will move the box along only the horizontal axis.) Repeat

100

Chapter 4

this process until you have a row of 5 boxes across the MacPaint window. Select this line of boxes and use the Shift-Option key to make a copy of the boxes directly below the first row. Do this until you have a 5 × 5 matrix of boxes. Select these 25 boxes with the lasso and choose *Copy* from the *Edit* menu. This puts the boxes into the Clipboard. Use the hand tool to move to another part of the picture and choose *Paste* from the *Edit* menu. Carefully line up the second set of 25 boxes. Repeat this process until you have 100 boxes in a 10 × 10 matrix.

Figure 4-37. Create Boxes

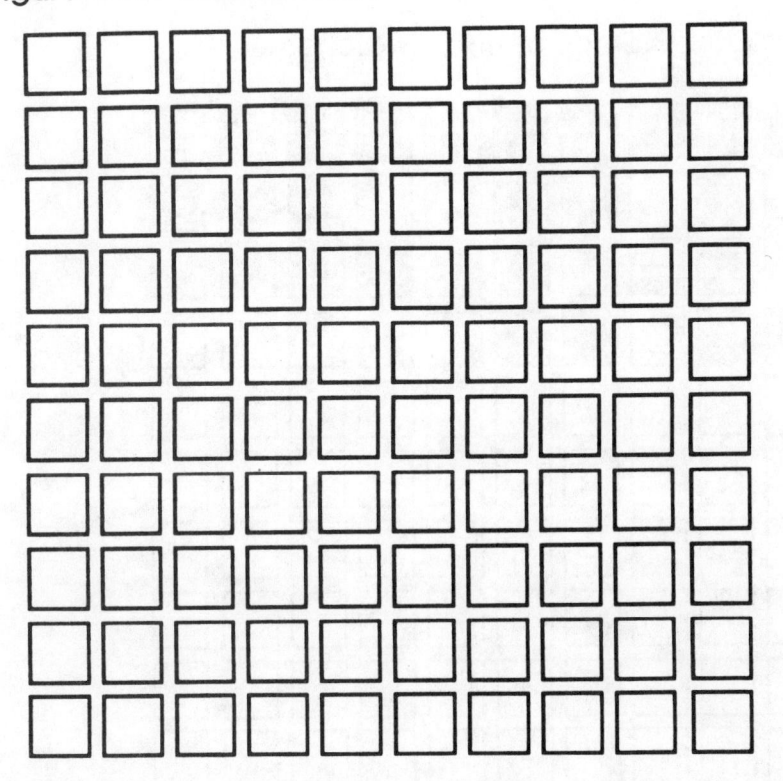

In the empty space at the bottom of the page, create some combined patterns and then spray paint with Command held down to combine them with other transparent patterns. Spray with white to open up some space. Now double-click on one of MacPaint's 38 patterns and pick up new patterns until you find

Chapter 4

one you like. Click *OK*. Repeat this process until all 38 standard patterns are replaced with your custom patterns.

Use the hand tool to go to the boxes at the top left part of your document. Next, use the paint can to fill each box with your custom patterns until you've grabbed them all. With the marquee, select the patterns you've been working with and choose *Invert* from the *Edit* menu. This will give you a negative image of your patterned areas. Pick up some of these new patterns. Now go back to your work area and create some more random patterns, pick those up, and fill more boxes. When you've finished, you'll have an entire document of pattern swatches.

Figure 4-38. A Document of Swatches

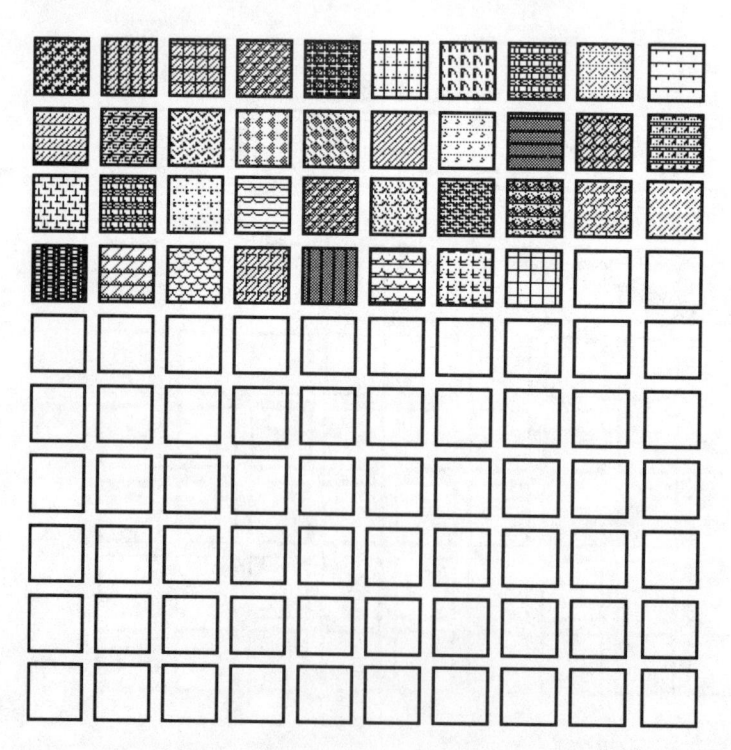

When you want to use some of your custom patterns, load this swatch document and select those you need. Keep some of MacPaint's standard patterns, such as white, black, and several dot-pattern grays. Clear the document by sliding it off the page in *Show Page* mode and start painting. (If you don't know how to clear a MacPaint document, read on.)

Chapter 4

Clearing a MacPaint Document

You can quickly erase a picture in MacPaint by double-clicking the hand icon to get into *Show Page* mode and then sliding your picture over until it disappears. Click *OK* and your picture is erased. Be careful—you can't retrieve a picture erased this way unless it was saved on disk. Besides clearing all or part of your picture, *Show Page* mode allows you to orient your picture on the page and to select the location of the MacPaint window.

Creating Bas-Relief

Bas-relief is a process that gives a three-dimensional look to an object. It does this by outlining one side of the object in white and the opposite side in black, giving the illusion that the object is projecting toward you from a flat surface. It looks as if it's casting a shadow. Photographers create bas-relief images by sandwiching a negative and a positive of the same subject slightly out of register. This is a tedious and time-consuming operation. But you can create bas-relief effects with your Macintosh in just seconds.

First, create a smooth, patterned background surface. Medium-to-light patterns with small units of repetition work best—dot-pattern grays, for example. Use the lasso to define the shape you want in relief. Now move this piece one or two pixels vertically and one or two pixels horizontally until you get the desired effect. The shadow can be placed on different edges of the shape by moving the lassoed shape in different directions.

Figure 4-39. Bas-Relief

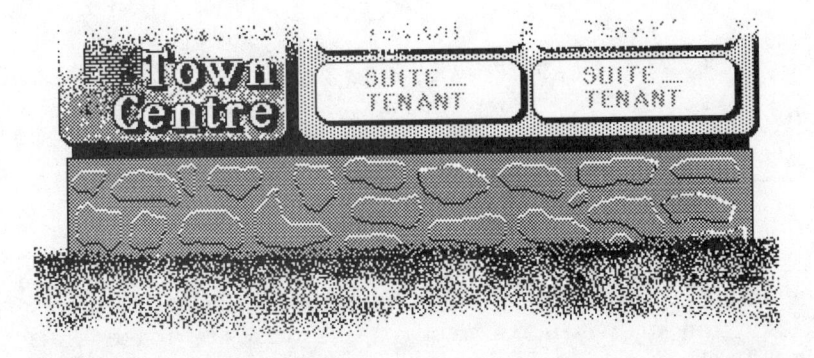

As you can see from Figure 4-39, this is an excellent way of creating structures like rock walls. Try this technique with other textures to get different effects.

Chapter 4

Shadowed Text

Have you ever wanted to create text that seemed to float on your page? It's easy with MacPaint. First, type your text in a large style. Outlined New York font in 18-point bold is a good choice. Duplicate it by selecting with the lasso and dragging with Shift-Option. Fill each outlined letter of one line of text with black.

Figure 4-40. Filling the Text with Black

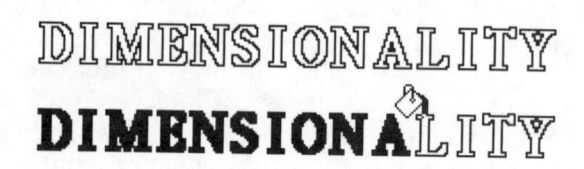

Choose a dot pattern and fill each black letter.

Figure 4-41. Filling the Text with Dots

Now select the unfilled text with the lasso, hold down the Option key, and drag the letters to the correct position over the filled text. (The Option key will make a copy of it in case you make a mistake.) Try to put the unfilled letters just above and to the left of the filled ones; that will best simulate shadowing.

104

Figure 4-42. Moving the Figure

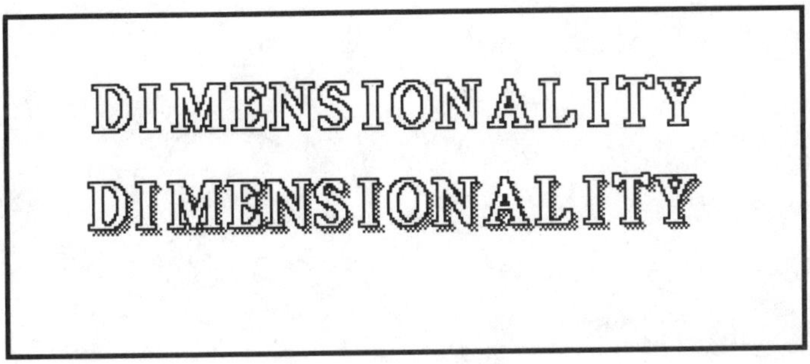

> DIMENSIONALITY
>
> DIMENSIONALITY

Experiment with a variety of font styles and patterns to design your own floating characters.

Concentric Circles

If you've tried to create concentric circles with MacPaint, you've probably discovered that it isn't easy. After you draw the first circle, how do you know where to position the cursor so that the second ends up precisely centered within the first? When you draw circles, it's very difficult to anticipate exactly where the circle will be located on the screen.

There *is* a technique for drawing as many concentric circles as you wish, quickly and easily.

Select the oval tool, place the cursor where you want to begin the first circle, and click once to create a dot as a point of reference. Starting at this dot, draw the circle by holding down Shift and dragging. Use the line tool to draw a 45-degree line running through the circle; the line will automatically go through the center of the circle (you can tell that the line is exactly 45 degrees when it's perfectly straight and has no "steps"). To get concentric circles, place the + cursor anywhere on this line. Again, press Shift while you drag the mouse along the line. Make sure the cursor is on the line before you release the mouse button.

Chapter 4

Figure 4-43. Creating Concentric Circles

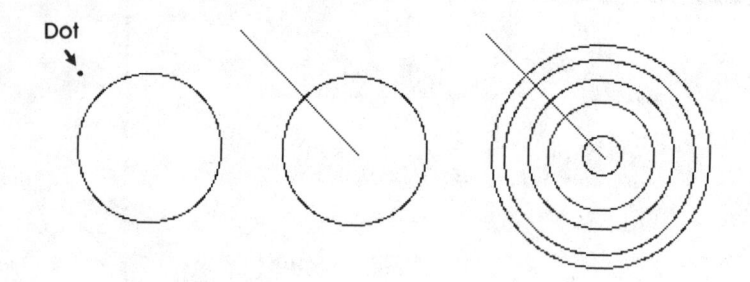

Shading

Here's a way to create shading by using some of MacPaint's advanced techniques. Outlined forms, such as block lettering made from simple geometric shapes, are good subjects for an example.

The first step is to cut a channel through the body of any letter containing an enclosed shape.

Figure 4-44. Channel Through All Enclosed Shapes

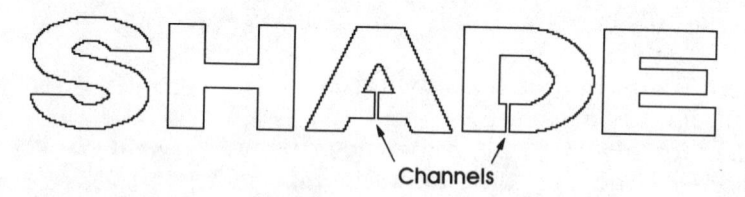

Now select the letters with the lasso and hold down the Option-Command keys while slowly dragging. You can drag in any direction, depending on what shading effect you want. If you don't like your result, press Tilde to undo and try again. Repair the channels with *FatBits*.

Figure 4-45. Create Shading

Chapter 4

You can use the shaded letter to produce still other effects. Select the letters with the marquee and press Command-E to trace their edges.

Figure 4-46. Trace Edges

Dig the channels, select with the lasso, hold down Option-Command, and drag to get another shadow in the same direction as the first.

Figure 4-47. Create a Second Shadow

Repair the channels and use the paint-can tool to fill this shadow with a pattern.

Figure 4-48. Paint the Shadow

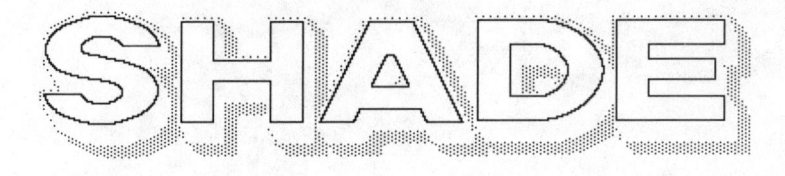

Again, cut channels into the first shaded result, lasso the shapes, cut them into the Clipboard, and paste them over what you got with the second pattern. That's the last step and should give you something like Figure 4-49.

Chapter 4

Figure 4-49. Finished

SHADE

Custom Lettering

You can design your own letterings and store them in the Scrapbook or in a MacPaint document for later use. The techniques outlined will allow you to create large, fancy letters for your special graphics projects. Here are some examples of completed custom lettering.

Figure 4-50. Custom Lettering

Bill Jonas, Artworks, Inc.

Chapter 4

Go through the procedure presented here for creating the *R* in Restaurant to see some of the techniques you can use in creating your own letter designs with MacPaint.

Font types. Start your custom-lettering designs with a choice from the *Font* menu. There are five classifications of font styles:

1. Roman (serif lettering). *New York, Toronto, Athens*
2. Gothic or block (sans serif lettering). *Geneva, Chicago, Seattle*
3. Italic (slanted, unconnected). Accessed through the *Style* menu
4. Script (slanted, flowing). *Venice*
5. Ornate (decorative). *London, Los Angeles*

Creating custom lettering. Most custom-designed lettering can be based on one of these fonts, then enhanced with MacPaint's features. For the Restaurant lettering, start with New York, bold, in 36- and 72-point sizes.

Figure 4-51. Start with an Available Font

Restaurant

Resize the letters if necessary by selecting them with the marquee, holding down Command-Shift, and dragging. In the example, the letters' heights were reduced somewhat. To make the letters bolder, you can use *Trace Edges* repeatedly and then erase the internal lines with the paint can with white.

Figure 4-52. Shrink and Make Bolder

Res Res Res

To customize the *R*, work on a copy of it which includes some of the surrounding letters. This insures that you have the original in case you make a mistake. Use the oval tool to sketch the position of the new top of the *R* as well as its scrolls.

109

Chapter 4

Figure 4-53. Start the Stroke and Scrolls

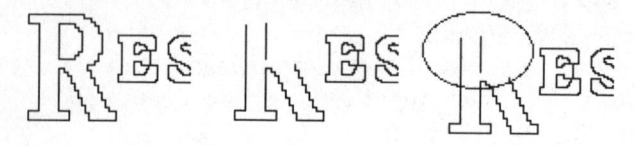

Use *FatBits* to erase unnecessary lines and enhance the scrolls.

Figure 4-54. Build the Scrolls

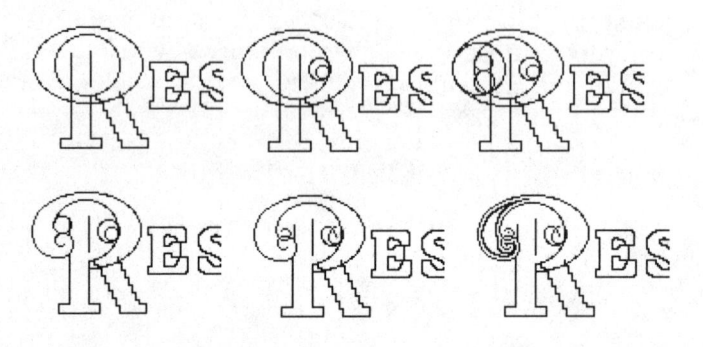

Erase the descender of the R. To make it easy to create a new descender, use the paint brush tool to draw it and then make it thin and bold by using Command-E to trace its edges. This may take several tries to get it right. If you make a mistake, press Tilde to undo, and try again.

Figure 4-55. Draw the Descender

Chapter 4

Add scrolls to the descender and enhance the vertical stroke. Clean up the ragged spots with *FatBits*. Use Shift-Command-E to trace edges with a shadow to complete the *R*.

Figure 4-56. Finishing the *R*

Now convert the other letters to your specifications.

Figure 4-57. Creating the Other Letters

E=E S=S T=T A=A
U=U R=R N=N

Put them all together to get the final result.

Enhancing custom lettering. MacPaint gives you many tools for enhancing the letters you create. The examples in this chapter have shown how you can use these tools for creating pictures and lettering. Figure 4-58 illustrates an example which shows the development stages of fancy lettering created by combining some of the techniques used in both the SHADE and Restaurant samples.

Chapter 4

Figure 4-58. Development Stages

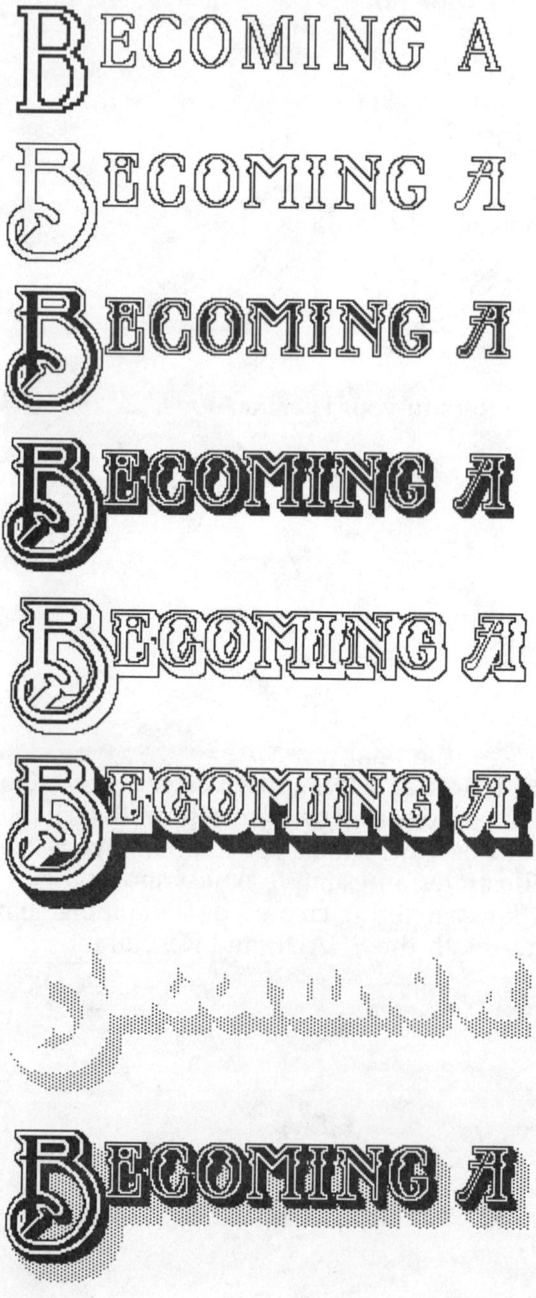

Chapter 4

Creating Custom Borders and Frames

If you aren't in awe of MacPaint's powers yet, perhaps this next section will win you over. By exploiting MacPaint's features, you can create an infinite array of fancy borders and frames for things like announcements and advertising flyers.

You first need to create a small portion of a border. Then use the lasso and the thickest line and drag with Option-Command-Shift to repeat it.

Figure 4-59. Creating Repeating Forms

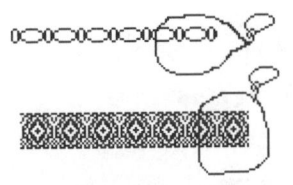

It's quite simple to design an almost limitless number of border patterns with this technique. Figure 4-60 shows just a few possibilities.

Figure 4-60. Repeating Border Samples

113

Chapter 4

To create larger border designs, you can draw a circle and repeat its form in different ways by changing the setting in the line thickness box.

Figure 4-61. Changing Line Thickness

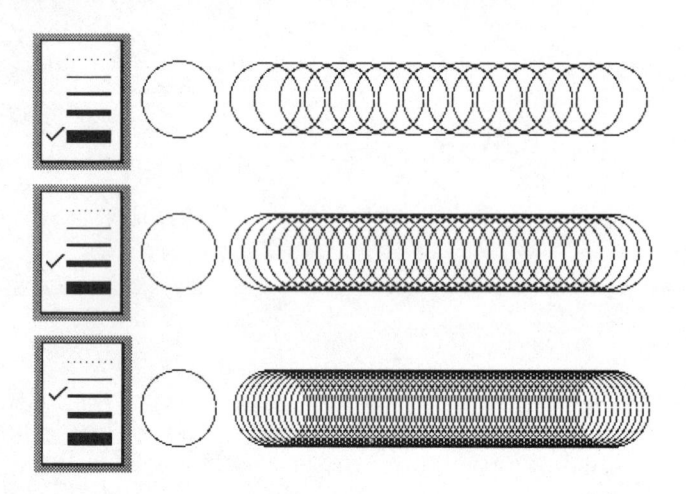

Let's try something a bit different. Draw a thick circle and cut a hole in it so that the area inside the circle is transparent as you drag to repeat its form. To make the corner, drag the repeating circle until you've created about three inches, release the mouse button, then hold down Option-Command-Shift and begin dragging in the new direction.

Figure 4-62. Creating Repeating Circles

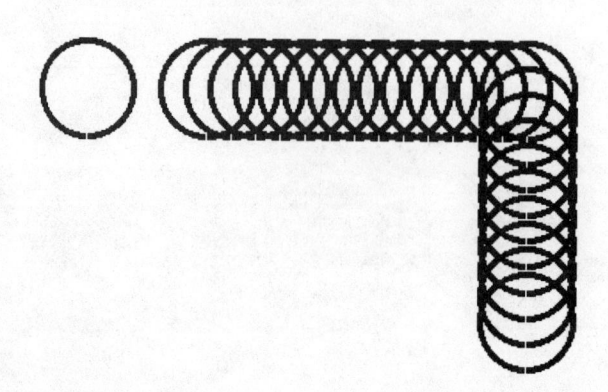

Chapter 4

To enhance your border pattern, select with the marquee and press Command-E to trace edges.

Figure 4-63. Trace Edges

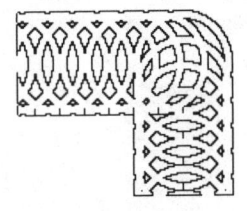

Use the paint can to paint the background.

Figure 4-64. Paint the Background

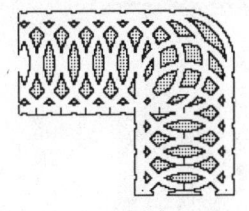

Or paint the foreground.

Figure 4-65. Paint the Foreground

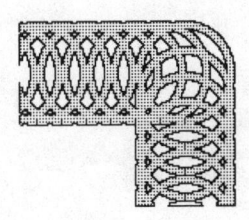

Some borders have a direction. The repeating pattern moves in one direction and then another.

Chapter 4

Figure 4-66. Borders with Direction

116

Chapter 4

Here are some more examples of borders and frames.

Figure 4-67. More Samples

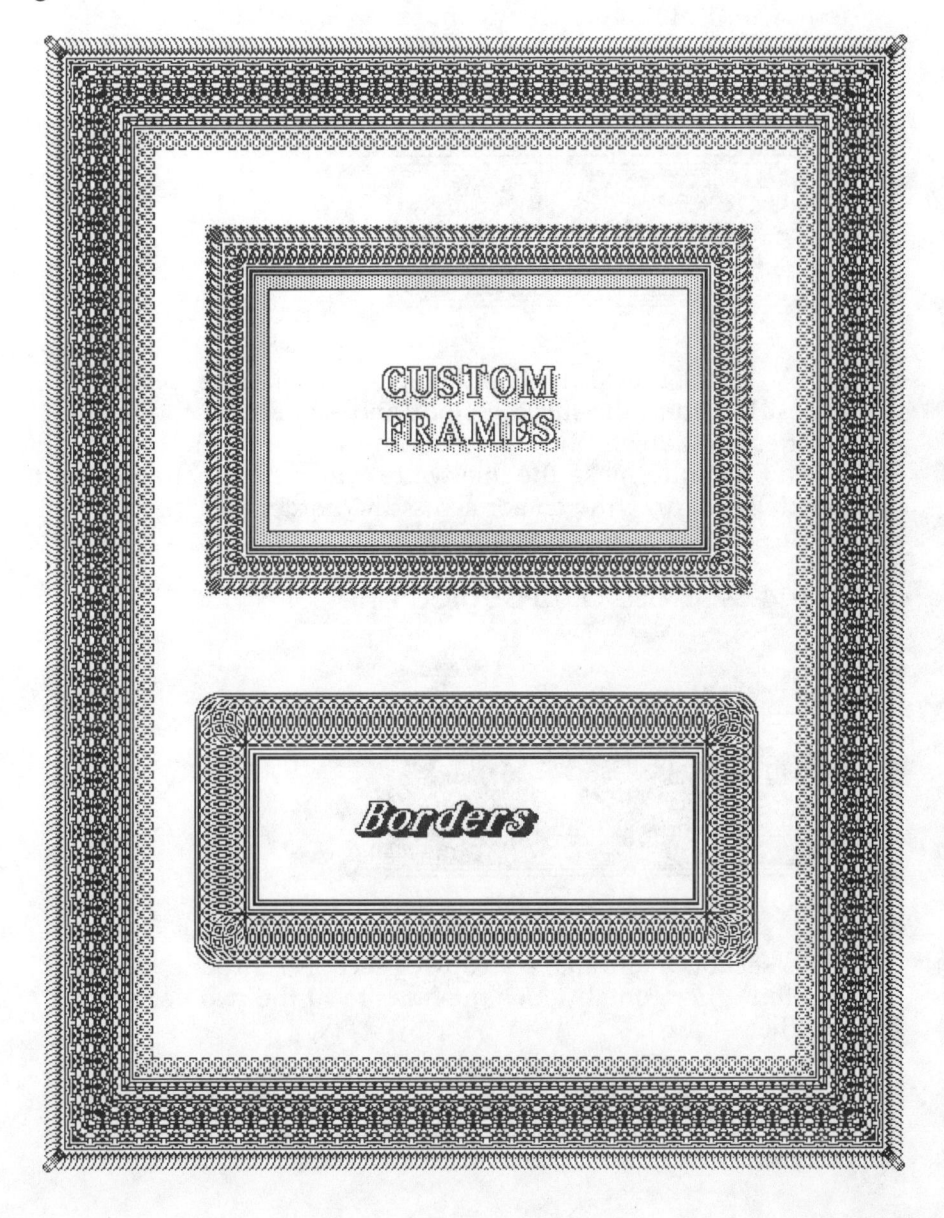

Chapter 4

Border designs can be made of extremely complex repeating sections. However, these sections must be spliced end to end; they cannot be extended with the lasso as smaller, less complex patterns can. Figure 4-68 shows an example.

Figure 4-68. Large Border Design

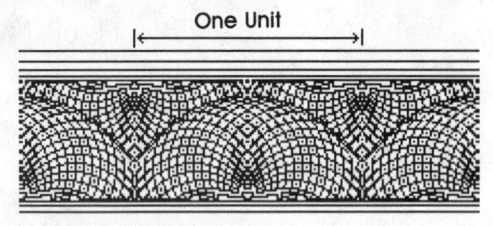

To create the corners of large patterns like this, select the widest line from the thickness box and white from the pattern palette. Hold down Shift to constrain the line to 45 degrees, hold down Option to make the line white (the current pattern from the palette), and drag the cursor across the border design. This will create sections A and B as shown.

Figure 4-69. Erase a 45-Degree Line

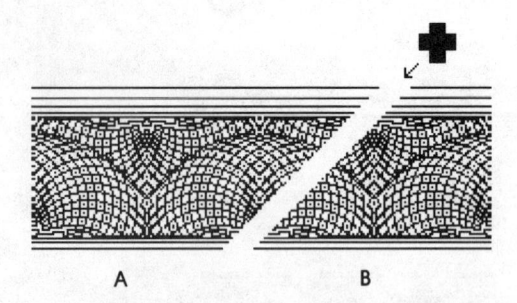

Erase section B and make a copy of section A. Rotate the latter and flip it horizontally. Use the lasso to fit the two versions of A together.

118

Chapter 4

Figure 4-70. Putting the Pieces Together

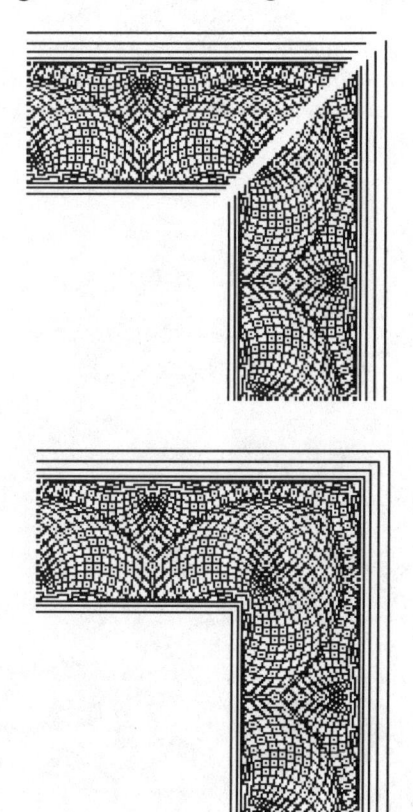

The point at which you cut your original pattern determines what the corner will look like. If you don't like the way it looks, try the procedure again but make the 45-degree erasure in a different place.

When you have a corner you like, copy the final result and rotate it to create the other three corners.

Creating Ornaments

Fancy, ornate details can easily be created with MacPaint. The following designs were created by starting with hand-drawn patterns. Enhancements were made by tracing the edges; sometimes the Shift key was used while tracing the edges to get a shadowed line.

Chapter 4

For the circular ornaments, the circle was created with a large outer circle and repeating circles inside it. To insure a symmetrical result, one-quarter of the result was copied, flipped, and joined to create a half circle. This in turn was copied, flipped, and joined to get the full circle. The other ornaments were constructed by joining flipped halves.

Figure 4-71. Ornaments

Much More

There's still a lot more to learn. Be adventurous. Try whatever pops into your head. It's this sort of creative play that will help you master MacPaint.

Chapter 5
MacDraw Tips and Advanced Techniques

Chapter 5

MacDraw Tips and Advanced Techniques

Working with MacPaint is somewhat like making pointillist paintings, where individual dots of paint are used to build a large work. You can use MacPaint's drawing tools to lay down patterns of dots in circles and squares, and you can use *FatBits* to alter your drawing at the individual pixel level. Working with MacDraw, on the other hand, is like working with a multipiece construction set that you first create and then put together to form larger shapes. In order to master MacDraw, you must keep this in mind.

MacDraw is a very powerful image processor, analogous to a word processor. A word processor lets you create and edit words and paragraphs—MacDraw allows you to create and edit picture elements. You can use MacDraw's tools to create geometric shapes, to move them from place to place, and to change their size and form. MacDraw even lets you write and edit text with the power of a limited word processor. It offers such a diverse collection of tools that it can be much more useful and efficient than conventional drawing methods.

Did you know that you can erase whatever you want from your MacDraw designs, or that you can use MacDraw like a roll of film? In this chapter you'll learn advanced MacDraw techniques like these, techniques that will make it easier for you to work with MacDraw. Open MacDraw and discover the intricacies of the electronic drafting table.

Using *Custom Rulers* and *Grid*

The accurate placement of objects within a MacDraw document is determined by two things: *Custom Rulers* and the *Grid* feature. *Custom Rulers* and *Grid* must be coordinated so that you can draw elements to size and move them to their proper locations easily and accurately.

Default ruler values. When you first open MacDraw, the rulers are set with major divisions of one inch. Each inch is subdivided into eight minor divisions of 1/8 inch. The *Align to Grid* feature is set on. MacDraw's grid is an invisible web, like MacPaint's, upon which objects can be hung.

To find out if MacDraw's grid is on, pull down the *Layout* menu—if *Turn Grid Off* is in the menu, the grid is on, if *Turn Grid On* is in the menu, it's off. With *Grid* on, the circles, rectangles,

123

Chapter 5

and polygons you draw will align themselves to the smallest divisions of your ruler—in our example, this would be 1/8 inch. You can move your pointer arrow from one of the eight subdivisions to another, but you can't make the arrow stop between them. Since the pointer arrow is restricted to working in 1/8-inch increments, it's easy to line up and overlap the shapes you draw. The *Align to Grid* feature makes your forms "drop" into place along the invisible grid. Fortunately, MacDraw offers you a lot of freedom in selecting both your rulers and the size of the grid divisions.

Turn Grid Off. When you want to move objects from place to place without restriction, choose *Turn Grid Off* from the *Layout* menu. This lets you move objects to any of 72 positions per linear inch—as fine a movement as one pixel. You can also start drawing your object at any pixel position on the document page.

Align to Grid. If *Turn Grid On* is selected from the *Layout* menu, you have access to *Align to Grid* in the *Arrange* menu. This feature allows you to align selected items to the grid. If an object was created with the grid turned off, you can use *Align to Grid* to line it.

Customizing the rulers. When you select *Custom Rulers* from the *Layout* menu, you'll see a dialog box which allows you to change the rulers. If you want to work in centimeters rather than inches, for instance, and you want to move the zero point to any location on the screen, you would make selections accordingly, choosing *Centimeter* and *Unlocked*, just as Figure 5-1 illustrates.

Figure 5-1. *Custom Rulers* Dialog Box

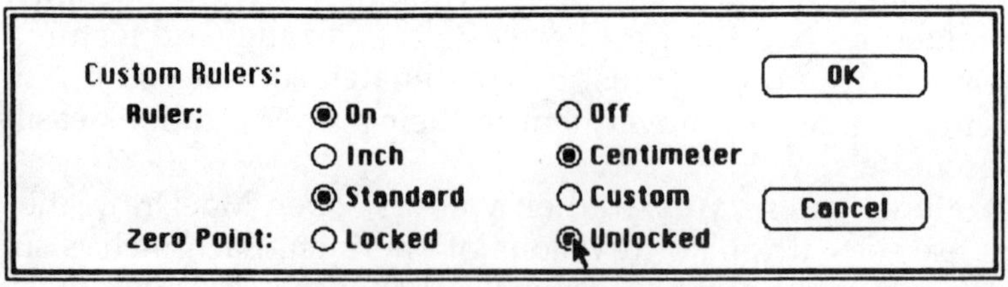

Custom Rulers:			
Ruler:	● On	○ Off	[OK]
	○ Inch	● Centimeter	
	● Standard	○ Custom	[Cancel]
Zero Point:	○ Locked	● Unlocked	

124

Chapter 5

Customizing *Grid.* You can customize ruler divisions by clicking *Custom* in the dialog box to reveal the rest of the choices. Now you can select the minor division increments. The dialog box will look like this when you choose 1/16-inch increments.

Figure 5-2. Customizing the Divisions

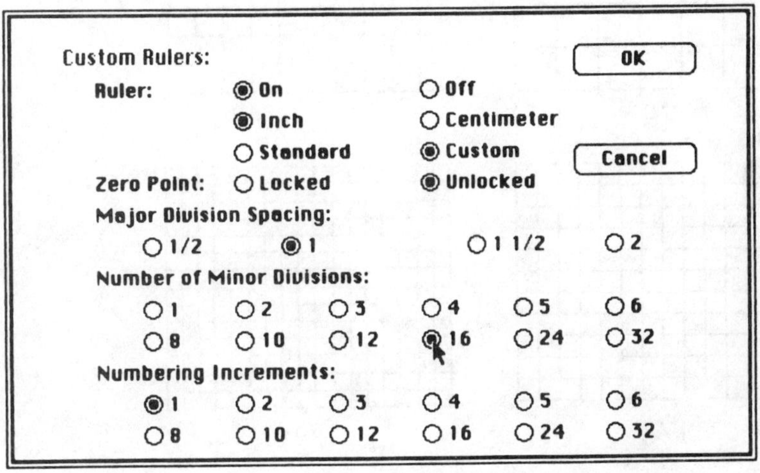

```
Custom Rulers:                              [  OK   ]
    Ruler:      ● On          ○ Off
                ● Inch        ○ Centimeter
                ○ Standard    ● Custom      [ Cancel ]
    Zero Point: ○ Locked      ● Unlocked
    Major Division Spacing:
        ○ 1/2      ● 1              ○ 1 1/2   ○ 2
    Number of Minor Divisions:
        ○ 1    ○ 2    ○ 3    ○ 4    ○ 5    ○ 6
        ○ 8    ○ 10   ○ 12   ● 16   ○ 24   ○ 32
    Numbering Increments:
        ● 1    ○ 2    ○ 3    ○ 4    ○ 5    ○ 6
        ○ 8    ○ 10   ○ 12   ○ 16   ○ 24   ○ 32
```

MacDraw doesn't restrict you to one grid size as MacPaint does. When you customize the rulers' minor divisions, it also determines the size of the invisible grid. The *Custom Rulers* option gives you 12 different grid sizes, 6 of which are represented in Figure 5-3.

125

Chapter 5

Figure 5-3. *Grid* Sizes

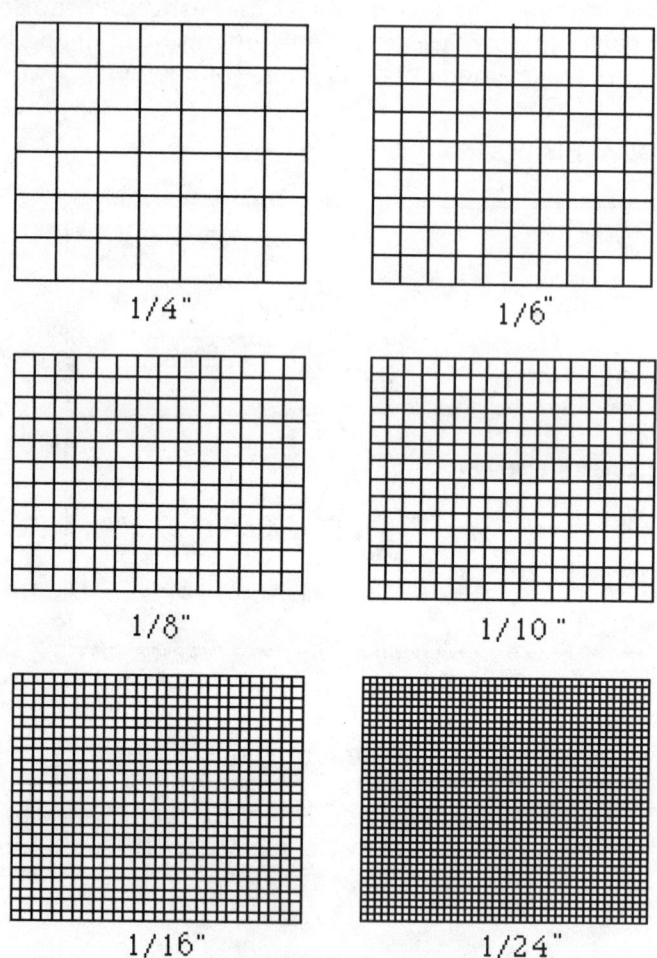

1/4"   1/6"

1/8"   1/10"

1/16"   1/24"

Draw Complete Elements

With MacDraw, you have to plan your drawing strategy before you start. Break the drawing into its components—then draw each as a separate element. This is the most important lesson you can learn about MacDraw.

More than likely, you learned how to use MacPaint before you started using MacDraw. You're probably in the habit of creating drawings spontaneously, without a plan, using any tool that

Chapter 5

gets the job done. And if your drawing didn't look right, *FatBits* was there to plant and pluck individual pixels.

But MacDraw demands a different approach. When you draw enclosed forms in MacDraw—such as rectangles with straight lines—you won't be able to fill them with a pattern, and you won't be able to move them from place to place easily. In MacDraw, something that looks right on the screen might not work well as an element of a document. As you learned in Chapter 2, MacDraw is an object-oriented graphics editor that makes it easy for you to manipulate distinct shapes. To use MacDraw properly, you must create your shapes according to how they'll be treated as part of a larger form.

An example will demonstrate the importance of the process of creating independent elements with MacDraw. Here's a drawing of a simple box with each surface filled with a different pattern:

Figure 5-4. A Simple Box

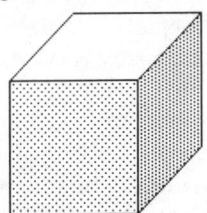

But it's not just a simple box. You can select its lid and drag it away:

Figure 5-5. Open the Box

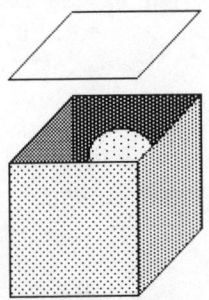

There's a small egg in the box. You can even drag the egg out of the box.

127

Chapter 5

Figure 5-6. Take Out the Egg

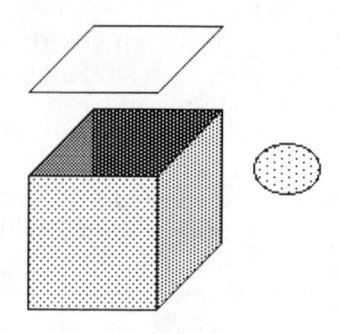

    This example illustrates the power of MacDraw: Each of the elements has its own position relative to all the other elements. MacDraw keeps track of the size and shape of each, as well as its position along x-, y-, and z-axes. (The z-axis position defines whether an object is on top of, or under, other objects, giving MacDraw picture elements a third dimension for arrangement.)

    To use MacDraw with any degree of flexibility and control, you must draw the design elements in a structured way. For example, if it's important to manipulate the sides of the box independently or fill them with different patterns, you must create each side as an individual element. Individual elements can also be manipulated along the z-axis for layering effects.

    To learn better how to effectively use MacDraw, take yourself through the following instructions. You'll end up with a box which seems to be three-dimensional.

An Example

Open MacDraw if you haven't already done so. The easiest way to draw the box is to start with its front and back surfaces. Since you're going to connect the corners of the front to the corners of the back, you must be able to see all sides of your two beginning squares—they must be transparent. But left to its own devices, MacDraw automatically fills rectangles and circular shapes with white. This white fill pattern prevents you from seeing the sides of the squares that a shape overlaps.

    To make transparent shapes, click the fill pattern box in the bottom left corner of the MacDraw window (just to the left of the scroll arrow) and then choose *None* from the *Fill* menu. You'll see an *N* in this box. From now on, each enclosed shape you draw will be transparent.

With the rectangle tool selected, you can get perfect squares every time by holding down the Shift key while dragging (the Shift key constrains the shapes you draw in MacDraw just as in MacPaint). Draw a square the size of one major unit and a second square on top, as shown in Figure 5-7.

Figure 5-7. The Front and Back

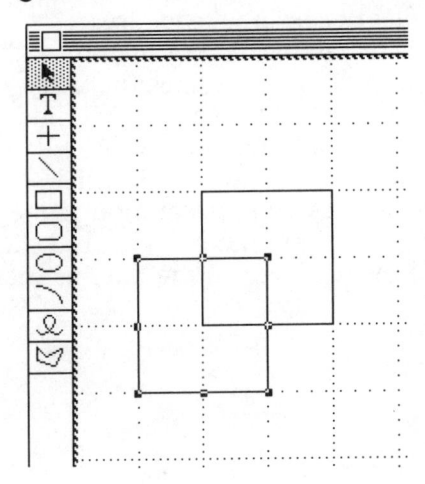

Looking at the overlapping squares, you might think the best way to complete the box is to use straight lines to join their corners. Figure 5-8 shows the lines you might add. (The lines are shown out of place so you can easily distinguish them from the two original squares.)

Figure 5-8. Don't Use Straight Lines

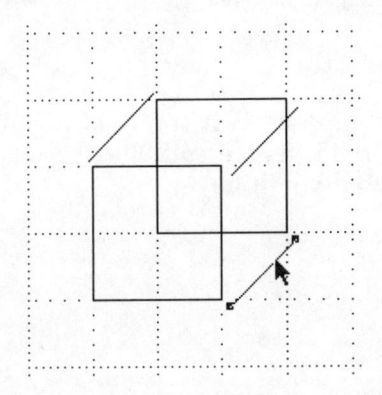

Chapter 5

This may be the easiest way to connect the corners, but it's far from being the best way to create a box with MacDraw. If you construct the side and top surfaces with straight lines, these surfaces can't be filled with patterns. And you can't choose the sides or top of the box and drag it to a new location, because the surface is composed of two straight lines, as well as two lines that make up one of the other two faces—the original squares. Sides constructed with lines have no integrity or independence.

The best way is to draw each remaining face of the box with the polygon tool. It will be necessary to go over lines that make up the faces you have already drawn. (You'll know when a line is exactly on top of an existing line because it will turn white.) If you make a mistake, there are two ways to eliminate it. Click twice to terminate the polygon—handles will appear around the incomplete shape. Press Backspace to delete the polygon and start again. Or use *Undo* from the *Edit* menu to return the lines as they were before the mistake was made.

Figure 5-9. One Line on Another

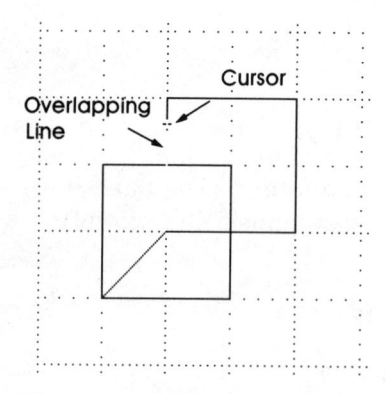

Don't forget; it's easy to draw the polygon if you hold down the Shift key to constrain the sides to 45-degree and 90-degree angles. When you're done, this is what you'll have:

Chapter 5

Figure 5-10. The Finished Polygon

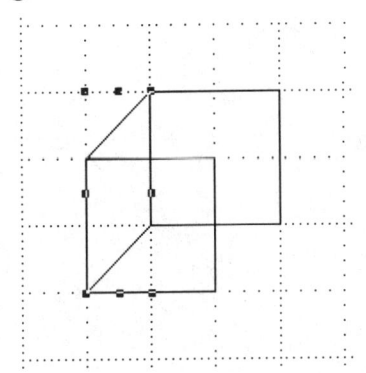

Now you must create an identical polygon for the opposing face. This is easily done by using Command-D to duplicate the first polygon. Move the second polygon into place at the right side of the box.

Figure 5-11. The Second Side

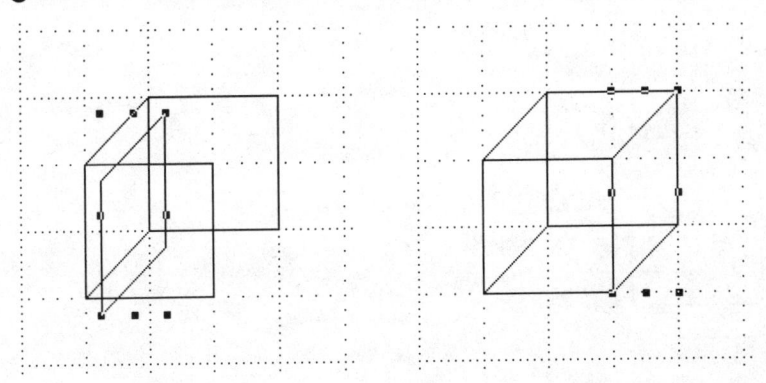

Finish the sides of the box by drawing the top and bottom faces. First, draw the top and then duplicate it to create the bottom. (You could also have used the first polygon you drew for the top face by flipping a copy of it horizontally and rotating it to the left.)

131

Chapter 5

Figure 5-12. The Top and Bottom

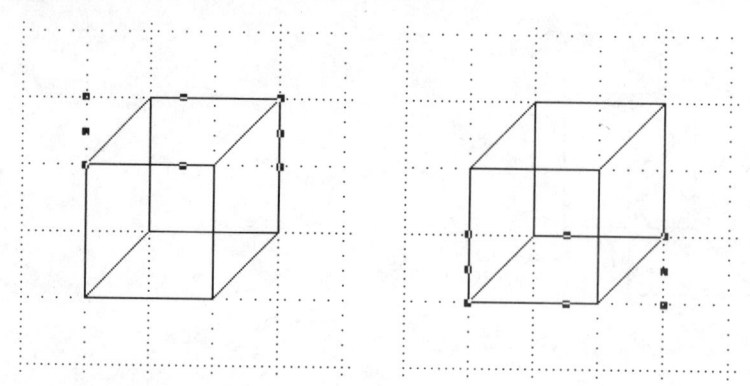

The box faces are now complete. Each is an independent shape and can be moved without disturbing the others. If you were to select each face and move it, you'd see something like this:

Figure 5-13. An Exploded View

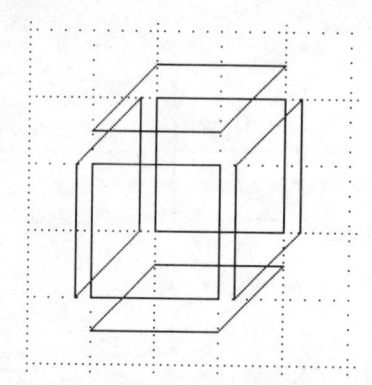

Chapter 5

Select the top, front, and right faces, one at a time, and fill them with the appropriate patterns. Fill the top surface with white. Be careful when you select the shape you want to fill—it's not always obvious which shape will be selected since they often have common sides. The position of the handles around the shape lets you know which one it is. You must click the perimeter of a polygon to select it, not the area inside. Click a side that's not shared by an overlapping shape to insure that the correct surface is selected. If you have trouble selecting a surface, don't worry; the next section will give you more details. After filling, the box should appear as in Figure 5-14.

Figure 5-14. The Colored Box

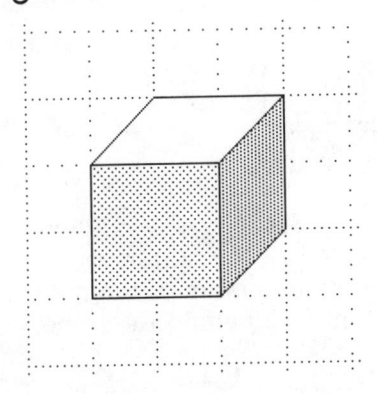

Layering—Organizing the Order of Shapes

The first four features of the *Arrange* menu make it easy to organize your shapes in any order you want along the z-axis. This lets you accurately layer your objects in a prescribed order.

Bring to Front and **Send to Back.** *Bring to Front* and *Send to Back* in the *Arrange* menu are absolute commands—they move the selected shape in front of, or behind, *all other shapes in the drawing.* If a shape is behind another, choose *Bring to Front* to move it to the top. The order of layering is chronological—the last shape drawn is in front of all other shapes unless you change the sequence with commands from the *Arrange* menu.

133

Chapter 5

Figure 5-15. Bringing a Face to the Top

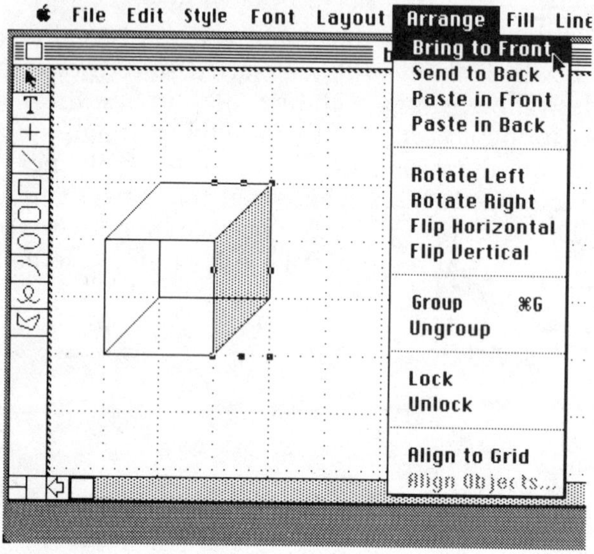

Since the front face of the box has sides shared with four other faces, it will be difficult to select. Click the bottom side of the square. This selects the polygon, or the bottom of the box. Choose *Send to Back* to send the bottom face behind the front.

Figure 5-16. Sending a Face to the Back

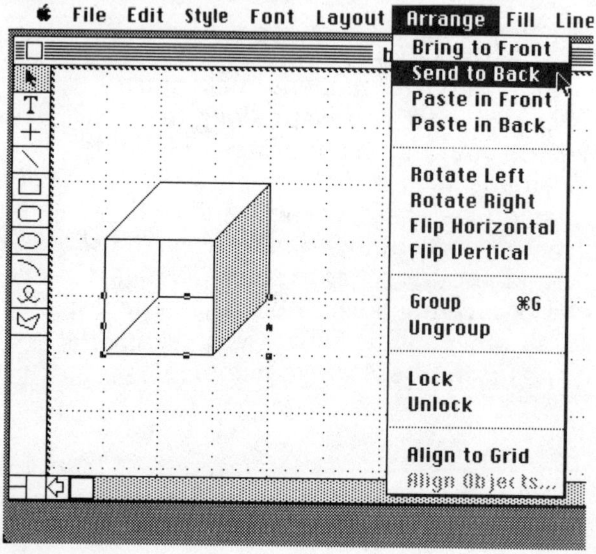

Chapter 5

The front face is now in front of the bottom polygon. Clicking the bottom side of the square selects it. Fill it with the dot pattern as shown.

Figure 5-17. Filling the Front Face

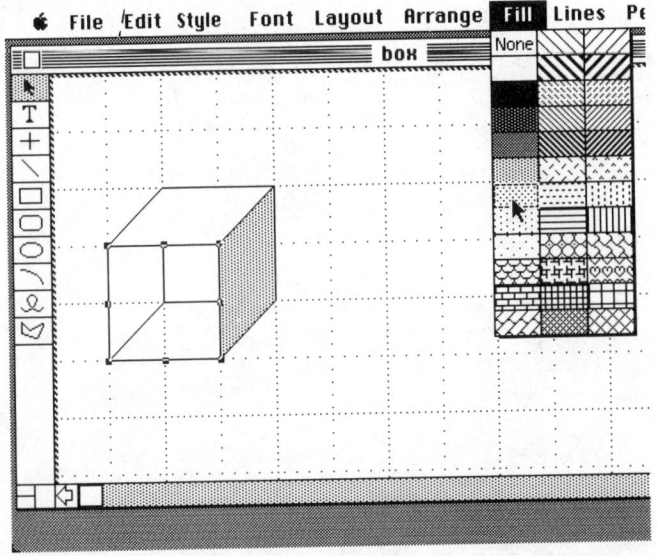

If the filled front face is not opaque, choose *Bring to Front*.

Figure 5-18. Bringing Front Face to the Front

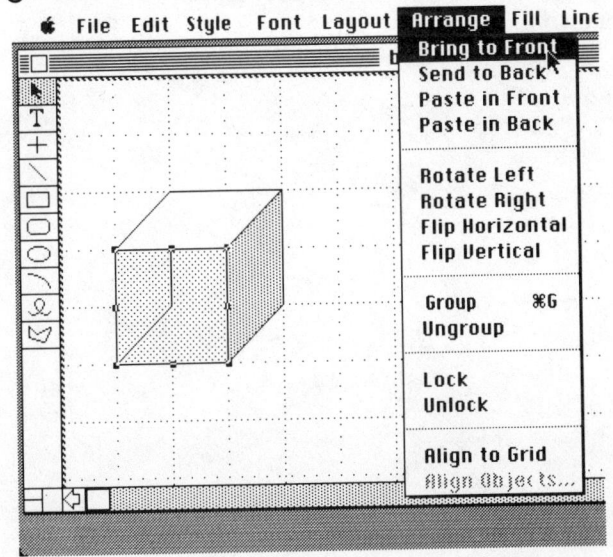

135

Chapter 5

You now have a box with three shaded sides—a white top, and patterned right and front sides. To work on the inside of your box, drag the lid away. Select the back side and fill it with the darkest dot pattern.

Figure 5-19. Filling the Back Inside Surface

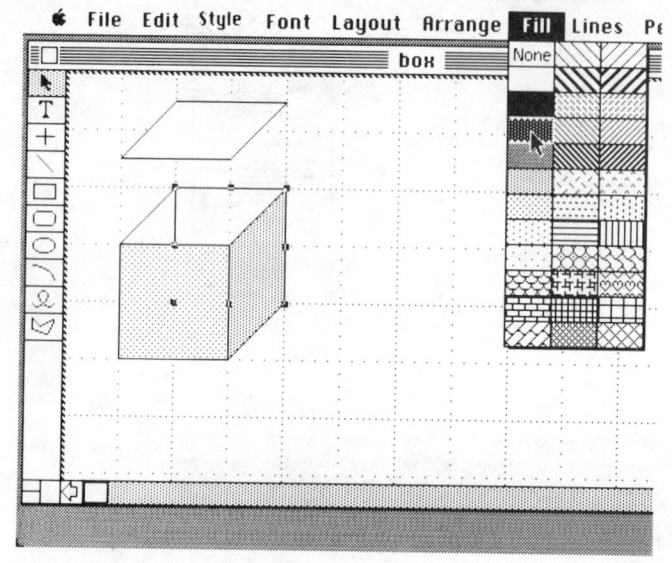

Select the left inside surface and fill it with the middle gray pattern.

Chapter 5

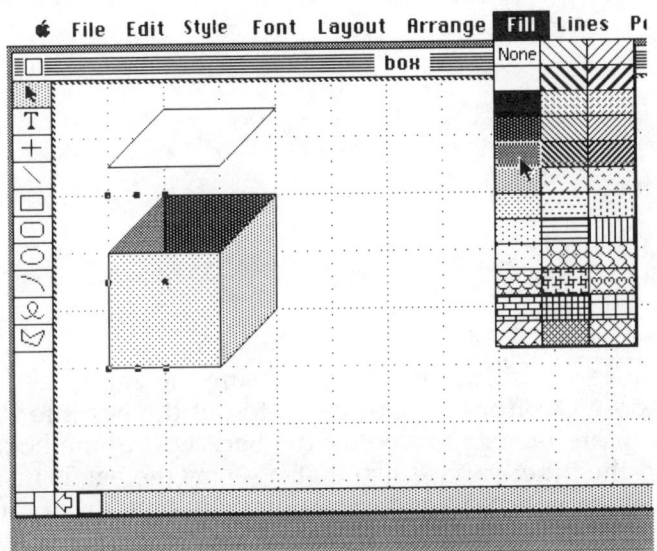

Figure 5-20. Filling the Left Inside Surface

The box is now complete.

***Paste in Front* and *Paste in Back*.** The *Paste in Front* and *Paste in Back* commands allow you to control exactly where an item will be pasted into your MacDraw document, relative to other shapes. First, the object you want to paste is copied or cut into the Clipboard. Then it's either pasted in front of or behind selected forms.

In the box example, draw an egg shape with the oval tool in a work space to the side of the box and fill it with a dot pattern. What happens when you drag the object to the box? It sits on top of all the faces of the box because the egg was drawn *after* the box's faces. Remember, the last item drawn is always on top of all other shapes unless you rearrange its relative position with commands from the *Arrange* menu.

Chapter 5

Figure 5-21. Egg on a Box

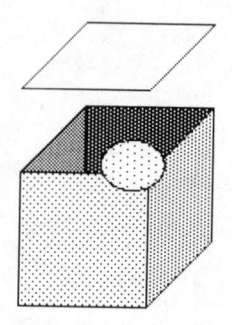

To put the egg "inside" the box, make sure the egg is selected and choose *Cut* from the *Edit* menu to put the egg into the Clipboard. To paste the egg in front of the back wall of the box, but behind all the other surfaces (so that it seems the egg is inside the box), select the back wall and choose *Paste in Front* from the *Arrange* menu. This puts the egg in front of just the back surface.

Figure 5-22. Paste the Egg

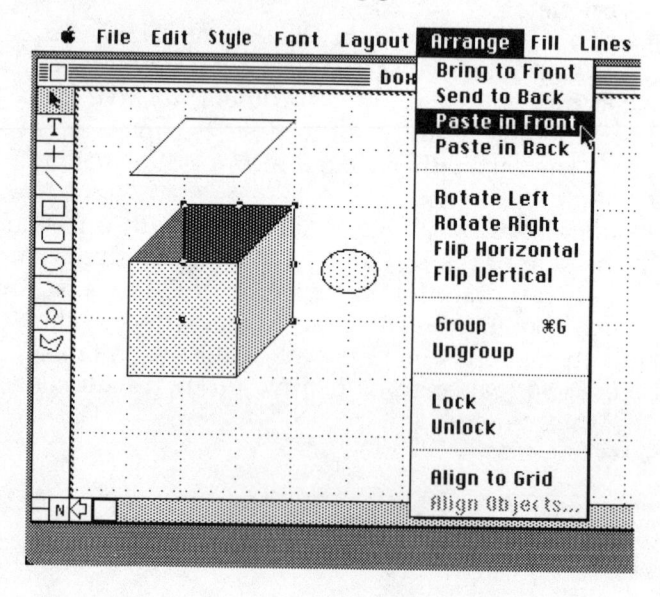

138

Chapter 5

Drag the top into position to close the box, hiding the egg.

The box example demonstrates how MacDraw's ability to remember and manipulate independent shapes gives you a great deal of flexibility in creating your drawings, allowing you to achieve complex layered effects.

Fill, Lines, and Pen

To see how to use the *Fill, Lines,* and *Pen* commands, take a few moments and go through the example below to create some simple shapes. This sample will be extended in the next few sections to demonstrate MacDraw's other features.

Fill. Draw a rectangle and fill it with the middle gray pattern. Inside the rectangle, create another rectangle, this one long and narrow, and fill it with black. To the side, create a polygon in the shape of an arrowhead and fill it with black. The result should look like Figure 5-23.

Figure 5-23. Two Rectangles and an Arrowhead

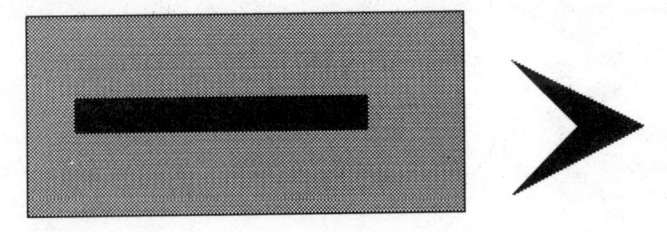

Drag your arrowhead to the rectangle.

Figure 5-24. Finished Arrow

The *Fill* command lets you fill any shape with the pattern of your choice. You can Shift-click several shapes and fill them all with one pattern. Refilling is easy—just select the shape and choose another pattern. If you decide you want to make a shape

139

Chapter 5

larger or smaller, the pattern fills the enlarged or reduced shape with no distortion.

Lines. You can use the *Lines* menu to choose one of four thicknesses for the outline of your shapes.

Figure 5-25. Various Outlines

By selecting the dashed line from the *Lines* menu, you can display shapes without outlines.

Perhaps you want to draw arrows for architectural drawings. It's simple. Draw a line (using the line tool) and select the arrow direction from the *Lines* menu.

Figure 5-26. Arrows

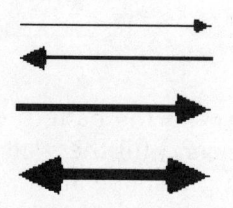

Chapter 5

Pen. The *Pen* feature gives you any one of 36 patterns as the outline for your shapes.

Figure 5-27. Arrow Variations

You can combine *Fill, Lines,* and *Pen* to create a wide range of different effects. Here's the arrow with a white outline.

Figure 5-28. White Outline

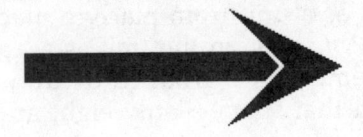

Chapter 5

Taping Items Together

Earlier you learned that you must create pictures from individual elements for the greatest control of drawings. Here's a car that was drawn from several independent elements.

Figure 5-29. Drawing from Elements

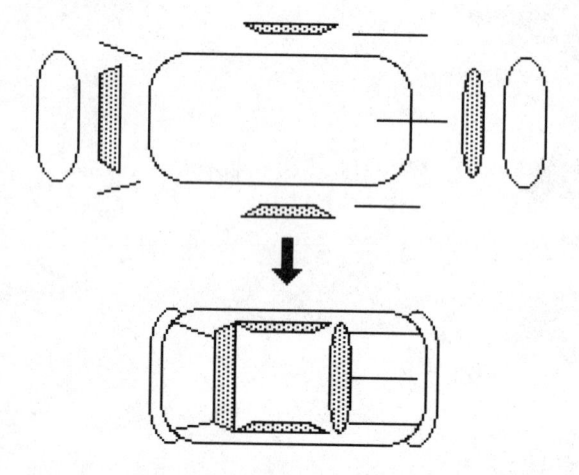

When one shape is constructed of numerous components, it can become difficult to work with. Each time you want to select the object, you must make sure to select *all* its pieces before you can drag it to a new position. If you're not careful, an unselected element may be left behind.

MacDraw's *Group,* from the *Arrange* menu, gives you a tool to blend individual elements into one shape. Once a shape's elements are grouped, it can be moved as a unit from place to place. Commands such as *Fill, Lines,* and *Pen* work on the unit as a whole. You can tell when several elements are grouped by the handles that appear when you select that shape—only eight appear around a grouped item.

Chapter 5

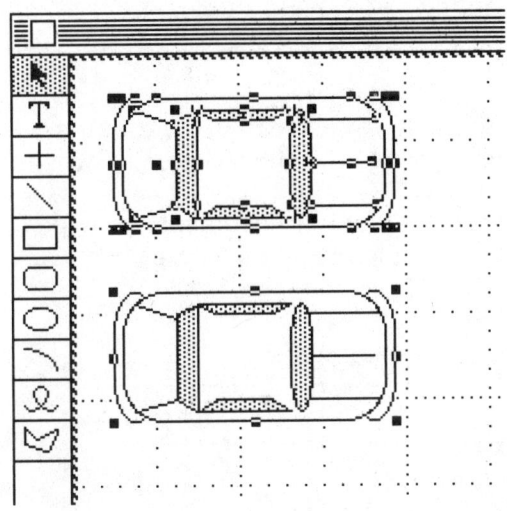

Figure 5-30. Before and After Grouping

One major convenience of a grouped item is that it can be altered in size and proportion by dragging just one handle.

Figure 5-31. Altering the Size of a Grouped Form

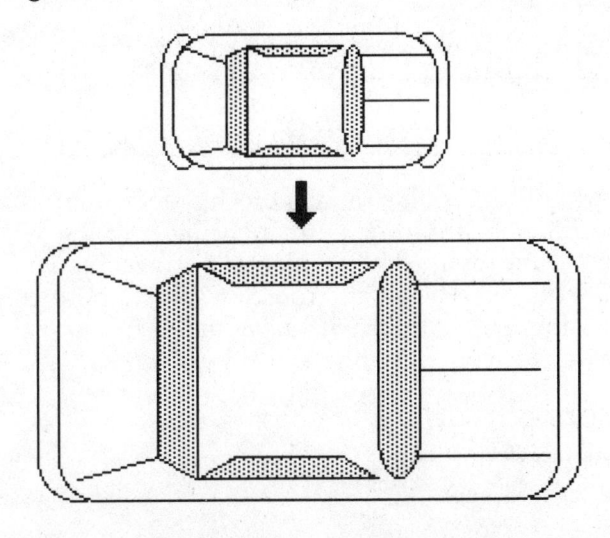

You'll notice that all individual elements, including the filled areas, are enlarged proportionally.

Chapter 5

The *Ungroup* command returns control of each element. This can be convenient if you want to alter just one piece of a grouped structure.

Taping Items Down

Sometimes it's necessary to move some elements without accidentally moving other, overlapping elements. There *is* a way to make some elements stationary.

Suppose you want to create a format document, on which you'll create page layouts consisting of three columns, like this:

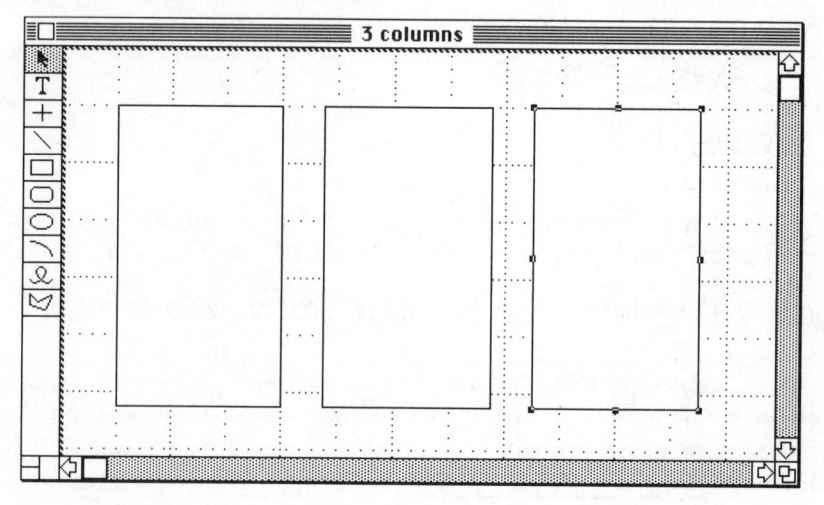

Figure 5-32. Three Columns

You'll create text and draw illustrations on this document. Since the column perimeters are to be permanent parts of the document, you don't want them to be accidentally moved as you click and select elements of your layout. You can "tape" these columns down by choosing *Lock* from the *Arrange* menu. If you try to move a locked element, you'll get this alarm box:

Figure 5-33. Item Locked

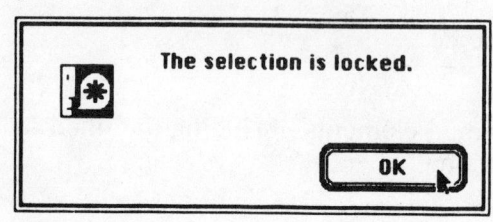

144

Chapter 5

You can click *OK* and then *Unlock* from the *Arrange* menu if you want to modify a locked item.

Perspective Drawings

Using MacDraw makes it easy to draw objects in perspective. After drawing a horizon line and vanishing points, for instance, you can hang objects with the aid of guidelines representing the rules of perspective. These guidelines allow you to convincingly show the foreshortening of objects as they get farther away from the observer. In this section, you'll learn how to draw three-dimensional objects with either one or two vanishing points.

One-point perspectives. By following these steps, you'll be able to draw two cubes in one-point perspective.

First, establish the horizon line and the vanishing point with straight lines. Also click the fill box at the bottom left and select *None* from the *Fill* menu so that the shapes will all be transparent.

Figure 5-34. Horizon Line and One Vanishing Point

Now draw the front surfaces of the two cubes.

Figure 5-35. Draw the Front Surfaces

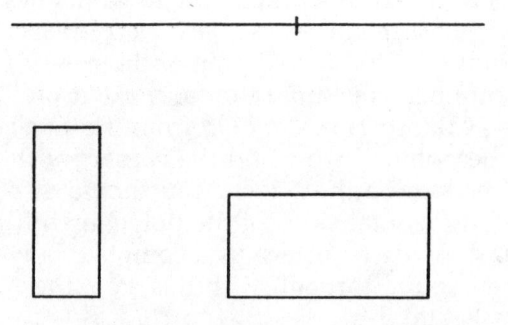

Keep the Command key held down while you join each corner of the front surfaces to the vanishing point. These perspective lines, the horizon line, and the vanishing point are your guides for creating the faces of the two cubes.

145

Chapter 5

Figure 5-36. Draw Perspective Lines

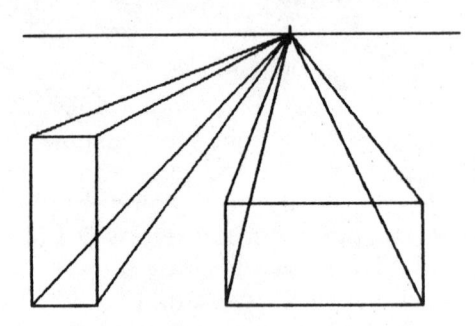

Holding down the Command key allowed you to draw straight lines without having to go back and select the line tool each time. When you release the Command key, all these lines appear selected, with handles around them. After the drawing is finished, you'll want to remove these guidelines, leaving only the three-dimensional structures you've drawn. What's the easiest way to get rid of these lines? If you group them now, you can later select them with one click, and you can delete them with a single press of the Backspace key. Since the perspective lines are already selected, Shift-click to select the horizon and vanishing point lines and choose *Group* from the *Arrange* menu.

To make sure that you don't accidentally move these lines as you create the cubes, secure the grouped perspective guidelines by choosing *Lock* from the *Arrange* menu.

The next step is to draw the top face of one of the cubes. Use a polygon. There are two things you should do to make it precisely draw the polygons. Choose *Turn Grid Off* from the *Layout* menu so you can place the pointer arrow and the corners of the polygon with the most freedom on the screen. You should also constrain the vertical and horizontal sides of the polygon with the Shift key. Make sure you draw each surface as a complete polygon with four sides. When you're through with this step, the drawing should look like Figure 5-37.

Chapter 5

Figure 5-37. The First Polygon

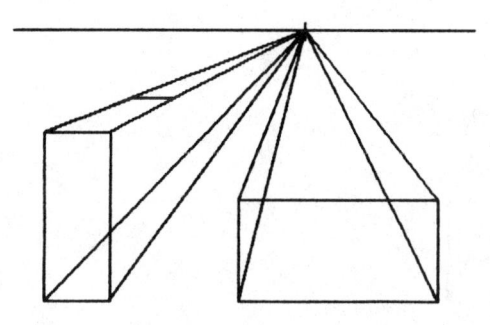

Figure 5-38 shows what the polygon would look like if it was moved away from the main structure.

Figure 5-38. Moved Away

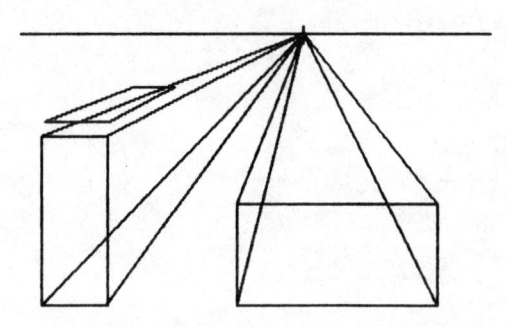

As you draw the surfaces of the two boxes, if the sides of the polygons and rectangles don't exactly drop on top of the perspective lines, you can double-click to stop and, when the handles appear, press Backspace to delete the incomplete shape, then start again. If the polygon you draw is close to correct, but has a slight flaw, use the *Reshape Polygon* feature in the *Edit* menu to fix it by carefully dragging the handles that appear at the corners of the polygon. Remember, when the line you are drawing or moving disappears, it means that the line is exactly on top of the one beneath it. Draw a polygon or rectangle for each face of the cube.

Chapter 5

Figure 5-39. Draw the Rest

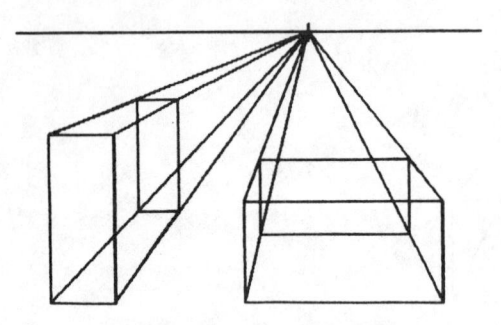

When you've finished drawing the remaining faces of the cube, click one of the perspective lines, choose *Unlock* from the *Arrange* menu, and press Backspace to delete them. Save your result and print it out.

Figure 5-40. The Finished Perspective

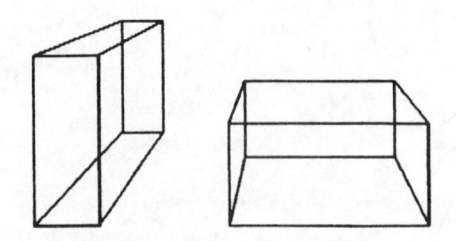

Two-point perspective. Drawings in two-point perspective, though not quite as easy as one-point perspective, can also be created with MacDraw. Try drawing two cubes in two-point perspective. First, start with the horizon line and two vanishing points.

Figure 5-41. Horizon Line and Two Vanishing Points

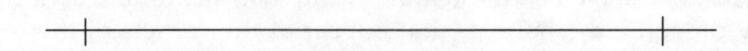

Draw two vertical lines to represent the forward edge corners of the two objects. Then draw four perspective lines for each object—from the ends of each vertical line to each of the two vanishing points.

Chapter 5

Figure 5-42. Vertical Lines

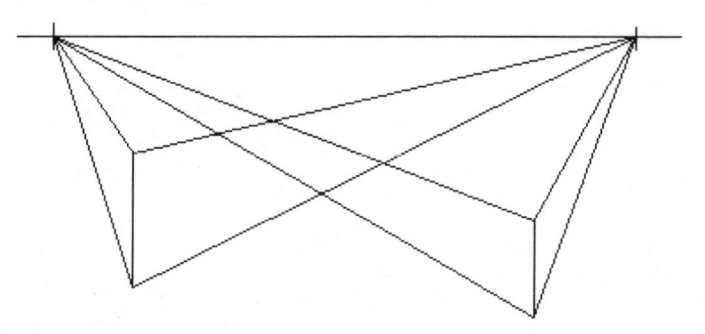

Now draw polygons for the two forward sides of each of the two cubes.

Figure 5-43. Polygons for Two Sides of Each Cube

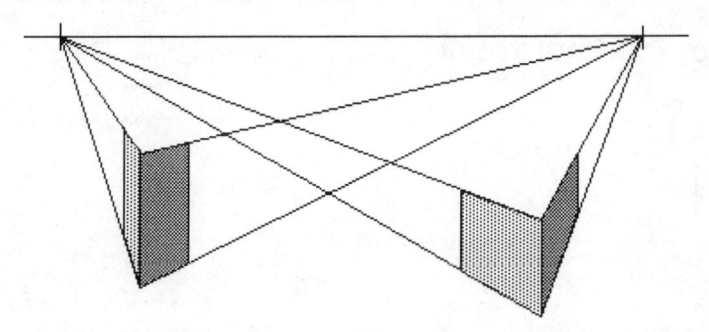

Extend perspective lines to the vanishing points and draw top and bottom polygons.

Figure 5-44. Tops and Bottoms

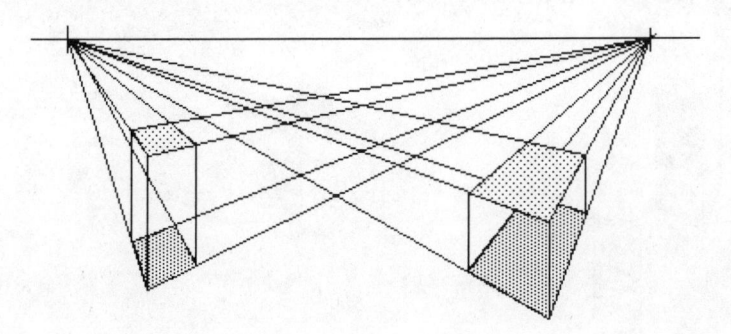

Chapter 5

The last two faces to draw are the rear ones.

Figure 5-45. Draw Rear Faces

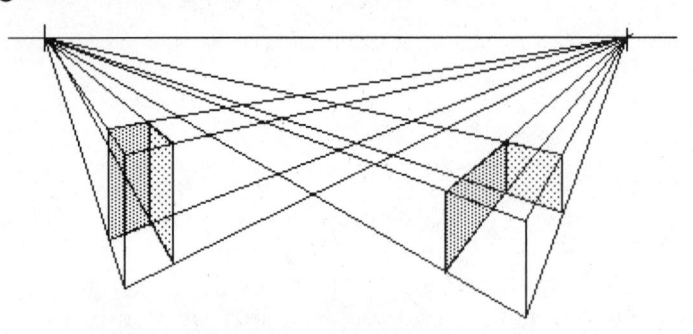

To remove all the guidelines, Shift-click until they're selected and press Backspace to delete them. Also, remove the vertical lines you started with. The end product looks like Figure 5-46.

Figure 5-46. The Final Result

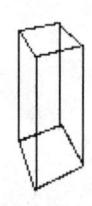

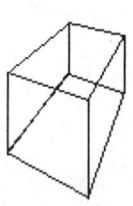

You can now fill the faces with the patterns of your choice. You can even lift off a surface and fill the inside back faces with darker patterns for a better effect.

Figure 5-47. Open Cubes

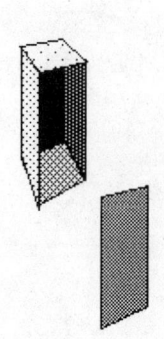

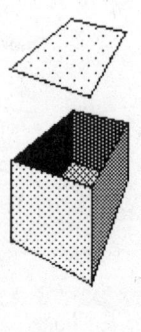

150

Chapter 5

Shadows. You can use the principles of perspective to draw shadows cast by objects.

Figure 5-48. A Shadow Cast

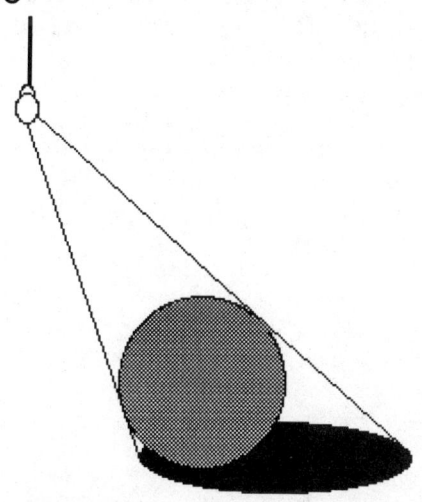

The shadow of the circle lets the viewer know that the circle is actually a sphere. But the circle looks flat because it's filled with a continuous pattern. There's no MacDraw tool that allows you to make part of the circle darker than the rest to give the circle a sense of volume. By transferring this picture into a MacPaint document, you can use MacPaint's spray-can tool to make the circle appear spherical.

Using Text

MacDraw also gives you the ability to create and edit words, either in the form of captions or as blocks of text.

Caption text. To create captions for your drawings, choose the text tool (signified by the box at the far left containing the *T*), click where you want it, and simply type. The insertion point, just as in MacWrite, is a blinking vertical line. You can vary the caption by selections from the *Font* and *Type* menus. After the text has been entered, you can edit with the Macintosh's standard text-editing techniques.

Dragging the I-beam cursor across the text selects it and is indicated by highlighted reverse text. Once selected, the text can be deleted by pressing Backspace or by choosing *Clear* from the *Edit*

151

Chapter 5

menu. Selected text can also be cut or copied into the Clipboard and later pasted elsewhere. Another way to select individual words is to double-click them. Deleting or inserting characters is easy—click to put the insertion point at the right place and use Backspace to delete characters to the left of the cursor or just insert characters at the cursor.

You can click on the text with the arrow to select it. You can't alter the size of your caption text by dragging the handles as you can with geometric shapes, but you can move it from place to place. If you move your caption to a patterned background, the text will be surrounded by a white area because the default fill pattern for text is white.

Figure 5-49. Text Area Is White

You can use the *Fill* menu to vary the look of your caption.

Figure 5-50. Text Background Filled

You can also change the style of any selected caption. When the background is a patterned fill, use outlined text for the caption.

Figure 5-51. Changing Text Style

152

Chapter 5

To get white letters on a patterned background, use outlined letters and choose *None* as the pattern.

Figure 5-52. No Fill

A MacDraw Caption

    Paragraph text. MacDraw gives you the ability to create text within blocks of various sizes, which you can define. If you want text in a 2 × 2-1/8 inch column, for instance, first draw a rectangle that size, then type your text. In *Paragraph Text* mode, you don't have to choose the text icon—MacDraw assumes that when you start typing after creating the rectangle, you want the text to be inside the shape. As you type, MacDraw wraps the words for you—that is, if a word cannot fit within the width of the block you've established, it's sent to the next line without being split.

Figure 5-53. Paragraph Text

Paragraph Text
gives you a lot of
text formatting and
editing tools.

    Fill the block with a pattern. You'll see that the text is shown on a white background.

Chapter 5

Figure 5-54. Fill Background of Text

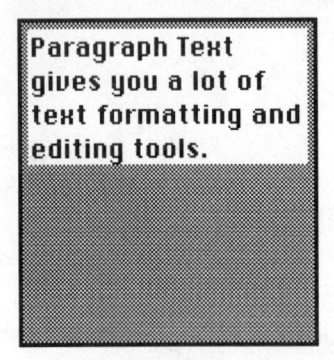

> Paragraph Text gives you a lot of text formatting and editing tools.

You can click the text (not the shape it's within) to select it; by dragging its handles, you can change the text's formatting. The word-wrap feature works as you change the text shape. This powerful feature of MacDraw allows you to alter the proportions of any text, whenever you wish.

Figure 5-55. Narrower Columns

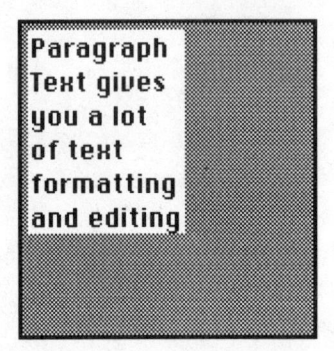

> Paragraph Text gives you a lot of text formatting and editing

You can center the text, or change its font, style, and size. By selecting *None* from the *Fill* menu, you can make the white area around your text disappear. Take a look at Figure 5-56; the text has been significantly changed by altering the font, the point size, and its style.

Chapter 5

Figure 5-56. Text Can Be Altered in Several Ways

> Paragraph
> Text gives
> you a lot of
> text creating
> and editing
> tools.

You can right justify the text and fill the area behind it with an entirely different pattern.

Figure 5-57. Fill the Text Background

> Paragraph Text
> gives you a lot of
> text creating and
> editing tools.

White letters on a black background can be attractive. Create this effect by choosing outlined characters, then fill both the text background and the rectangle with black.

Chapter 5

Figure 5-58. White on Black

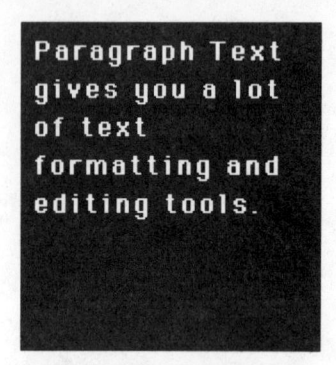

```
Paragraph Text
gives you a lot
of text
formatting and
editing tools.
```

You can also change the shape of both text and background by grouping them together, then by dragging one handle to change the size of both. The text is automatically reformatted as you drag it.

Figure 5-59. Group and Change the Size

```
Paragraph
Text gives
you a lot
of text
formatting
and editing
tools.
```

The Roll of Film

MacDraw lets you create drawings in sizes from 8 × 10 inches to 4 × 8 feet. To view an entire drawing, enter the *Reduce to Fit* mode, selected from the *Layout* menu. Your drawing appears on the screen, each page outlined—you can think of it as a roll of film. Figure 5-60 shows a *Reduce to Fit* window made up of 21 pieces. If these sheets were filled with parts of a drawing, printed

Chapter 5

out, and taped together, the final drawing would be 30 × 56 inches.

Figure 5-60. 21-Sheet Drawing

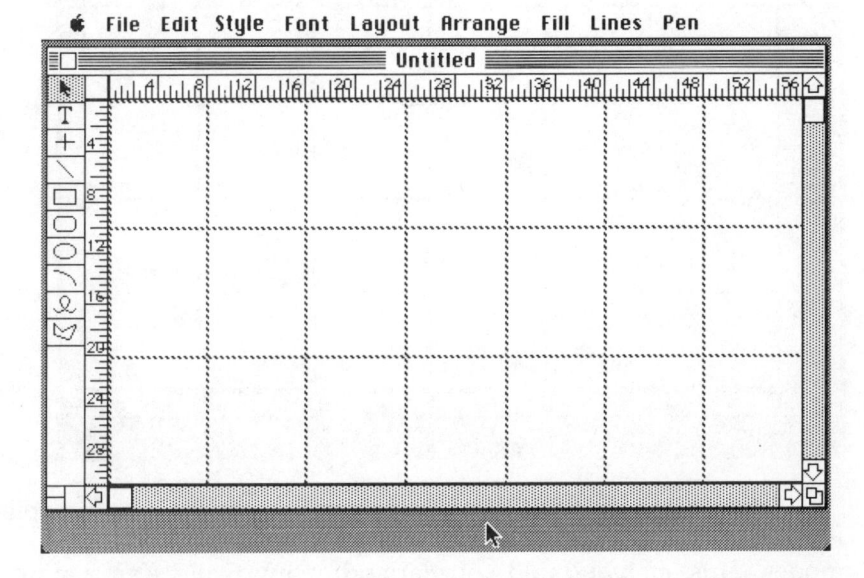

Horizontal layouts. If you want your sheets to be laid out horizontally rather than vertically, choose *Page Setup* from the *File* menu and click *Wide*.

Figure 5-61. *Page Setup* Dialog Box

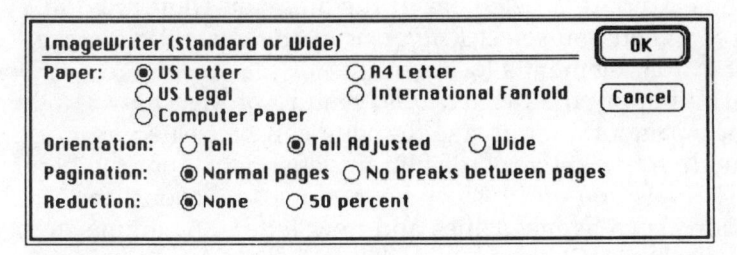

The drawing is now 32 × 60 inches and is made up of 24 sheets of paper.

Chapter 5

Figure 5-62. 24 Horizontal Sheets

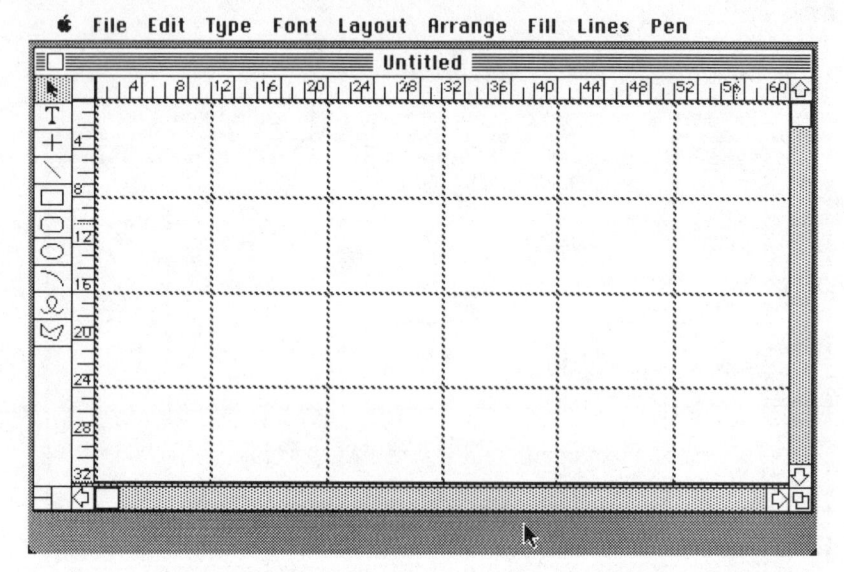

Zooming in and out. With MacDraw's large-drawing capability, you can create and edit both text and pictures in reduced modes. This lets you build your large drawing while seeing more of it than fills the window. If a detailed change has to be made, you can go back to normal mode to work on a single part of the drawing.

How can you control the location you'll arrive at in a large drawing when you zoom in and out with the *Reduce* and *Enlarge* commands? Choose an element in the area you want to go to by clicking it. When you select *Reduce* or *Enlarge*, you'll enter the drawing at that element's location.

You can apply the *Reduce to Fit* feature of MacDraw to other uses. Each page of a multipage drawing can be treated as a cell, like a single frame on a roll of film, independent from the other pages. This lets you create story boards or page layouts for publications such as magazines and newsletters. A sample story board is shown in Chapter 6.

Masking with MacDraw to Erase, Enhance, and Repair

Many reviews of MacDraw in the popular magazines bemoan the fact that a tool like MacPaint's eraser is not available. Although such a tool is absent, (because MacDraw can't forget part of a shape), there *is* a way of erasing portions of the shapes you create.

Chapter 5

Erasing. To erase a portion of a shape with MacDraw, cover it with a shape of the opposite value—if you want to erase a white structure, cover it with a black object; if you want to erase something that's black, cover it with something white. This may seem like sweeping the dust under the carpet at first, but it *is* a useful and valid technique. The process of making a form disappear by covering it with a white form is called *masking*.

A few examples can easily demonstrate the procedure. Suppose you want to change a rectangle so that it has openings in it like this:

Figure 5-63. A Rectangle with Openings

Draw the rectangle, then two short lines at least as thick as the rectangle's perimeter. Drag the lines to the shape.

Figure 5-64. Two Lines in Place

Select both lines by Shift-clicking and choose the white fill pattern from the *Pen* menu. Now the lines make the parts of the rectangle they cover disappear. The rectangle seems to have two openings in it.

Since the open rectangle is actually made up of three independent components (the rectangle and two short lines), if you select the rectangle and move it to a new location, the masking lines will not accompany it. To make the masking lines a fixed part of the rectangle, use the selection rectangle to select all three parts and *Group* from the *Arrange* menu. Now the masking lines are "taped" to the rectangle.

One advantage of this masking process is that since the

Chapter 5

rectangle is really an intact form rather than a form with openings, it can be filled with a pattern.

Figure 5-65. The Filled Masked Rectangle

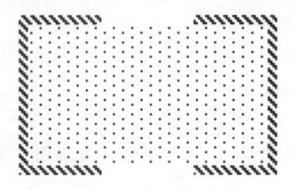

Enhancing. How could you represent a two-lane road with MacDraw? It's easy if you use a masking technique. First, draw a rectangle and fill it with black to represent the roadway. Now add narrow, white lines to represent the lane dividers.

Figure 5-66. A Two-Lane Highway

Repairing. Sometimes you'll make small errors in creating shapes with MacDraw. If the error is detected only after a drawing is finished, or if the shape that contains the drawing is too difficult to re-create, you can mask to repair the damage.

If you wanted to remove the trailing line on the polygon below, it's easier to mask it out than to redraw the whole shape.

Figure 5-67. Polygon with a Tail

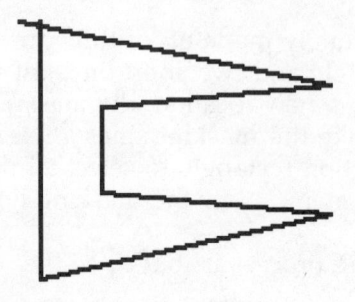

Chapter 5

Draw a rectangle large enough to cover the tail and drag it into position. Turn the *Grid* feature off to make it easy for you to get the rectangle in the proper place.

Figure 5-68. Cover the Tail with a Rectangle

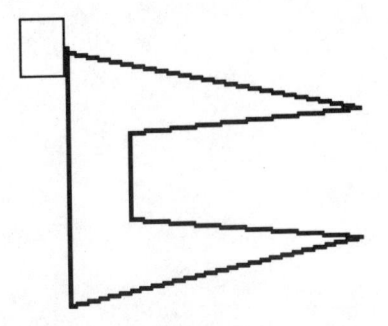

Make the rectangle disappear by choosing white from the *Pen* menu and, like magic, the tail vanishes.

Figure 5-69. The Final Result

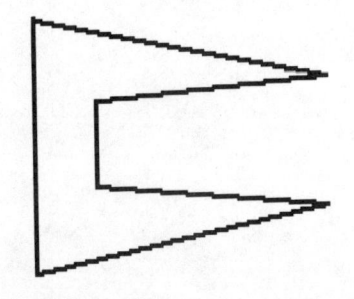

An Expert

In this chapter you've learned some of MacDraw's advanced features. It will take some time to master the intricacies of this graphics editor, but learning about it can be fun and certainly rewarding.

Chapter 6
The Many Uses of Mac Art

Chapter 6
The Many Uses of Mac Art

Professionals are finding that the Macintosh's graphics features can make them more productive. Graphic artist Richard Bloch of Boston, Massachusetts, uses the Mac extensively for his graphic design business. "As a graphic designer, I feel that the Macintosh is worth every penny I paid for it. I do sketch after sketch, revision after revision, and this is where the Mac earns its keep. It saves me a lot of time because I rarely have to redraw." In Bloch's view, Macintosh sketches are better than hand-drawn ones for several reasons.

- I can make changes to a design and still retain the original if I want to. If I want to show a client two sketches, one slightly different from the other, I don't have to draw two separate sketches—I can just save one, alter it, and save the modified version as a separate document.
- I save money on transfer lettering by using Mac's fonts to lay out copy. I also save money on pattern sheets by using Mac's pattern palette, customizing the patterns when necessary.
- I can accurately rough out blocks of text using Mac's fonts. This gives me a visual representation of the space that will be taken up by a block of text without having to do complex character counts and calculations or having to pay for typesetting.
- My clients are impressed by the Mac's printouts. They suggest changes and we make them directly on the Mac until they're happy with the result. There are no surprises—they know exactly how their work will look before someone inks the final drawings from the Mac sketches.

This chapter shows you ways to use the Macintosh for a variety of visual art applications. Business graphics, design, and the preparation of slides are all covered. Each section is illustrated with examples actually created with MacPaint and MacDraw. Procedures not covered in earlier chapters are usually described step by step.

Graphic Arts

Even if you're not artistically inclined, MacPaint and MacDraw will enable you to give form to visual ideas for your business. In a surprisingly short time, you can be designing logos, business cards, announcements, and advertising flyers.

Chapter 6

Logos

Everybody loves a logo. Logos represent ideas much more succinctly than words do. A logo is a pictorial distillation of the traits that characterize an individual or an organization.

The Mac makes it fairly simple to design a logo. If your logo requires freehand elements, use MacPaint. If the elements that make up the logo are simple geometric forms, use MacDraw. After you've created a logo, you can put it into documents such as business cards, letterheads, and announcements.

The three logos presented here were created with MacPaint. MacPaint's *FatBits* and eraser features gave the artist the control that was needed to prepare custom lettering and to create fine details.

Figure 6-1. Three Logos Produced with MacPaint

Bill Jonas, Artworks, Inc.

Chapter 6

You can use MacDraw to create logos if you're not planning on using custom lettering and fine hand-drawn details. Another advantage of MacDraw is its *Custom Rulers*, which help keep exact proportions in a logo.

The next logo was done with MacDraw. Two intermediate steps are also shown.

Figure 6-2. A Logo Created with MacDraw

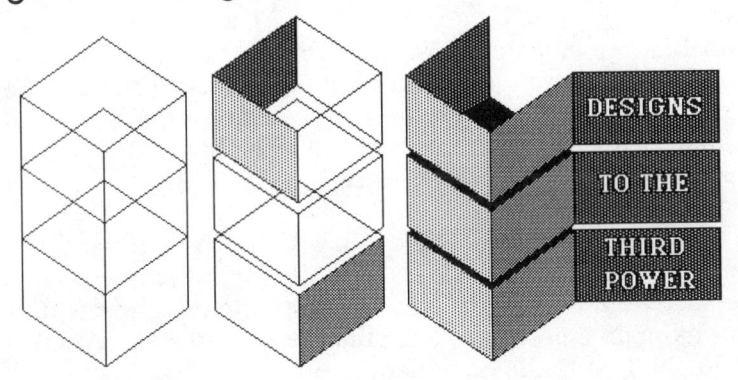

Remember, when creating geometric forms with MacDraw, draw them as complete, individual elements. The faces of the cubes in Figure 6-2, for instance, were not constructed by the juxtaposition of simple straight lines. Instead, MacDraw's polygon and rectangle tools were used. They were drawn this way because, as you'll remember from Chapter 5, MacDraw can fill polygons, ovals, arcs, free-form drawings, and rectangles with a pattern, but it cannot fill enclosed spaces made up of straight lines. To save yourself lots of redrawing, just avoid using MacDraw's straight-line tools in creating enclosed forms.

Business Cards

The next time you need a new business card, you can use your Macintosh to design it. When you've finished, you can take your design to a graphic artist and have it inked and the lettering typeset. You'll be pleasantly surprised at how little time it takes to communicate your design ideas when you have a well-executed sample that displays everything just the way you want it. You don't have to look through sheets of hundreds of typefaces and type styles, and you don't have to decide on various type sizes. With the Macintosh, you can come close to a final design and

Chapter 6

type selection—all the graphic artist may do is make suggestions for putting it into final form.

To design a business card, begin by drawing a 2 × 3-1/2 inch rectangle (the size of a standard business card) with MacPaint and create your design inside it. If you've already designed a logo with MacPaint, you can paste it into the card format. And if the logo is too large to fit, just use the shrink feature to make it smaller. *FatBits* can clean up the reduced logo if necessary.

With MacDraw, it's easy to move the card's elements from place to place until you get the desired look. *Show Size* from the *Layout* menu will help you get the correct size for the card's outline. Remember, however, that you won't be able to design a freehand logo easily with MacDraw—use MacPaint instead for cards that need such a drawing.

To maximize flexibility, you can use both MacPaint *and* MacDraw to design your business card. Just follow these steps.

Step 1. Use MacDraw to create the outline of your business card and its main elements, such as name and address. When you've finished, save the document.

Figure 6-3. Design the Business Card Elements with MacDraw

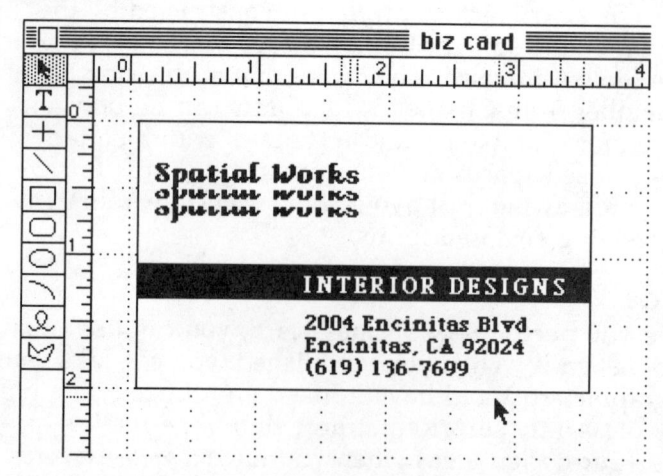

Step 2. Select your design with the selection rectangle and choose *Copy* from the *Edit* menu to put it into the Clipboard.

Step 3. Quit MacDraw and open MacPaint.

Chapter 6

Step 4. Choose *Paste* from the *Edit* menu to paste your design into the open MacPaint document.

Step 5. Create your logo in a work space to the side of your card design. (If you already have a MacPaint document with your logo in it, close the business card document, saving the changes; open the logo document; copy the logo into the Clipboard; open the business card document again; and paste the logo into it.)

Step 6. Move the logo into the proper position within your design.

Figure 6-4. The Finished Business Card Design

```
Spatial Works
opuciuu nuino
opuciuu nuino

        INTERIOR DESIGNS
          2004 Encinitas Blvd.
          Encinitas, CA 92024
          (619) 136-7699
```

Here's an example of another business card, this time produced with MacPaint.

Figure 6-5. MacPaint Business Card Design

```
≡□≡  Mac Artist for Hire  ≡
        GRAPHIC DESIGN
           James Fine
         1122 Left Bank
         Paris CA 94128
         (666) 123-4444
```

The two application icons for MacPaint and MacDraw were obtained by screen dumps from the desktop. With the MacPaint working disk directory on the desktop, Command-Shift-3 results in a MacPaint document entitled Screen *n*, where *n* is a number.

Chapter 6

You can then produce a screen dump of this document by selecting *Print* from the *File* menu. You can do the same thing with MacDraw. The appropriate application icons were cut from these documents and pasted into the business card document and moved into position. The title bar was obtained from another screen dump of a MacPaint window.

Letterheads

You can use the power of the Macintosh's graphics to create a letterhead design with either MacPaint or MacDraw. It's so easy to create attractive letterheads with the Mac that you'll probably make several—one for your business letters, one for your invoices, one for your letters to friends, and one for a club or professional organization. Two example letterheads produced with MacPaint follow.

Figure 6-6. Two Letterheads Created with MacPaint

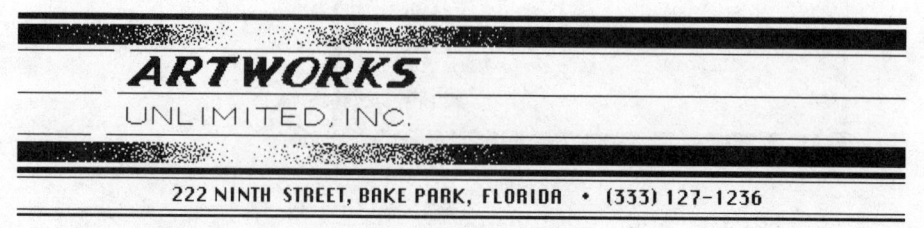

From the desk of...

Majie Alley

10000 Harpo
Interlochen, MA
49999

ARTWORKS
UNLIMITED, INC.

222 NINTH STREET, BAKE PARK, FLORIDA • (333) 127-1236

You may want to take your letterhead design to a graphic artist for typesetting and final inking, or you may want to reproduce

Chapter 6

the letterhead yourself. In order for the letterhead to print each time you want to create a letter on the Imagewriter, paste the design into MacWrite's Scrapbook. This way, you'll be able to paste your letterhead into any MacWrite document and type your letter below it.

To put a MacPaint letterhead into a MacWrite document, just go through these steps.

Step 1. Select the letterhead and copy it into the Clipboard.
Step 2. Quit MacPaint and open MacWrite.
Step 3. Choose the Scrapbook and paste your letterhead into the Scrapbook.

Now your letterhead can be copied from the Scrapbook and pasted into a document whenever it's needed. Using the letterhead is just as easy.

Step 1. Open MacWrite, choose Scrapbook from the Apple menu, and use the scroll bars to locate your letterhead.
Step 2. Choose *Copy* from the *Edit* menu to put the letterhead into the Clipboard. Put away the Scrapbook.
Step 3. Choose *Paste* from the *Edit* menu to put the letterhead into your MacWrite document.

Now you're ready to type your letter.

Figure 6-7. Letterhead Pasted into a MacWrite Document

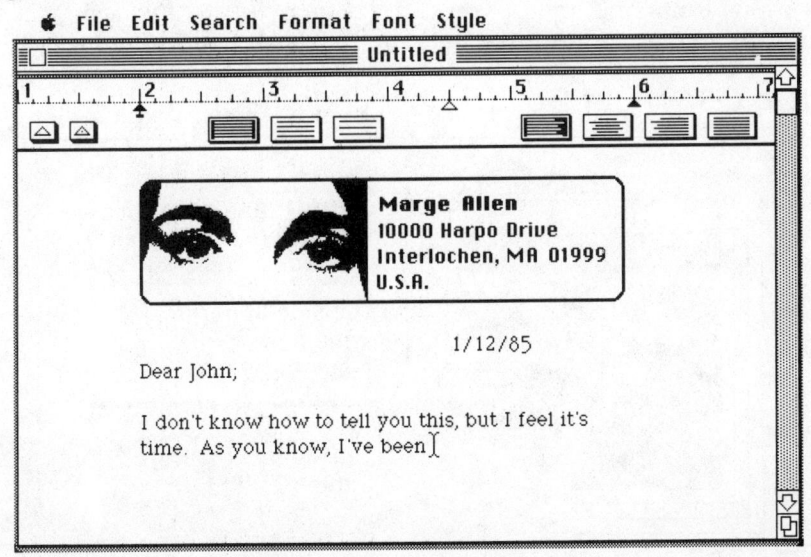

When you've finished typing your letter, you can print it on quality stationery with the Imagewriter.

Chapter 6

Letterheads transferred from MacPaint to MacWrite can only be as large as the MacPaint window. If you need a wider letterhead, use MacDraw to design it. You can move pictures as wide as seven inches from MacDraw to MacWrite.

A large letterhead can be drawn with MacPaint, but it can't be moved to MacWrite if the letterhead is larger than a window. To get around this problem, you must type your text below the letterhead in the MacPaint document. To make editing the text easier, turn MacPaint's *Grid* feature on before you start typing. This aids in finding the proper position for the insertion point at the beginning of a line in case you want to retype it. The problem with writing text with MacPaint is that if you make a mistake, it's very difficult to go back and correct it. Remember that with MacPaint, once the characters are typed, they are remembered not as letters, but as a series of dots, and for this reason the text editing available with MacDraw is not possible with MacPaint.

Type carefully. If you make a mistake, use the Backspace key. To change the font or style of your text, you must retype it unless you make the font change before clicking somewhere.

Announcements

Most Macintosh owners will someday use the computer to make a printed announcement. With Mac's graphics as illustrations and its various fonts and styles, you can design eye-catching text. You can design a single announcement, such as is shown in Figure 6-8:

Figure 6-8. An Art Gallery Announcement

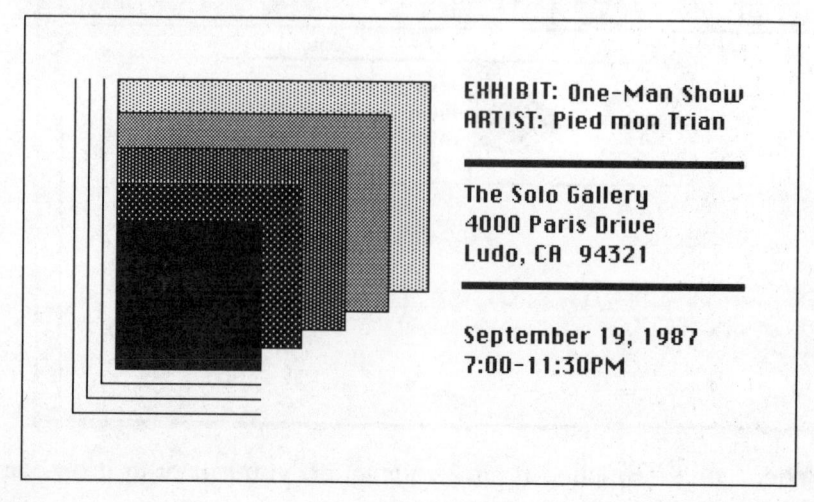

EXHIBIT: One-Man Show
ARTIST: Pied mon Trian

The Solo Gallery
4000 Paris Drive
Ludo, CA 94321

September 19, 1987
7:00-11:30PM

Chapter 6

Or you can create the framework for an announcement format, which you'll use to build several announcements:

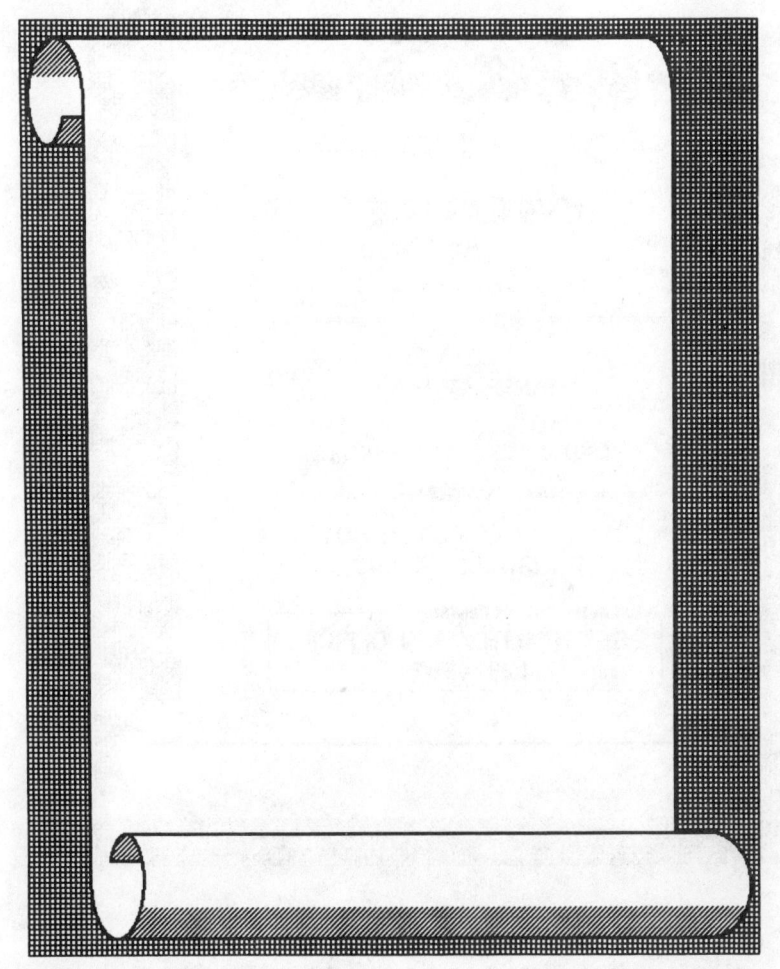

Figure 6-9. An Announcement Format

When you want to prepare an announcement based on such a framework, open the format document and enter the relevant information. If you create several format documents, you'll have a small library to choose from. Figure 6-10 shows a finished announcement which uses the above format.

Chapter 6

Figure 6-10. A Finished Announcement

> Palm Beach County
> **Sheriff's Office**
>
> ———— PRESENTS ————
>
> ## K-9 BANQUET
> ### FOR
> *Graduating Class #4*
>
> ══════ JOIN US ══════
>
> **FRIDAY**
> **JUNE 29TH 1984**
>
> 6:15 PM..................................OPEN BAR
> 7:30 PM..................................DINNER
>
> ══════ AT THE ══════
>
> **COLONNADES BEACH HOTEL**
> **ON SINGER ISLAND**
>
> ┌─ FOR RESERVATIONS CONTACT: ──────
> **SGT. SMITH / K-9 OFFICE**
> **123-4567**

Post Cards

You can even use the Macintosh to make post cards. Buy some continuous-feed post cards from your local computer supply store. You can purchase 3-by-5-inch cards that come in either one- or two-card widths. Also available are 4-by-6-inch continuous-feed post cards.

Following the layout and size of the cards, design a MacPaint page of cards and print them out. This can make it very easy to prepare a large number of cards in a short period of time. They can serve as greeting cards or business announcements.

Figure 6-11. A MacPaint Document Prepared for Post Cards

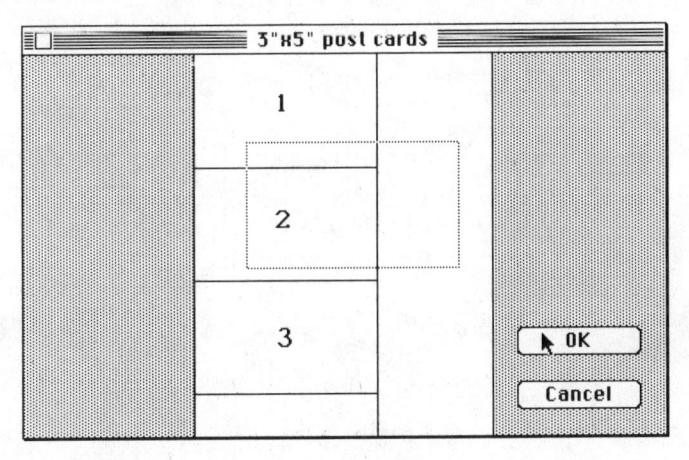

Advertising Layouts

If you're laying out advertising for personal or business ads, the Macintosh can make the work a snap. Open MacPaint and put your ideas on the screen. When you're satisfied with your preliminary sketch, have your client examine it and make suggestions. Working with your client, when you're both sitting down in front of the Macintosh, makes it easy to incorporate ideas and suggestions.

Take a look at the example in Figure 6-12. It's actually a rough sketch put together with individual items, such as couches and chairs, that were drawn once and then stored in the Scrapbook. The advertising copy is represented by the horizontal line pattern.

Chapter 6

Figure 6-12. Ad Layout—Economy Furniture

Richard Bloch

  Layouts like this can quickly give concrete form to your visual ideas. In a few moments you can have a printout to show. Changes are easy to make if editing is required.

  The Macintosh can also be used to design camera-ready advertisements. You can save a lot of money by designing your own ads for newspapers and magazines. Make sure you use fonts and font sizes that give you clear, legible results. Use only font sizes that appear as outlined in the *FontSize* menu—they'll look the best.

Chapter 6

Figure 6-13. Camera-Ready Ad

```
        New in town

   SMALL WORLD
    auto parts
  Featuring parts for your
  foreign or domestic auto
  ═ Call: (777) 122-9696 ═
      Weekdays: 9 to 6
      Saturday:  9 to 3
   4651 HOPE BLVD - Suite G
```

Advertising Flyers

If you plan to sell something like a car or a home, use MacPaint to create an advertising flyer. If you have a lot of text for your ad, enter it as a MacWrite document. Make the visual component of the ad with MacPaint and paste it into the MacWrite document. Photocopy the ad on colored paper and distribute the copies.

If you're selling a house, use MacPaint's drawing tools to show buyers what it looks like. You'll be pleasantly surprised at the response.

Chapter 6

Figure 6-14. Advertising Flyer for a House

HOUSE FOR SALE

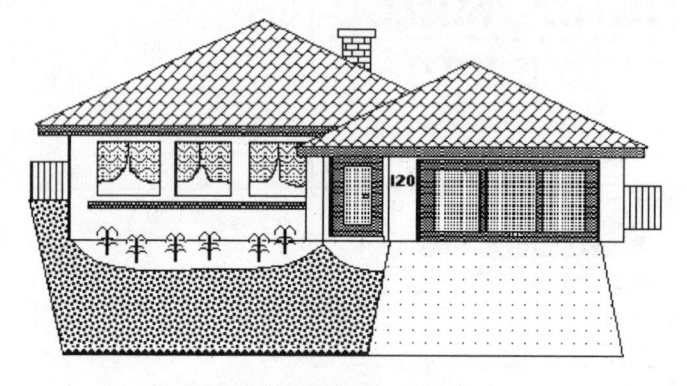

- 3 Bedroom, 1-3/4 Bath
- for sale BY OWNER
- redwood deck and spa
- large covered shade patio
- separately fenced orchard

All this for $ 99,950

For more infomation call 136-7777

Chapter 6

The next ad shows how you can use MacPaint to create a flyer to post on the bulletin boards you often see at supermarkets, coin-operated laundries, or corner drugstores. First, though, let's look at the tear-offs, the small pieces of the flyer that interested buyers can take with them.

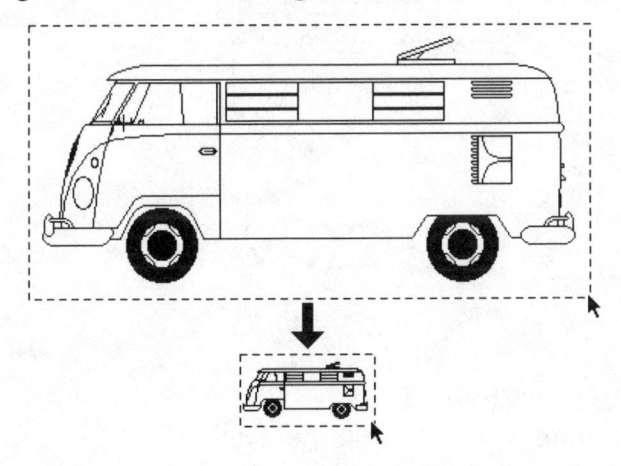

Figure 6-15. Creating the Tear-Offs

The tear-offs (which will go at the bottom of the ad) were made by selecting the outline of the bus with the marquee and shrinking it. Shrinking is done by holding down Shift-Command while dragging the right corner of the selection rectangle toward the middle of the drawing.

179

Chapter 6

Figure 6-16. Flyer for a VW Bus

FOR SALE

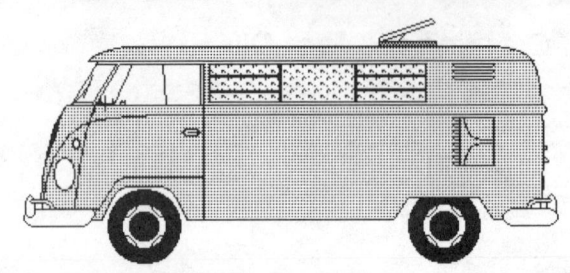

1964 CAMPER VAN

* Seats 7 & Rear seat folds
* AM / FM / Cassette Stereo
* 2 Burner Stove
* 10 Pound Vented Propane Tank
* Ice Box, Dining Table
* Clothes closet
* Storage for 2 milk crates +
* Good Karma
* 1500 cc Engine w/35 K miles
* Oil cooler & filter, Air scoops
* $1600 / or best offer
* call 123-4567
  Ask for Mike

Mike Heckrotte

| VW Bus $1600
Mike 123-4567
eves 987-6543 | VW Bus $1600
Mike 123-4567
eves 987-6543 | VW Bus $1600
Mike 123-4567
eves 987-6543 | VW Bus $1600
Mike 123-4567
eves 987-6543 | VW Bus $1600
Mike 123-4567
eves 987-6543 |

Here are two more examples of ads created with the Macintosh. Figure 6-17 was created with MacPaint and Figure 6-18 was created with MacDraw.

Chapter 6

Figure 6-17. Air Man

John Kohlenberger

Figure 6-18. Computer Art and Design

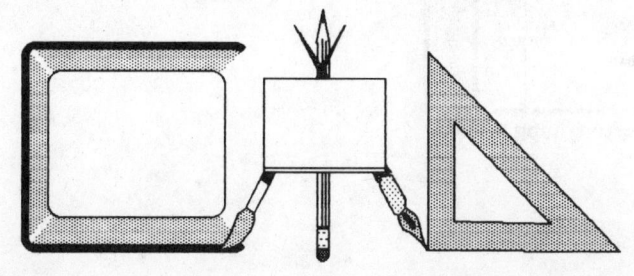

Chapter 6

Business Graphics

You can produce attractive charts, graphs, and maps with the Macintosh. MacDraw, which helps you draw objects to scale, as well as create indicator arrows, is the ideal tool for such illustrations. In graphing, charting, and mapping, you can also take advantage of MacDraw's *Align Objects* and *Align to Grid* features.

MacPaint can be used to generate acceptable charts, graphs, and maps, too, but you'll have to work hard to size the elements accurately. MacPaint's *Grid* feature can at least help line up your elements.

Graphs

It's easy to draw graphs with the Macintosh. The following examples were created with MacPaint.

Figure 6-19. Three Graphs from MacPaint

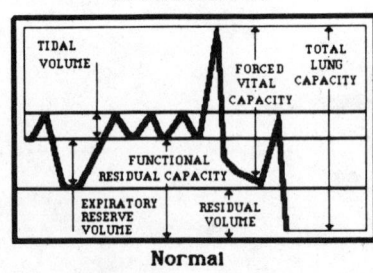

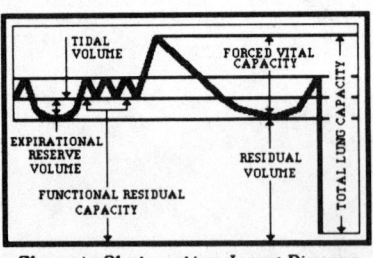

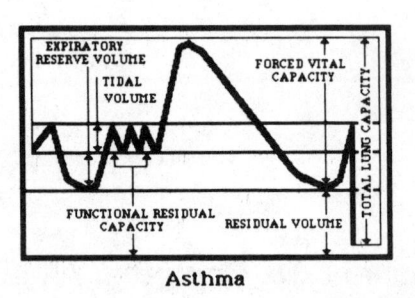

Chapter 6

Figure 6-20. A Bar Graph

RESPIRATORY VOLUMES

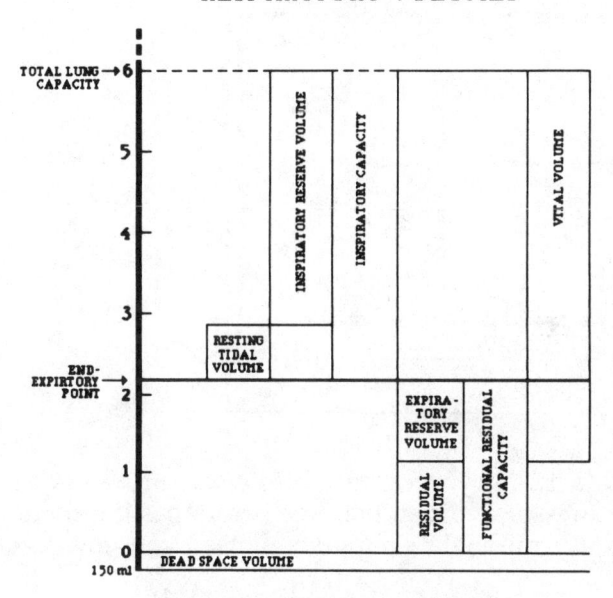

The different volumes of air that can be voluntarily drawn into or expelled from the lungs. Note that at the end expiratory point, when all muscles are relaxed and elastic forces balanced, the lungs contain 2.2 litres of air and a further 0.15L is accommodated in the rigid trachea and bronchi.

Once the rectangular format for the three graphs was created, it was copied into the Clipboard and pasted into documents as needed. The *Rotate* option was used to create labels for the y-axis.

Since MacPaint doesn't give you a tool for drawing arrows, you'll have to draw several thicknesses with *FatBits* and copy them three times each. Use the *Rotate* and *Flip* commands to orient the arrows in all four directions. Store these in the Scrapbook and paste them into documents whenever they're needed.

Chapter 6

Figure 6-21. Arrows in MacPaint's Scrapbook

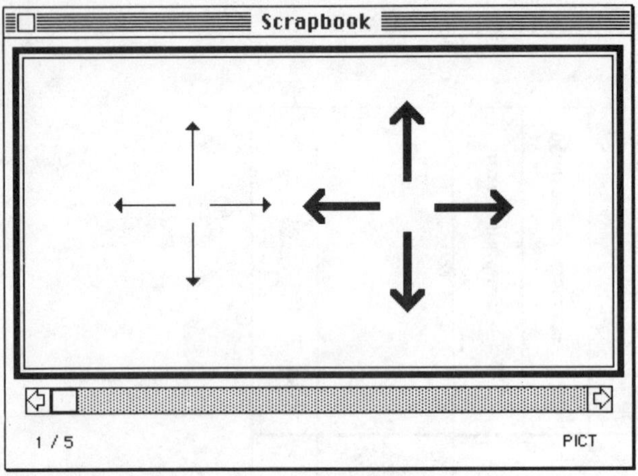

If you have MacDraw, you can use it to create arrows with different line thicknesses and pen patterns before pasting them into your MacPaint Scrapbook. Chapter 3 showed you how to do this.

Charts

Charts are just as easy to design with the Macintosh as graphs. Once you create a chart format, you can save it on disk and recall it for later use. Programmers, for example, can use the Macintosh to construct flow charts to represent program logic flow.

First, the various elements of the chart were built, then put into the Scrapbook. Constructing the chart itself is thus only a matter of pasting the elements in as required.

Chapter 6

Figure 6-22. Scrapbook Entry for the Flow Chart

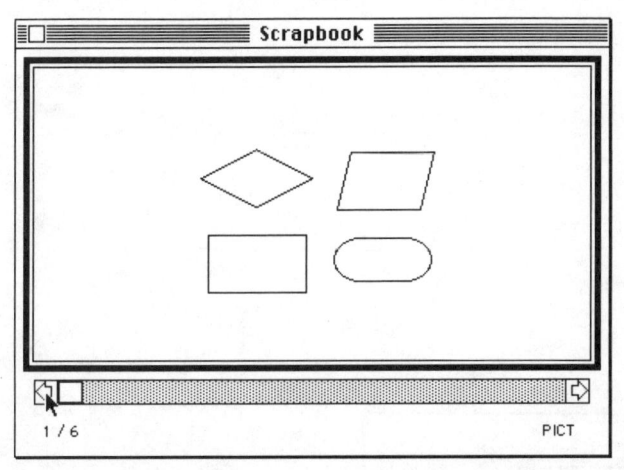

The following chart was created with MacDraw, using the symbols shown above. MacDraw's arrow-drawing tools and its ability to align objects were extremely useful.

Chapter 6

Figure 6-23. Program Flow Chart

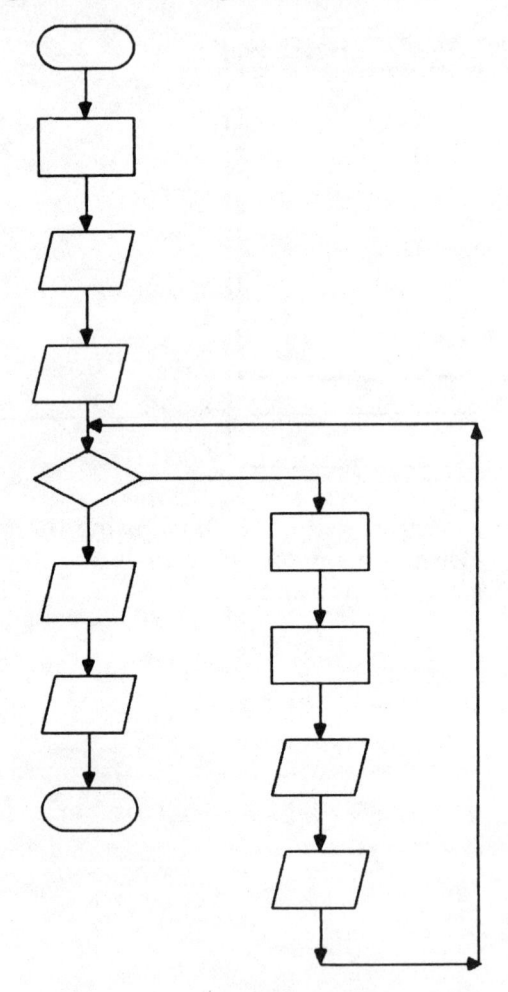

Each element of the flow chart was put into the Scrapbook and pasted in as needed.

An organizational chart can be created and modified in much the same way. Since these charts usually take up a full page and require the alignment of elements both vertically and horizontally, it would be best to use MacDraw. Figure 6-24 shows just such a chart.

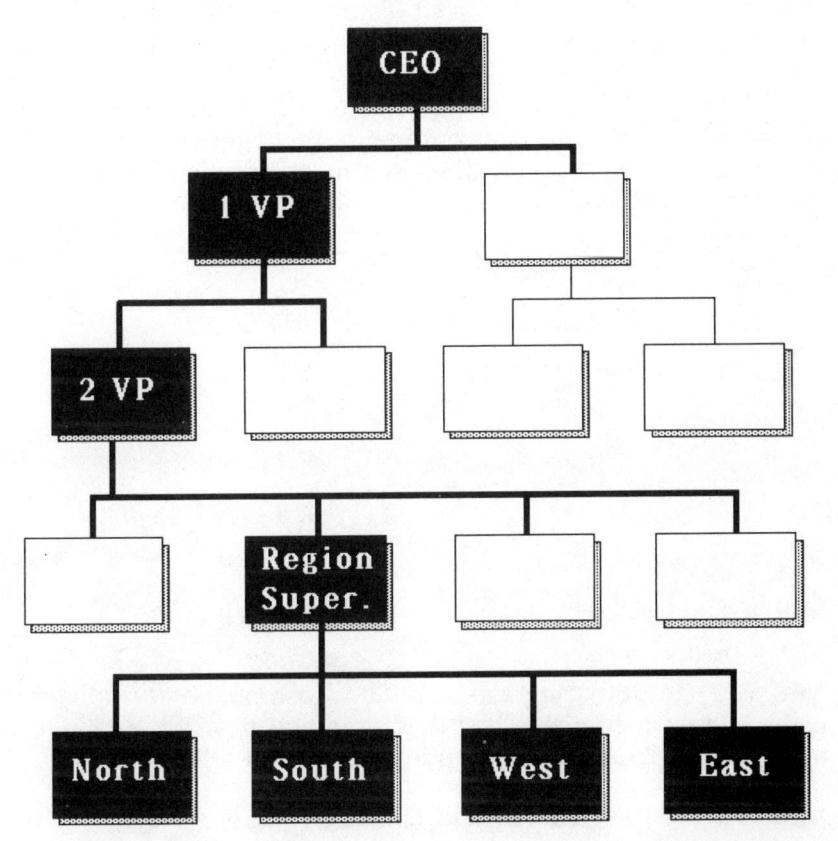

Figure 6-24. Organizational Chart

To put together a chart like this, design a box (your choice of size) with a drop shadow and then paste it into the Scrapbook. The *Duplicate* command will create all the boxes you need. Use the text tool to create labels within the boxes.

If you want to reproduce the look of Figure 6-24 (white letters on black), follow these steps:

Step 1. Type the label outside your drawing area in a bold, outlined type style.

Step 2. Choose the Selection arrow and click the text.

Step 3. Drag it into position in a box.

Step 4. To get rid of the white background around the letters, choose *None* from the *Fill* menu while the text is still selected. This will make the area outside your letters transparent, allowing the pattern underneath to show through.

Chapter 6

Maps

Maps with contours and labeled features can be produced with MacPaint's pencil tool and *FatBits*. It's easier to draw an accurate map if you first trace an outline of a published map with a felt marker on a piece of acetate (available from an office or graphic arts supply store). Tape this outline to the screen and trace it with the mouse. This process is described more fully in Chapter 8. Finally, save your outline on disk.

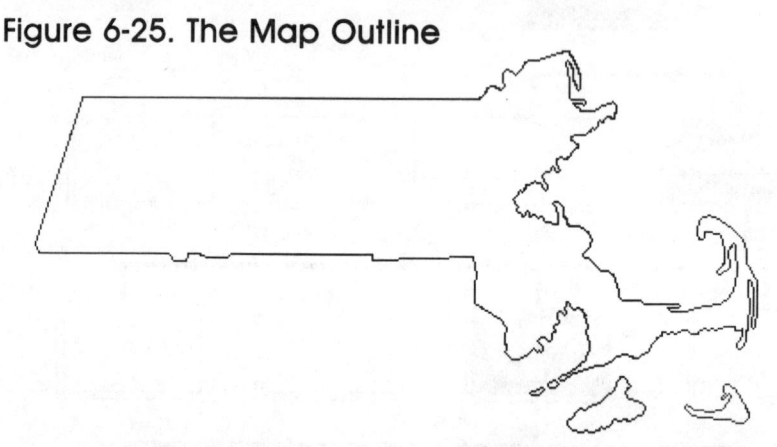

Figure 6-25. The Map Outline

Now you can draw physical or political contours and fill them with different patterns. Label them and you have an attractive map showing changes in altitude or statistical relationships.

Figure 6-26. Finished Statistical Map

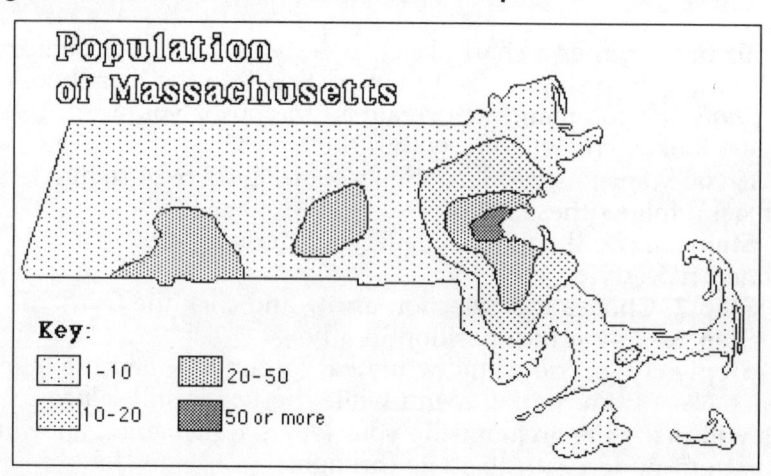

Chapter 6

You can use the same outline to prepare other maps.

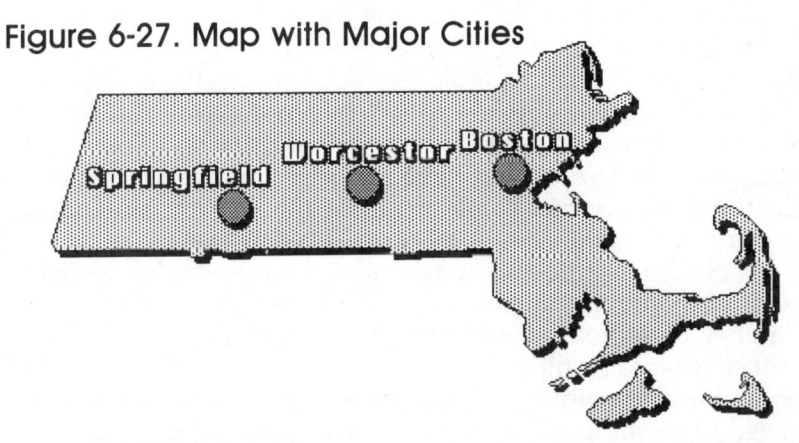

Figure 6-27. Map with Major Cities

MacPaint can be used to draw quick sketches of road maps for ads or flyers to guide your clients, customers, or friends to your office for business or to your home for a party.

Figure 6-28. A City Map

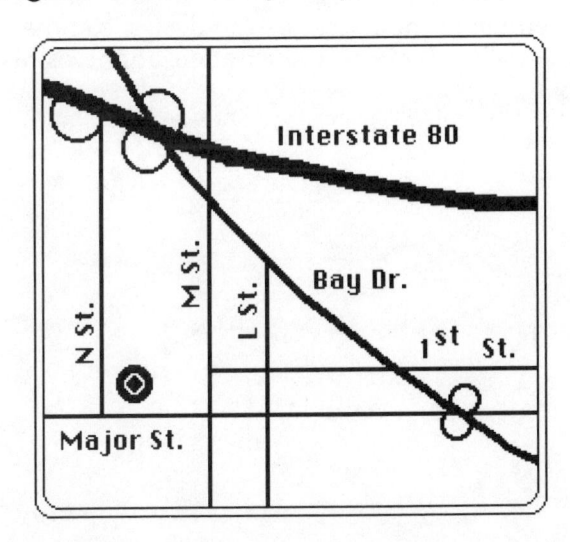

Chapter 6

Design Work

The Macintosh can be a valuable tool for anyone who has a product to design, whether it be a better mousetrap or an architectural landmark. You can make quick sketches with MacPaint or MacDraw and develop them into full-blown designs. You can store your designs and modify them without having to redraw all the elements. And when you have a working representation of the product, the Imagewriter printout can be traced by a pen-and-ink artist to put the design into final form. This process makes it possible for designers to focus their creative energies and financial resources on the development of designs, rather than spending time and money on tedious sketching and resketching.

Since it takes so little time to move from an abstract idea to a working drawing with the Macintosh, designers will be encouraged to be more adventuresome. The Mac will make it comfortable for you, the designer, to draw boldly, unafraid to experiment.

Product Design

Any type of product can be designed with the Mac, from circuit boards to furniture. Bill Jonas of Artworks Unlimited, Inc. in Jupiter, Florida, has been using the Macintosh to design commercial signs and murals. Here's a MacPaint illustration of one of his typical installations.

Chapter 6

Figure 6-29. An Illustration of a Three-Dimensional Structure

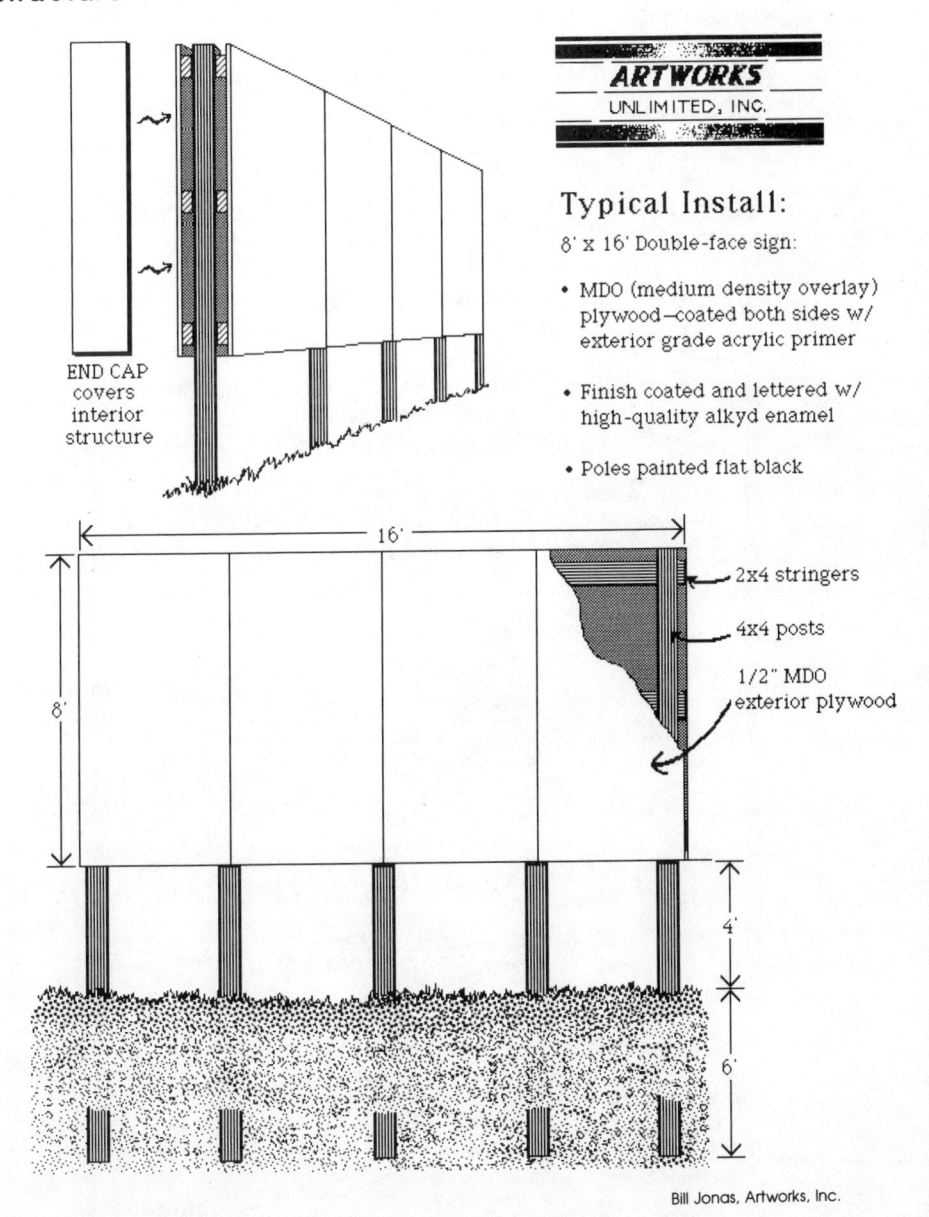

END CAP covers interior structure

ARTWORKS UNLIMITED, INC.

Typical Install:

8' x 16' Double-face sign:

- MDO (medium density overlay) plywood—coated both sides w/ exterior grade acrylic primer

- Finish coated and lettered w/ high-quality alkyd enamel

- Poles painted flat black

16'

2x4 stringers

4x4 posts

1/2" MDO exterior plywood

8'

4'

6'

Bill Jonas, Artworks, Inc.

Chapter 6

Jonas also uses the Macintosh to create sketches of signs that his clients have commissioned. When the client examines the sketch and suggests changes, Jonas makes a few sweeping gestures with the mouse, and in a few minutes, a new, edited version of the design is in his client's hands. Here are three more examples of Jonas's work:

Figure 6-30. Three Designs of Signs Produced with MacPaint

GEORGIAN PARK/MAIN I.D. SIGNS

5'4"x 6' MDO/ WHITE BACKGROUND
"GEORGIAN PARK": RED w/ GREY SHADOW
"GLOBE USA" DARK BLUE
LOGO IN FULL COLOR
PHONE # RED
BORDER & SCROLL DARK BLUE

Bill Jonas, Artworks, Inc.

Chapter 6

SABAL RIDGE/TEMPORARY PROMOTIONAL SIGN

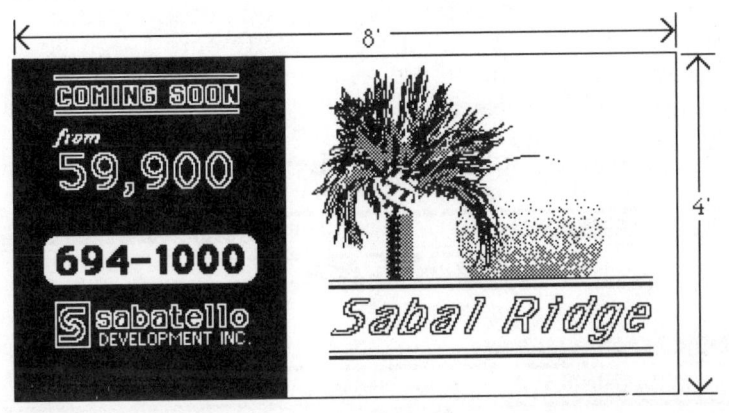

White lettering on
Black background

Black lettering
Pale Grey background
Black & Dk. Grey tree

Bill Jonas, Artworks, Inc.

Jupiter Town Centre/Directory Sign

Hand-carved and sandblasted main I.D. sign in full color
Redwood panels w/ incised and gilded lettering
Mounted on natural stone base

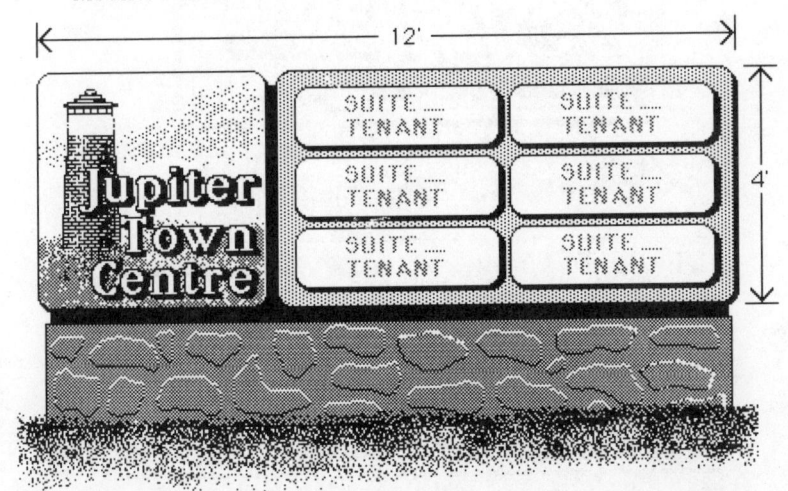

Bill Jonas, Artworks, Inc.

193

Chapter 6

When the client accepts Jonas's design, the printout becomes the work order that goes to the shop. Sometimes an opaque projector is used to project the design directly onto a sign board so that it can be traced in the proper size. This assures fidelity to the plan approved by the client.

Figure 6-31. Invoice Including the Design

ARTWORKS
UNLIMITED, INC.

222 NINTH STREET • BAKE PARK • FLORIDA • 33403
(333) 127-1236

Purchaser: Phone: Date:

Address: Job name or number:

City, State, & Zip   Job location:

Job description:

[Sign design: BONITA ISLE AT THE LAKES OF SHERBROOK]

DEPOSIT.............................$_____
BALANCE............................$_____

ACCEPTED BY:_____ DATE:_____

Make checks payable to.
ARTWORKS UNLIMITED, INC.
222 NINTH STREET, BAKE PARK, FL. 33403 • (333) 127-1236

Bill Jonas, Artworks, Inc.

194

Once the sign is finished and ready for delivery, Jonas uses MacPaint to create the invoice as shown in Figure 6-31. The design itself appears on the invoice. This sort of visual invoicing assures that complex orders made up of several signs are properly billed.

Engineering Design

Engineers can use the Macintosh for creating engineering drawings. One advantage of a MacDraw-derived drawing over one produced on a drafting table is that the Mac's can be altered with a click of the mouse, without tedious redrawing. Another advantage is that a Mac drawing need not carry the mark of an artist's personality. The idiosyncratic style of an artist's rendering can sometimes make it difficult for the job supervisor to make sense of the details. Because engineering drawings created with the Mac are machine-generated, structural details are drawn in a standard manner.

One of the best uses of the Macintosh in mechanical design is that the illustrator can take advantage of the Macintosh's Scrapbook to paste frequently used elements into plans and elevations. Here are two examples of plans produced with MacPaint.

Figure 6-32. Structural Design Using MacPaint

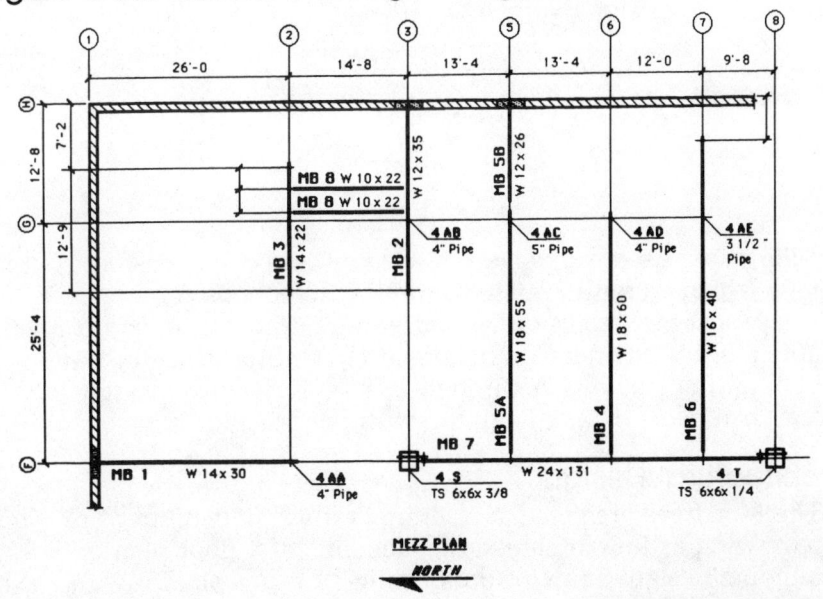

Chapter 6

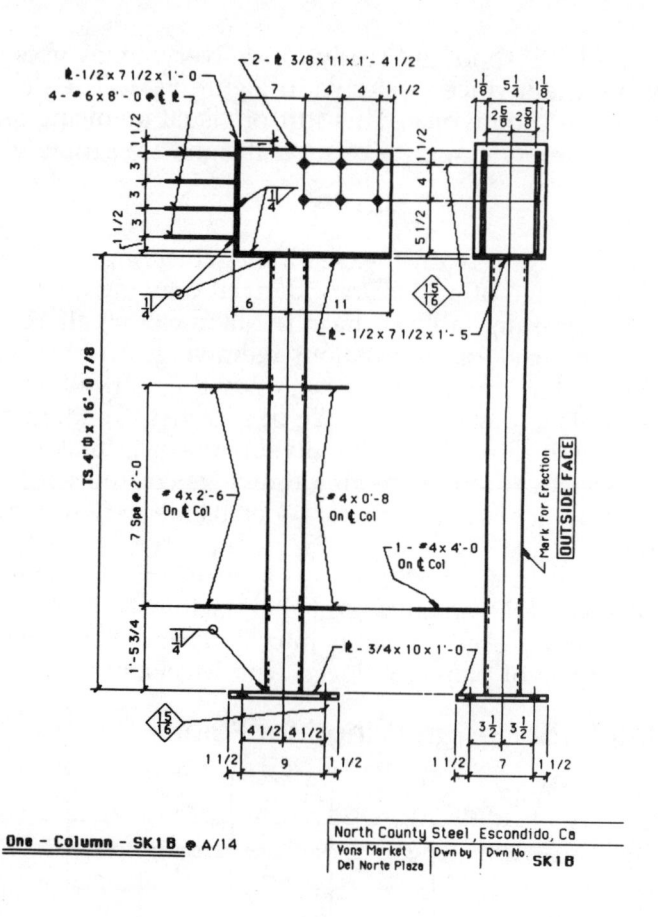

FatBits was used extensively to create some of the custom characters, which were then pasted into the Scrapbook for later use.

MacDraw's ability to produce large drawings makes it a valuable tool for engineers accustomed to creating such illustrations. Standard documents A through F (8 × 10 inches through 4 × 8 feet) can be drawn and printed with the Macintosh.

Architectural Design

The Mac frees architects and drafters from the tedium of repeated redrawing as they organize the elements of a floor plan or a building design. Some of the benefits of using MacDraw might be:

Chapter 6

- MacDraw's built-in rulers eliminate the need to lay a ruler on the drawing to get its dimensions each time you need to size an item.
- You can customize the units that make up MacDraw's rulers.
- If you need to know the dimensions of an item, *Show Size* will give it to you on demand.
- The ability to draw in various sizes, from 8 × 10 inches to 4 × 8 feet, will be important for architectural renderings.
- When you draw frequently used elements for the first time—symbols of doorways, windows, appliances, and furniture, for example—you can store them in the Scrapbook for use in other drawings. You'll never have to draw them again.

Figure 6-33. Sample Scrapbook Item

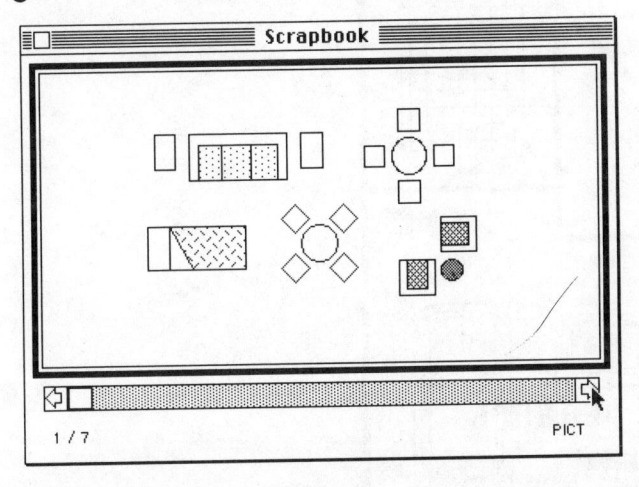

- If you need to "tape" items together, or "tape" items to the "drafting table," you can use MacDraw's *Group* and *Lock* features. No tape is required.

   Enough of the benefits of MacDraw. Let's look at some actual designs. Figure 6-34 shows one architect's Macintosh rendering.

Chapter 6

Figure 6-34. Ground-Floor Design Created with MacDraw

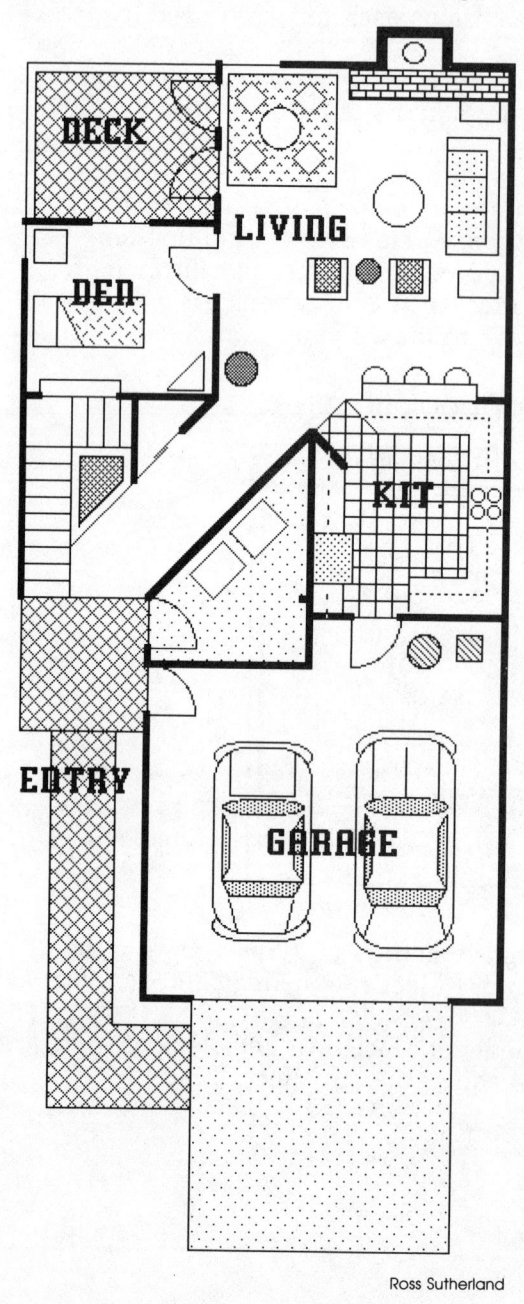

Ross Sutherland

Chapter 6

Isometric drawings provide architects with a way of representing three-dimensional structures.

Figure 6-35. An Isometric Drawing

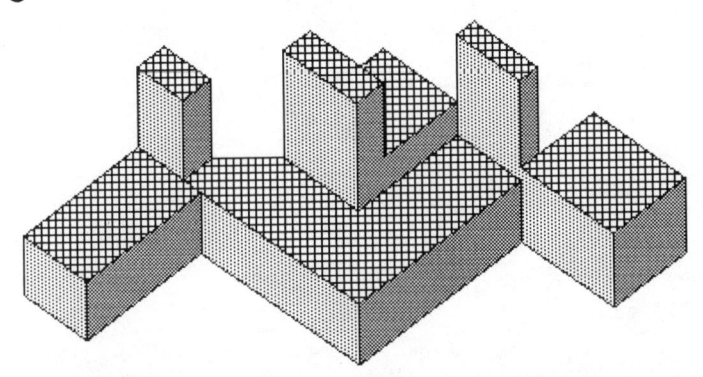

You can use either Macpaint or MacDraw to create such views. If it's important to show how the structure is put together, use MacDraw. Create each part of the structure as a complete unit, and then drag elements apart for display. To move part of the design, click the element you want to move and drag it to a new location. It's simple, and can give a completely different type of illustration.

Figure 6-36. Pieces Moved

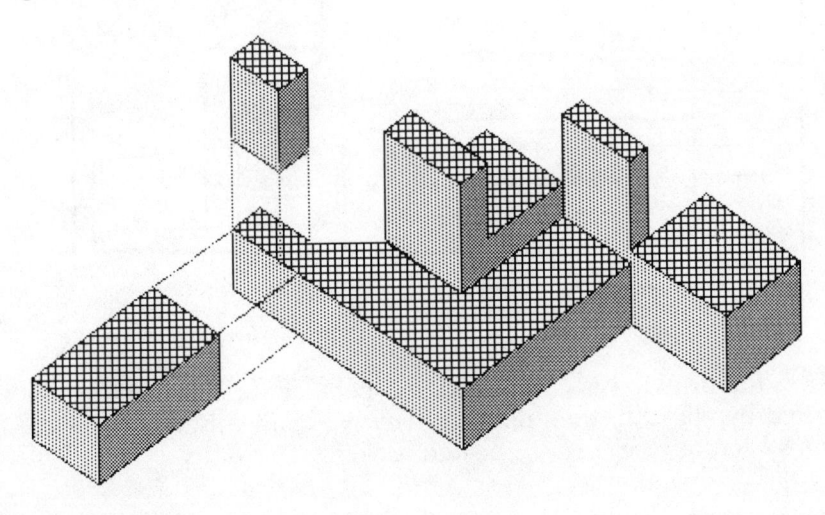

Chapter 6

Architects can use the principles of perspective to sketch building designs that communicate a sense of depth. You'll remember from Chapter 5 that you can use MacDraw to create perspective lines to help you draw objects in three dimensions. An architect could use this to create something like Figure 6-37.

Figure 6-37. Two Stages of a Perspective

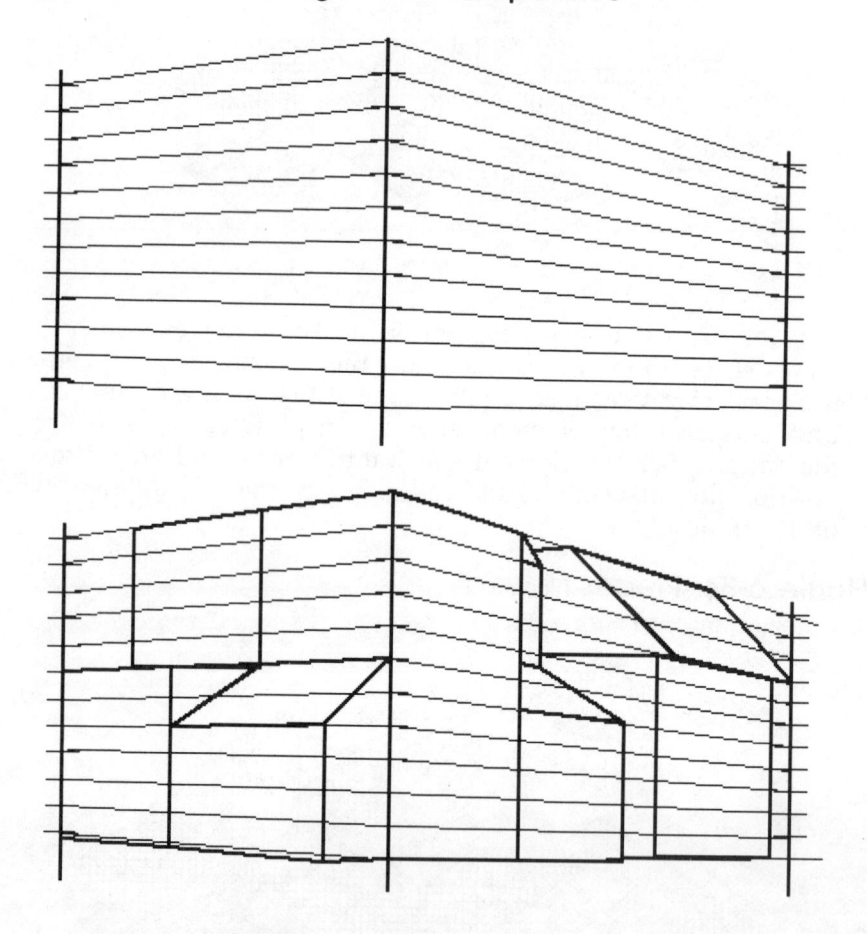

After the drawing is completed, the perspective lines can be selected by clicking, then deleted. Now you can fill the surfaces of the structure to give it a finished look.

Chapter 6

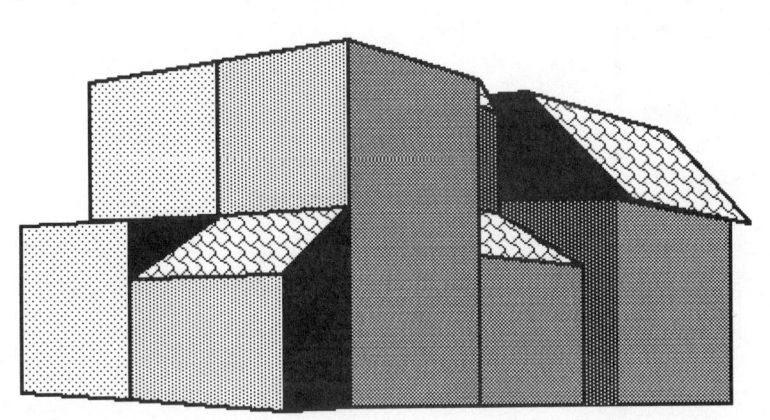

Figure 6-38. The Completed Sketch

When you use MacDraw's electronic drafting table, you'll never have to sweep eraser crumbs from your drawings or have pieces of masking tape hanging from every corner of your table. Everything is kept neat and tidy—inside the computer.

Interior Design

If you're an interior designer, the Macintosh will save you a great deal of time in preparing sketches for your clients. With MacDraw, you'll be able to enter a floor plan, consult with the client about what decorating changes are to be made, and quickly prepare a sketch of what the rooms will look like after walls and other structures are removed or added.

Chapter 6

Figure 6-39. Before and After with MacDraw

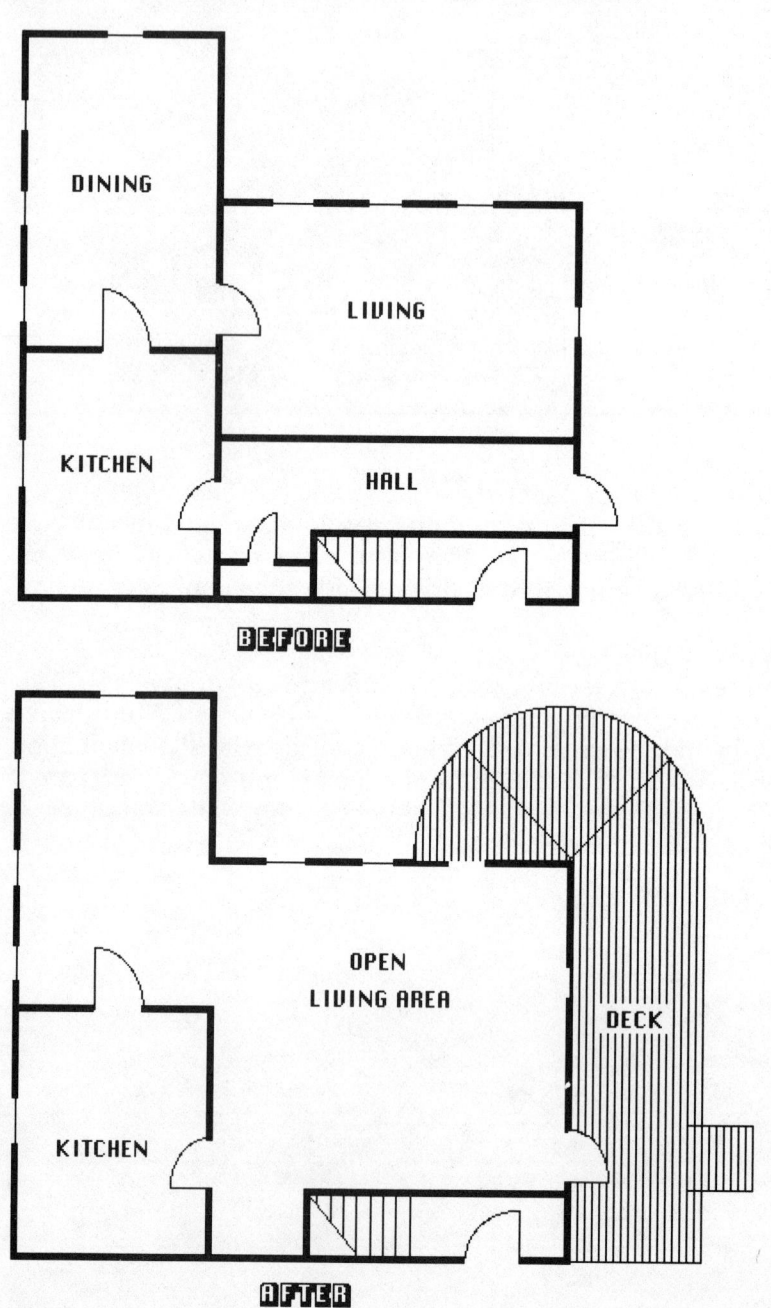

Chapter 6

You don't have to be an interior designer to take advantage of MacDraw's powers to create before-and-after sketches. You can use the Mac to help plan a furniture arrangement that fits your lifestyle and the space available.

You can create a "before" sketch—to help you put your planned changes into perspective—by first drawing a floor plan with MacDraw or MacPaint. MacDraw's rulers make it easy to get the proper scale for your drawing. Paste this floor plan into the Scrapbook for future use. Just create symbols for the furniture and appliances you have in your home or would like to add, and paste these into the Scrapbook, too. Move the furniture symbols into their present locations on the floor plan.

To start working on your "after" design, paste your floor plan from the Scrapbook into the document under the "before" sketch. Now paste the furniture and appliance symbols from the Scrapbook into a work space to the side. Move them into position. This will give you a way of testing several decorating ideas until you arrive at the design you like best.

Landscape Design

Landscape design is another application of the power of Macintosh graphics. Clients can view early sketches and make suggestions until the final version is completed. And just as important, the landscaper won't have any trouble following the sketches.

But you don't have to be a professional landscape designer to use the Mac for this type of design work. Designing landscaping for your own property is as simple as using your computer. You can place flower beds, fences, and walkways wherever you want in the design, move them around, even eliminate them entirely, until you like what you've got. If you create plans which show several stages of landscaping, you can visualize how the property will look as trees and bushes grow and new plants are added. Don't forget to store frequently used items, such as tree and bush symbols, in the Scrapbook for use in later designs. As long as you have those symbols available, you can just erase a design and start over if you don't like what you've done.

Chapter 6

Figure 6-40. MacPaint Landscape Sketch

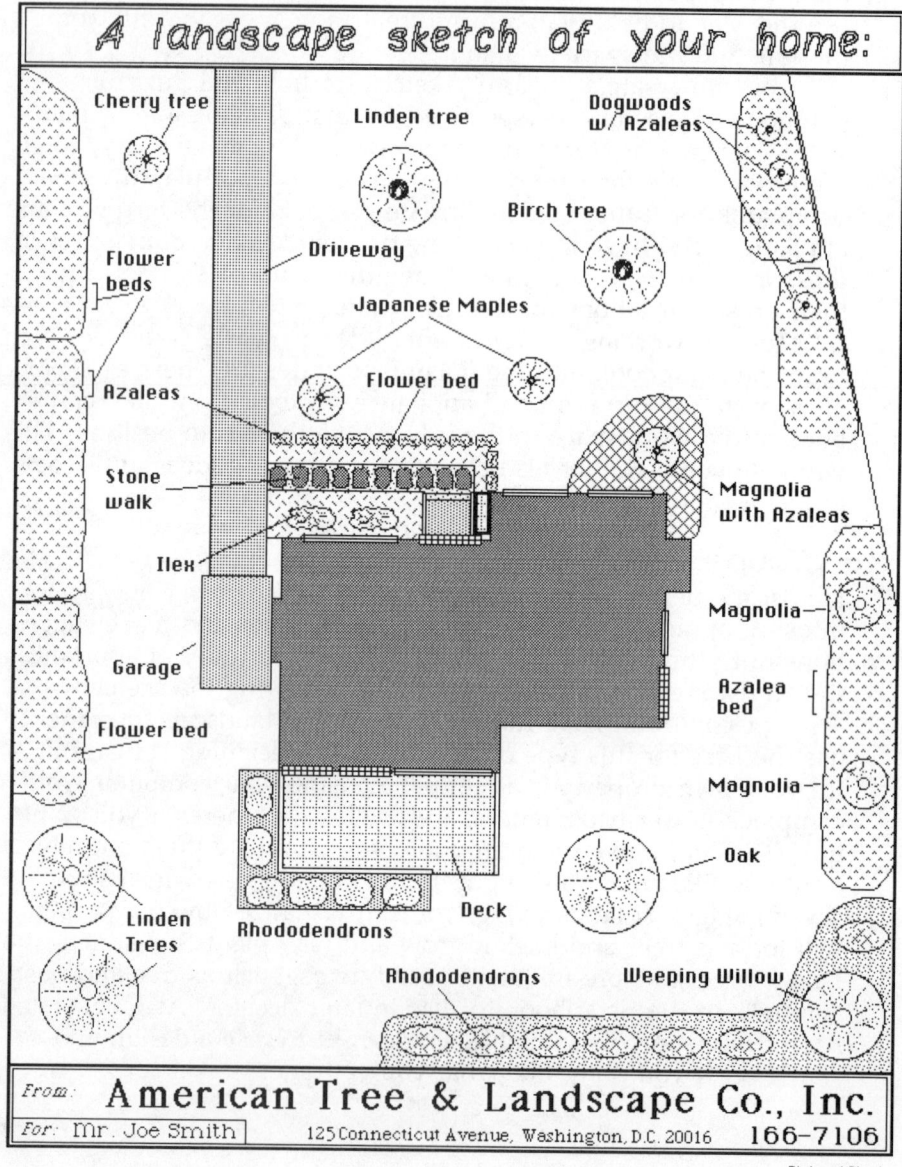

Chapter 6

Printing and Publishing

Printers and publishers, large or small, can save a lot of time by automating their layout and design operations with a graphic computer like the Macintosh. Much of the work of preparing pages for printing is repetitious, requiring the same procedures each time a new edition is created. The Macintosh can make this process easier, allowing editors and layout artists to direct energies to the more creative aspects of their jobs.

Page Layouts

If you publish a newsletter, a small journal, or a magazine, your Macintosh can provide a blank, accurately sized format for laying out pages. This format can be altered or filled in to incorporate each issue's changes—without having to redraw the format itself each time. Here's a sample layout for a small newspaper.

Figure 6-41. Format Document for a Newspaper Layout

Chapter 6

The format size, header, and columns are marked. The layout artist simply inserts the elements for each issue and in a short time, a rough sketch of the page is ready with all components clearly shown.

Figure 6-42. Newspaper Layout

Chapter 6

The Macintosh can also help lay out and design pages for magazines, newspapers, other periodicals, and even technical manuals. The first step is to store a format for the standard page size and the columns within the page. The layout artist can then organize each page with a quick sketch, using either MacPaint or MacDraw. Here's an example of a magazine page layout done with Macpaint.

Figure 6-43. Magazine Layout

Cover Design

MacPaint can even design covers. Once you're happy with your results, just have an artist complete it.

Chapter 6

Figure 6-44. Two Sample Book Cover Designs

Chapter 6

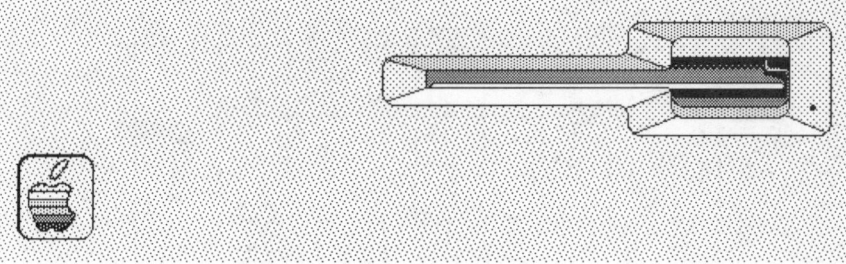

Bill Jonas, Artworks, Inc.

Chapter 6

Book and Manual Illustrations

With MacPaint and MacWrite, you can prepare an entire manual, booklet, or pamphlet. Use MacPaint for the illustrations and MacWrite for the copy.

Bob Kovacs of Rak-Ware used Macpaint to create the illustrations for a manual that accompanies a printer interface he designed. Here are pages from the manual he created.

Figure 6-45. Pages from a Manual Prepared with MacPaint

Part II Chapter 10   ELECTRICAL SPECIFICATIONS

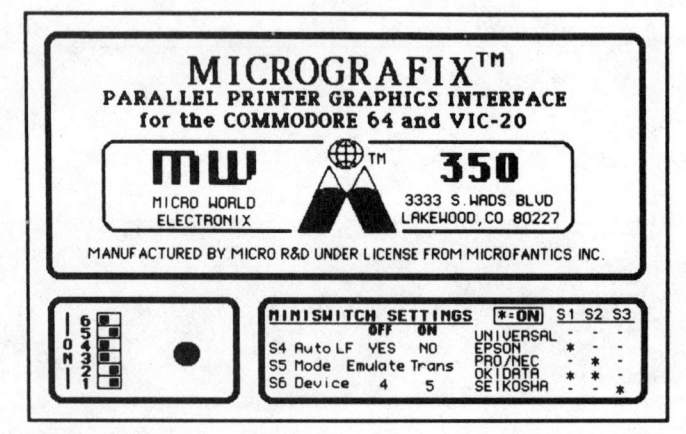

```
         MICROGRAFIX™
  PARALLEL PRINTER GRAPHICS INTERFACE
    for the COMMODORE 64 and VIC-20

   m w              ™      350
  MICRO WORLD             3333 S.WADS BLVD
  ELECTRONIX              LAKEWOOD, CO 80227

 MANUFACTURED BY MICRO R&D UNDER LICENSE FROM MICROFANTICS INC.

  MINISWITCH SETTINGS  [*=ON]  S1 S2 S3
              OFF   ON       UNIVERSAL  - - -
  S4 AutoLF  YES   NO        EPSON      * - -
  S5 Mode  Emulate Trans     PRO/NEC    - * -
  S6 Device    4    5        OKIDATA    * * -
                             SEIKOSHA   - - *
```

Figure 10-5

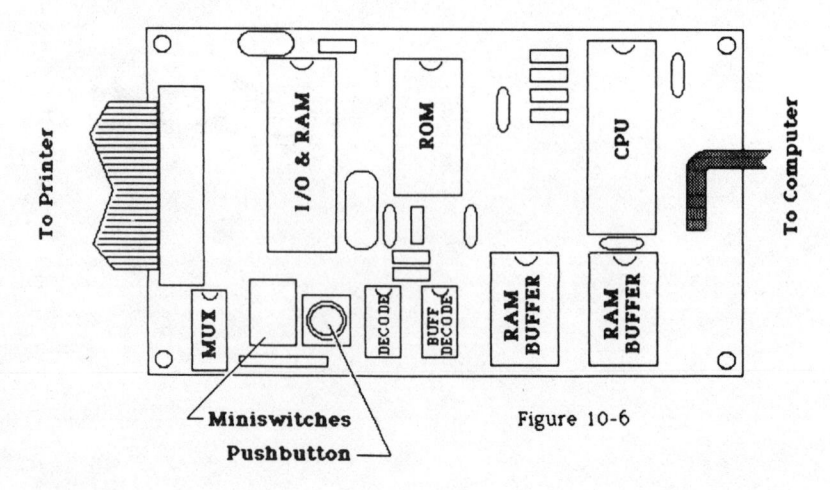

Miniswitches
Pushbutton
Figure 10-6

Labels: To Printer, MUX, I/O & RAM, ROM, DECODE, BUFF DECODE, RAM BUFFER, RAM BUFFER, CPU, To Computer

210   Page 10 - 4

Chapter 6

Part II Chapter 10   *ELECTRICAL SPECIFICATIONS*

Printer   **Computer**

MicroGrafix Interface
Figure 10-1

Commodore Serial Bus Connector
Figure 10-2

Parallel Printer Connector
Figure 10-3

To Interface   **To Cassette or Joystick Port**

Power Cable
Figure 10-4

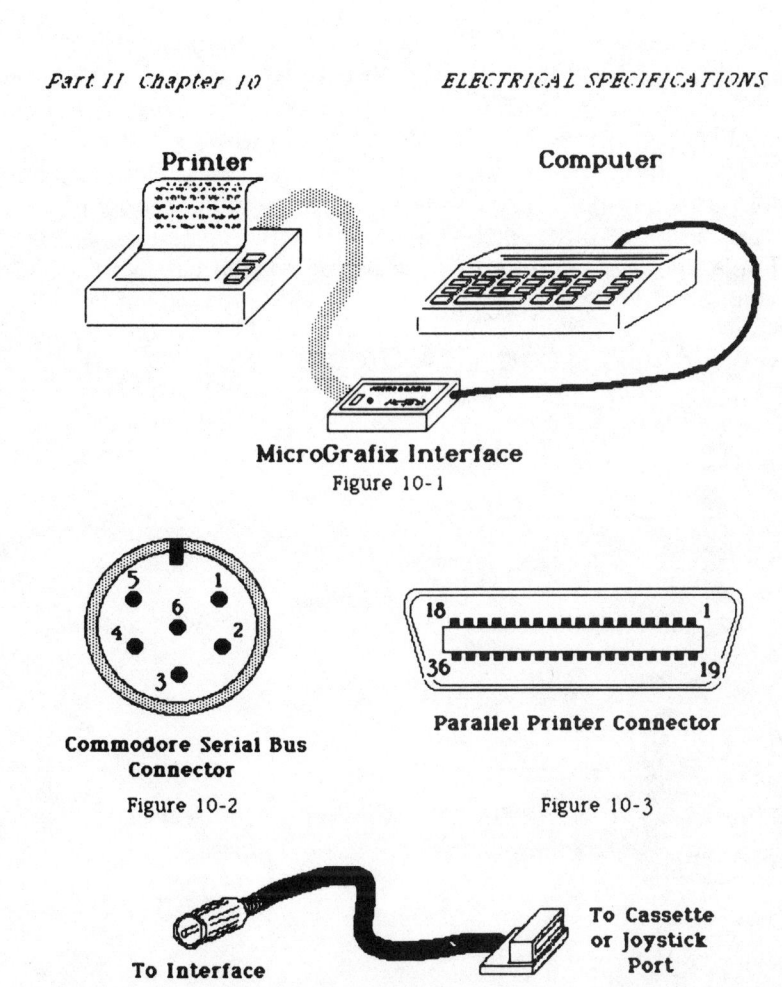

Page 10 - 3

    Kovacs reduced the Imagewriter printouts photographically and had the results printed by a professional. Reducing an original makes the Imagewriter output look less coarse. If the quality of the Imagewriter output is not adequate for your purposes as camera-ready art, you can still design the illustration with MacPaint and then have an artist ink it. For the finest results, use

Chapter 6

a typesetting service that can work directly from documents stored on disk. Refer to Chapter 7 for more information on producing high-quality, camera-ready art with the Macintosh.

A video-digitizer can make it very easy to create illustrations for books and manuals. Look to Chapter 8 to find out how digitizers can help you put together more attractive visuals.

Here's another example of an illustration that can be drawn with MacPaint.

Figure 6-46. An Exploded View Created by MacPaint

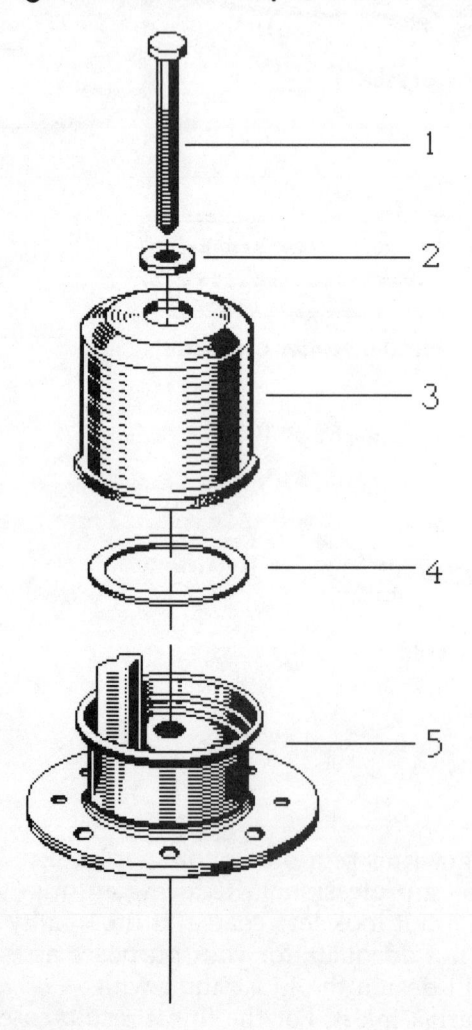

Chapter 6

Project Development

Anyone involved in the visual arts will benefit by using the Macintosh in project development. You can sketch ideas quickly and casually. Later, you can develop the successful aspects of your sketches into complete works.

Visual Diary

Artists can use the Mac to keep a record of their visual ideas on a regular basis. They can use MacPaint to produce working sketches with explanations next to them. This way, inspired ideas can be given form quickly.

Here are some sample sketches produced by Robert Fichter which give concrete shape to the critters that visit the corners of his mind.

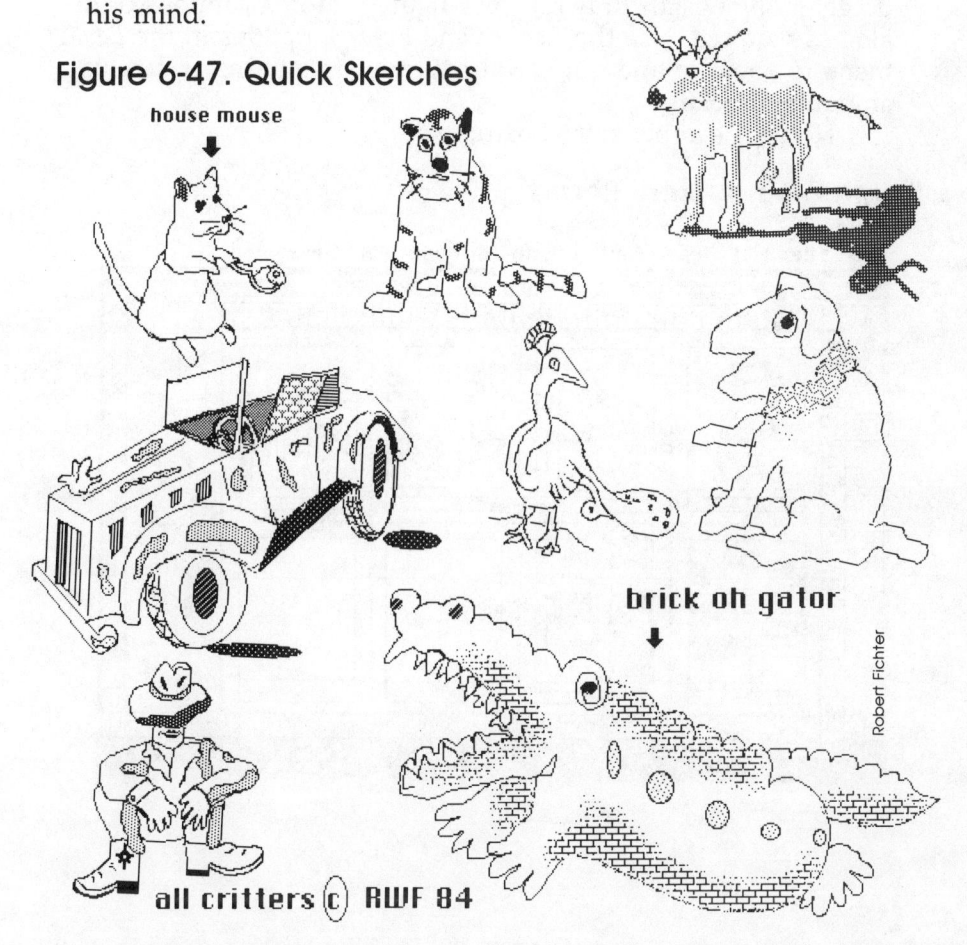

Figure 6-47. Quick Sketches

213

Chapter 6

More of Fichter's work appears in Chapter 10.

Story Boards

Artists who need story boards—from directors of commercials to cartoonists—will delight in using MacDraw. Animators and script writers will find that this makes planning all that much easier.

Choose *Drawing Size* from the *Layout* menu and click the appropriate box to select the number of cells you want to work on in one document. By choosing *Reduce To Fit* from the *Layout* menu, you'll see the entire set of cells on the screen. Set up a format for your story board that outlines the margins for the visual and verbal components. Make sure you use the *Lock* feature in the *Arrange* menu to "tape down" your format to avoid accidental dragging. Now start drawing your figures, adding captions or dialog as required. Use the *Reduce* and *Enlarge* options in the *Layout* menu to zoom in and out of your story boards to insert various amounts of detail.

Here's a sample story board.

Figure 6-48. A Story Board

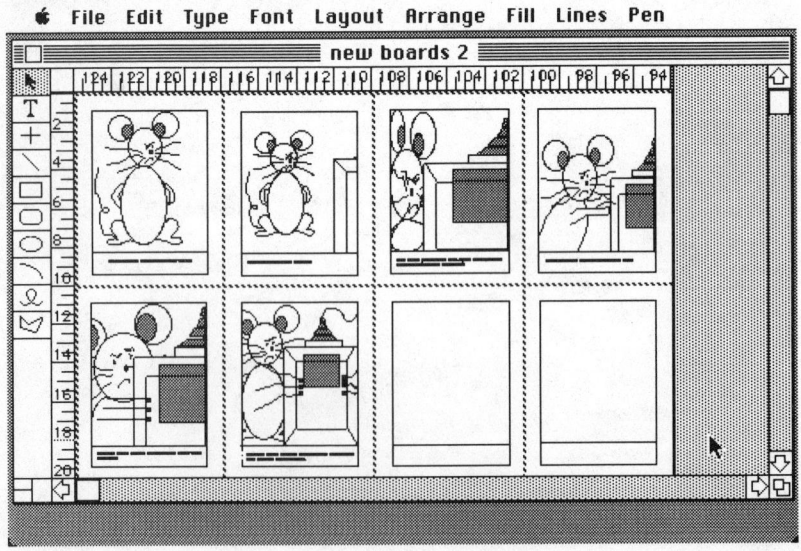

Bob Lee

Chapter 6

Slides

It's expensive to have slides professionally prepared. The Macintosh makes it easy for you to design your own presentation-quality slides for titles, maps, graphs, and illustrations.

Use MacPaint or MacDraw to design the slide. Since the proportions of the screen windows of these application programs are approximately the same as those of a 35 mm slide, you can design your slide within them. When you have the results you want, print the document in high-quality mode on your best paper. You may want to use a colored ribbon and colored paper to coordinate your results with other slides in the presentation.

When you've completed the printout, photograph it using even lighting and a camera on a tripod. Use a macro lens for best results. If you don't have a macro lens, use a normal 50 mm lens. Photograph in an open, shaded area if you're working outdoors. For better control over the illumination, use photofloods as shown below.

Figure 6-49. Photographing Imagewriter Printouts

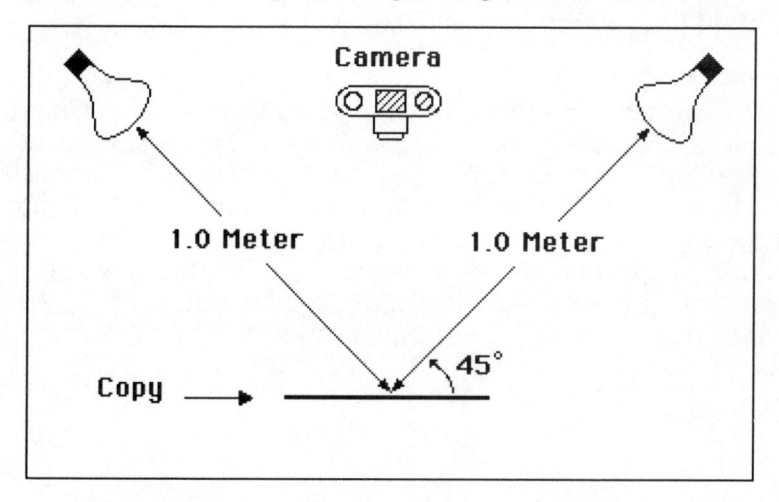

A film like Kodachrome 25 will give you the clearest, sharpest results. This film can be processed only by Kodak, so it may take more than three days for you to receive your processed slides. Ektachrome 100 slide film is also acceptable and can be processed by your local film-processing lab. Make sure the film is right for your source of illumination. If you're photographing outdoors, use

215

Chapter 6

Daylight film; if you're shooting with photofloods, use Tungsten film.

Black-and-white originals can be photographed with color slide film, but the results are sometimes unacceptable. The blacks are never a true, rich black, and the whites are usually slightly clouded. For the finest black-and-white slides, use Kodak Precision Line Film LPD4. It's available in 150-foot rolls. Your local photo dealer can tell you about bulk loading your own film from such long rolls—it's not very difficult. With photoflood lamps (RFL-2), make a series of exposures of three seconds each, opening your shutter in one f-stop intervals from f22 to f2 (all the way closed to all the way open).

Process the film for two minutes in Kodak Dektol developer diluted 1:1 at 68 degrees Fahrenheit (20 degrees Celsius); use a stop bath, fix, and wash as recommended by the manufacturer. The blacks will be deep and the whites will be clear.

After some experimenting, you'll be able to produce slides with the Macintosh quickly and easily. Slide production combined with a video-digitizing process for creating images can open a new world of pictures and designs.

Take It from Here

This chapter has shown you how the Mac can be used to generate sophisticated visuals quickly and painlessly. Obviously, there are more applications of the Mac's graphics capabilities than are listed here. You'll probably think of several that I didn't mention. After all, how you use the Mac is best left up to you. With a little trial and error, you'll soon be using its power to complete tasks efficiently. And the result will probably look far better than if you'd just done them freehand. With the Macintosh, almost everyone can be an artist.

Chapter 7
Getting the Most Out of Your Imagewriter Printer

Chapter 7

Getting the Most Out of Your Imagewriter Printer

The Imagewriter

The computer will not make the printed page obsolete. No revolutionary advances in disk drive or diskette technology are likely to push newspapers, paper correspondence, or printed books out of our lives. Documents on paper are immediate and transportable—to read them you don't have to insert them into a computer.

When you show someone what you've created with the Macintosh, you usually show them something on paper—it's not always practical to bring your audience to your home or office so they can admire your work on the screen. The work you do with your computer is thus ultimately judged by the quality of the printed output. Just as good speakers demonstrate the capabilities of a good sound system, a good printer is the display medium of a computer system.

The Macintosh can produce high-resolution graphics combined with text in a variety of fonts, styles, and sizes. To keep up with the Macintosh's ability to display more than 175,000 dots on its screen, you need a printer that can print high-resolution graphics quickly and clearly. And because constant graphics mode printing can shorten the life of a print head, you need a printer that can withstand this sort of intensive use.

The Macintosh's Imagewriter printer performs beautifully. It can accurately reproduce anything displayed on your computer's screen. Quiet, fast, and reliable, the Imagewriter provides a choice of three print quality modes.

Printer Characteristics

The Mac's screen displays square pixels, but the Imagewriter produces round dots. This reduces the similarity in appearance between a screen display and a printout. The Imagewriter compensates for this by being able to print more than double the density of dots that the screen can display—160 dots per linear inch rather than 72.

The Imagewriter's three modes—high-resolution, standard, and draft—allow you to choose a compromise between print quality and speed. If you want the highest quality printouts, you must sacrifice print speed. High-resolution printing involves a double pass over each line, which effectively smooths out the fills in the spaces between dots so that solid areas appear darker and richer.

Chapter 7

Screen Size and Page Size

If scale and proportion are important, you should note that there may be a discrepancy between the size and shape of a form on the screen and the way it prints out with the Imagerwriter printer. If you draw a 2 × 2 inch circle, following the rulers in MacDraw, and measure the actual screen size of the circle, you may find that the circle is actually elliptical—2-1/16 × 1-5/16 inches, for example.

Figure 7-1. Screen Size Versus Actual Size

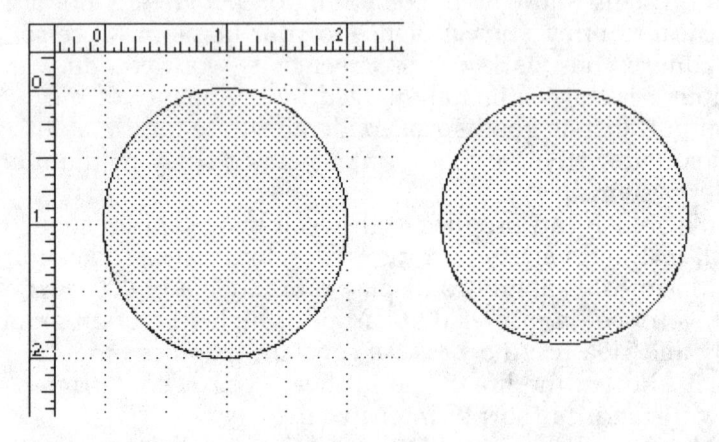

Your circle may appear as an oval on the screen, but when printed out it will be exactly 2 × 2 inches. Run a test to see if your Macintosh's screen distorts images. Draw a perfect circle by using the Shift key to constrain the oval. Measure the horizontal and vertical dimensions on the screen. Now print out the circle and compare the printed circle's dimensions with the screen dimensions.

The discrepancy between how a shape looks on the screen and how it looks on paper won't affect your work in MacDraw. You'll size your shapes according to the rulers built into the application itself, not according to the actual measurement of the shapes on the screen. But if you're using MacPaint, you may have some difficulty getting accurate sizes. If you hold up a ruler and draw a shape to size on the screen, it will probably print out differently. One solution to this problem is to use MacDraw whenever size is important. If you must use MacPaint for drawings in

Chapter 7

which size relationships are crucial, take your Macintosh to your dealer and ask the technician to adjust the video output so the dimensions of the video image correspond more closely to the dimensions as they appear in the printout.

Avoiding Paper Jams

After your Imagewriter has remained inactive for four hours or more, the first sheet of paper that's printed is curled from having been wrapped around the platen. When you print out this first sheet, the curled paper will hit the clear paper cover and may be deflected into the feed slot for cut paper. This will cause a paper jam. If the Imagewriter is left unattended, it may become damaged as it continues to print after the paper reenters the printer.

You can avoid this problem by lifting the clear plastic paper cover when you print the first sheet of paper. The paper cover is there to muffle the sound and reduce the amount of dust that enters the printer. If you want to keep the cover down to reduce the noise level, lift the cover for the first sheet and then put it back down.

Printing Printouts

There are several ways to get printouts with the Macintosh. This freedom of choice gives you considerable flexibility.

Printing from the Desktop

You can print documents from the desktop without having to open an application. This allows you to choose several documents to print and have them produced one after the other. When you come back to your computer, they're all done.

Select the documents by Shift-clicking or by surrounding your choice of documents with the selection rectangle, or with a combination of both techniques. Choose *Print* from the *File* menu. Note that version 1.3 of MacPaint always prints from the desktop in high-quality mode. This will take more time than printing in draft mode. Also, this will unnecessarily shorten the life of the ribbon and Imagewriter print head. Version 1.0 of MacPaint prints from the desktop in draft mode. It's a good idea to acquire all versions of application programs so that you can use features one has that the other doesn't. Your Apple dealer will probably have both versions of MacPaint.

Chapter 7

Printing from Applications

Most applications have a *Print* option in the *File* menu. When you choose to print, MacWrite and MacDraw present you with a dialog box.

Figure 7-2. *Print* **Dialog Box**

```
ImageWriter (Standard or Wide)                    [  OK   ]
Quality:     ○ High      ● Standard   ○ Draft
Page Range:  ● All       ○ From: [  ]  To: [  ]   [Cancel]
Copies:      [1]
Paper Feed:  ● Continuous  ○ Cut Sheet
```

After you make your decisions about print quality, number of copies, and type of paper feed, the current active document is printed out.

When you choose either *Print Draft* or *Print Final* from the MacPaint *File* menu, you're not shown a dialog box. Instead, you just have the choice between *Print Draft* and *Print Final*. (Version 1.0 of MacPaint does not have a *Print Final* mode—all printouts are in draft mode.)

Figure 7-3. *Print* **Options from MacPaint 1.0 and 1.3**

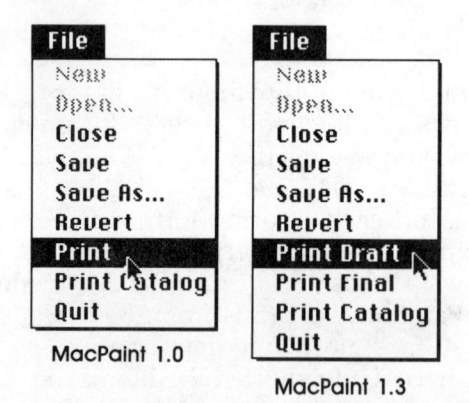

```
File                    File
New                     New
Open...                 Open...
Close                   Close
Save                    Save
Save As...              Save As...
Revert                  Revert
Print                   Print Draft
Print Catalog           Print Final
Quit                    Print Catalog
                        Quit
MacPaint 1.0
                        MacPaint 1.3
```

Screen Dumps

You can print out everything that appears on the screen simply by pressing Command-Shift-4. Many of the illustrations in this book were generated with this feature.

Chapter 7

Window Dumps

To get a printout of just the active window on the screen, press down Caps Lock, then press Command-Shift-4.

Print Catalog

MacPaint gives you the ability to print out a catalog of all the MacPaint documents on a disk. Choose *Print Catalog* from MacPaint's *File* menu to get your list of documents. The results are greatly reduced in size, but usually there's enough detail to help you identify the documents. The title of each document also appears, making it very easy for you to locate the document you're looking for. It's a good idea to keep a notebook of the catalogs of all disks that contain MacPaint documents.

Figure 7-4. A Printed Catalog

MacPaint documents on disk Bones and others

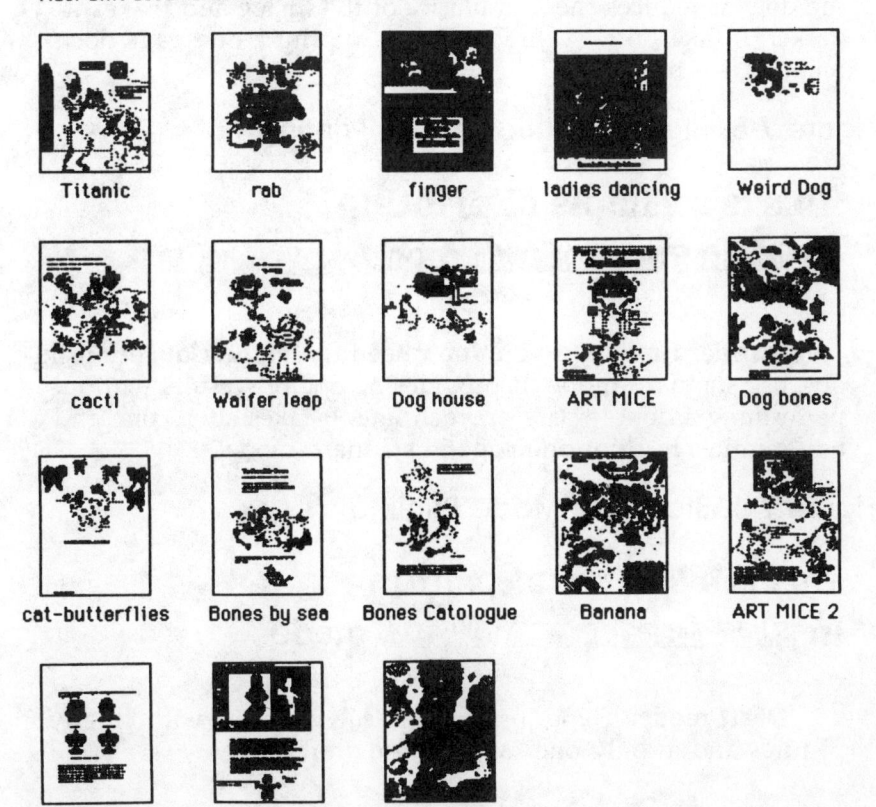

Titanic	rab	finger	ladies dancing	Weird Dog
cacti	Waifer leap	Dog house	ART MICE	Dog bones
cat-butterflies	Bones by sea	Bones Catologue	Banana	ART MICE 2
silhouette	Woman man source pix	Naturalist		

223

Chapter 7

Verson 1.3 of MacPaint will print out the catalog in high-quality mode. Again, this unnecessarily wastes ribbon and puts wear on the print head. Use MacPaint version 1.0, if you have it, to print catalogs in draft mode.

Printout Quality

The print mode you choose, the life of the ribbon, and the quality of the paper are all factors that affect print quality.

Print Modes

The Imagewriter can print in three modes that vary in speed and quality.

High-resolution mode. Obviously, this mode provides the highest quality output with the Imagewriter printer. The print head passes over each line twice. By filling the spaces between the dots, it reduces the granularity of the image and makes it darker. It takes almost three minutes to print a one-page document in this mode.

Figure 7-5. High-Resolution Mode Printing

This is a sample of printing in high resolution mode.

Standard mode. If you don't need the highest quality printout, use standard mode. It provides acceptable results without performing a double pass on each line. It takes about one and a half minutes to print one page in standard mode.

Figure 7-6. Standard Mode Printing

This is a sample of printing in standard resolution mode.

Draft mode. If you just want to see your text without any pictures and in only one font, choose draft mode.

Chapter 7

Figure 7-7. Draft Mode Printing

```
This   is  a  sample    of  printing
in   draft     mode.
```

Horizontal Streaks

The Imagewriter is an excellent companion for the Macintosh, but it isn't perfect. The feed mechanism has some inherent functional problems that result in horizontal streaking across printed pictures. This is most noticeable in dense dot-patterned areas.

Figure 7-8. Horizontal Streaking

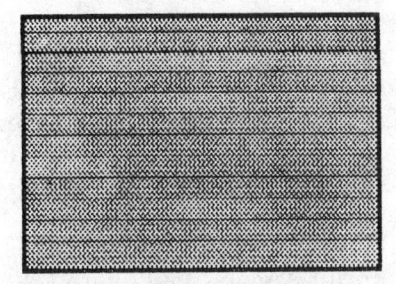

50% dot screen

You can't eliminate this streaking, but you *can* reduce it by using a higher quality paper, as discussed in "Paper Quality," later in this chapter. You can avoid these horizontal lines by using less dense dot patterns—those less than the 50 percent gray pattern used for the background of the desktop seem to work fine.

Figure 7-9. Less Dense Gray

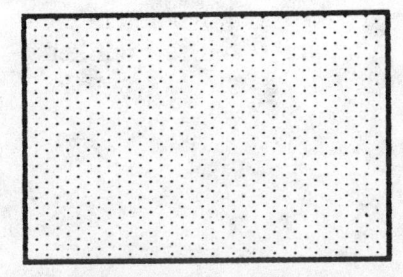

10% dot screen

Chapter 7

Ribbons

Don't try to economize too much on ribbons. If your printouts are light gray rather than black and your ribbon is beginning to look like the dog chewed it, buy a new one. An excellent MacPaint drawing printed in faint grays leaves a lot to be desired.

You can buy high-quality ribbons at discount prices if you do a little shopping around. Look for those small ads in the back of computer magazines. You should be able to find ribbons for less than $8 each. Make sure that the ribbons you order are for the C.Itoh 8510 and the NEC 8023A printers. They should be nylon ribbons—cotton ribbons sometimes fray, causing damage to the pins of the Imagewriter's print head.

You can extend the life of a ribbon with a two-ribbon system, one for drafts and one for final printouts. If you're printing rough drafts before completing an illustration, a well-used ribbon is sufficient. But when you're ready for a final printout, use a new ribbon. When your draft ribbon is too worn even for draft printouts, throw it out and use your old "final" ribbon for drafts, and a new one for the final picture or manuscript. Since the Imagewriter cartridge is very easy to change, this system is a practical solution to the problem.

Note that a new ribbon is likely to cause some smearing at the edges of dark areas. Before you print camera-ready copy or pictures with a new ribbon, break it in with a few repeated printings of a dark illustration.

Don't throw away your used ribbon cartridges. There are services that will refill used cartridges with newly inked ribbons and sell them back to you for about 25 percent of what a new ribbon costs. Look in the yellow pages or the back of computer magazines for the names of companies that offer this service.

If you're going through ribbons quickly, buy a reinker. This will allow you to add ink to a spent ribbon. You can get two or three additional uses out of each ribbon this way. You can even ink ribbons with a variety of colored inks. Look for ads in computer magazines for the names of companies that sell reinkers, inks, and blank cartridges.

Chapter 7

Paper Quality

The quality of your printed results is certainly affected by the type of paper you use. You'll probably use fanfold, form-feed paper most of the time. It's tempting to buy the cheapest—after all, "paper is just paper." But if your finished product will be seen in the form of Imagewriter printouts, you must consider the quality of the paper you use. If you're using Imagewriter printouts as finished or camera-ready art, for instance, you should use high-quality paper. Even if you're just printing something for yourself, keep at least a small stock of high-quality paper for final printouts. You don't have to print everything on high-quality paper, just those items that need that extra look—announcements, proposals, and resumes, for example.

Fanfold paper. The cheapest fanfold papers are lightweight and sometimes difficult to tear along the perforations. You might end up with rough edges after the pin-hole margins are torn off. This kind of paper can also deposit a great deal of paper dust in your printer, which may eventually cause problems if you don't regularly remove it. Also, cheaper papers can turn yellow after several weeks of exposure to daylight.

You can purchase something called laser-perf fanfold paper, which has a 25 percent cotton rag content. It's heavier than the cheaper papers and has finer perforations that are almost invisible after the margins are torn. In addition, the extra weight limits horizontal streaking somewhat, and the cotton content virtually eliminates yellowing.

Cut paper. For your special printouts, use single-sheet cut paper. You can print on your own letterhead if you wish. You'll obtain the best results with papers that have a hard, smooth finish. Rice paper and some light Bristol papers will give you excellent results. The best way to decide on a paper is to try some tests yourself. Experiment with a variety until you find one that gives you the effect you want. To conduct your testing systematically, design a printer test document with MacPaint. Use patterns of lines spaced close together and 50 percent gray areas to test for misfeeding and paper slippage. Use text of small and normal sizes. Include a picture that exemplifies the type of work you do most frequently. Here's a printer test document I created.

Chapter 7

Figure 7-10. Printer Test

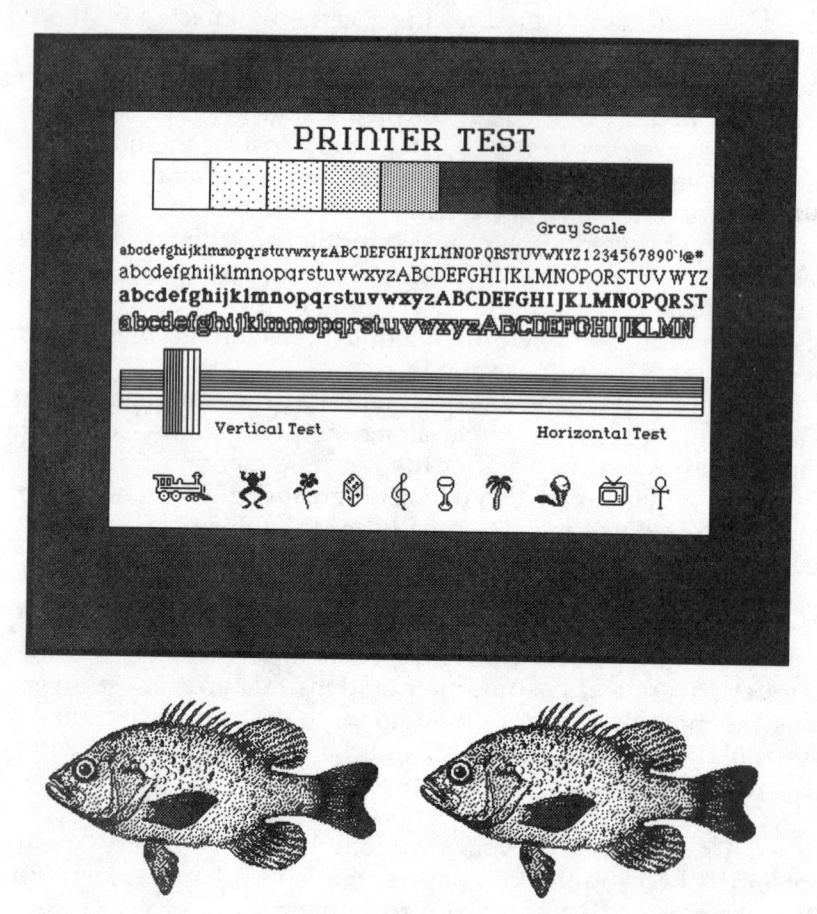

Go to an art supply store and buy samples of a wide variety of papers. Stay away from very heavy papers, such as those that are two-ply—they cause a great deal of slippage.

Figure 7-11. Thicker Papers Cause Slippage

Avoid papers with a lot of texture—they can create a softness to the dots and make the picture look fuzzy. Maybe this is what you're after; in that case, test some of the softest, most textured papers.

Matching Quality and Function

There are no easy rules for getting the best possible print quality. Before you decide the best way to print something, you have to know what you'll be using the printout for.

Most of the time, high resolution yields the best results. If you compare the results from *Print Final* and *Print Draft* modes of MacPaint, you'll see that *Print Final* produces a sharper-looking image with greater contrast. Take a look at Figure 7-12 for just such a comparison. The *Print Final* version is at the bottom.

Figure 7-12. *Print Final* and *Print Draft*

Chapter 7

If you photocopy your printouts, the copying process itself will yield a darker result than the original. When you compare photocopied material in *Print Draft* and *Print Final* modes, you may find that they're virtually indistinguishable, depending on the characteristics of the photocopy machine. If this is true, you don't have to use high-quality printing for printouts that will later be photocopied. Draft mode with MacPaint and a well-used ribbon is usually adequate. This will help economize on ribbons and reduce wear on your printer. You can also save money by using a lower quality paper. Experiment with the lightness and darkness controls of the copy machine to get the best results.

If you plan to reduce the size of the original when you photocopy it, make sure you use only *Print Draft* mode. When you reduce *Print Final* printouts, text and fine lines get a little thicker, making them appear less sharp.

If you're doing camera-ready work, use your best ribbon, paper, and print mode. If you're using fanfold paper, keep the friction switch at the left of the printer set forward. This can reduce paper slippage.

Laser Printers

Laser printers give much better results than the Imagewriter printer because they provide more than three times as many dots per inch. This makes the image much sharper. Laser printers typically are very expensive, but as they become more common, costs will probably decrease.

A Macintosh system consisting of a laser printer and a professional-quality word processor can give you the capabilities of a typesetter. Such a system can cheaply produce camera-ready mechanicals of graphics and text.

As the use of laser printers becomes more widespread, it may be possible for the Macintosh (with appropriate software) to create half-tone prints of photographs. Dots smaller than the pixels on the Macintosh screen would be used for fine grays, and these tiny dots would be grouped to create denser dot screens. Self-publishing books and magazines with your Macintosh? Exciting prospect, isn't it?

Printing in Color

Many owners of the Macintosh may want to create announcements and greeting cards as finished MacPaint printouts. Try using papers of different colors. Go to an art supply store and buy

Chapter 7

a variety of colored paper samples. Try printing some of your MacPaint documents on this paper. Which colors and typefaces work best?

You can also purchase color ribbons for the Imagewriter. This will let you choose the color for your pictures. If you take some time to plan your pictures, you could put a piece of paper through the Imagewriter several times to get multicolor printing. Try combining different colored inks with different colored papers.

Working Directly from Disks

The best possible printed results can be produced by services that connect the Macintosh to typesetting equipment. Working directly from disk, this technique produces photographically generated output that closely matches what you see on the screen. For each pixel, the typesetting machine lays down a perfect, clean square. The illustrations in this book were done in this way.

Other Printers

A letter-quality printer can be connected to the Macintosh with the proper cable and software. This will let you produce conventional, fully formed characters rather than dot-matrix-quality results. Business users may want to have this capability. It's apparent, however, that the Macintosh's Imagewriter output is quickly establishing a new aesthetic for computer printouts. Sometimes dots have a charm all their own.

Chapter 8
Working from Originals

Chapter 8
Working from Originals

Those gifted with an artist's eye and a steady hand can create elaborate and beautiful drawings with MacPaint and MacDraw. But what about the rest of us? How can we create those works of art when our hand-eye coordination or patience is just not up to it? Is there a way of transferring already existing pictures into the Mac? Can you take instant snapshots of objects with the Mac? The answer is definitely *yes*. This chapter shows you how to use various mechanical methods to transfer existing art into the Macintosh computer.

Tracing with the Mouse

Professional artists frequently trace outlines for their graphics projects. Sometimes they use overhead projectors to project original art work onto paper, then trace it. This insures fidelity to the original and saves the artist time.

Tracing can make it easy even for nonartists to copy originals into Mac documents. The mouse is an excellent input device for pointing and dragging, but it's not the best tool for creating detailed drawings. Even gifted artists have to practice before they can draw freehand designs smoothly with the device.

You've probably thought of using the mouse to trace an original picture into a MacPaint document. You could put the picture under a piece of glass or plastic and trace the outlines with the mouse. If you've tried it, you've probably found that this technique doesn't work very well. The problem with the mouse device is that it registers the movements you make in a relative way—there isn't a direct relationship between the space in which the mouse travels and the space it maps on the screen. For this reason, the mouse is almost impossible to use in tracing original art. Any slight shift in the angle of movement or slip of the mouse ball on the surface it moves across will produce irregularities. No matter how hard you try, the starting and ending points will rarely meet.

As a solution, some writers have recommended that users mount the mouse into a holder or strap it to the mechanical rulers of a drafting table. These solutions are really not worthwhile. You can save yourself hours of frustration by abandoning mouse tracing in favor of one of the techniques discussed below.

Chapter 8

Using Transparencies

This is probably the cheapest and easiest way of working from an original. A transparency is taped on the Macintosh screen and traced with MacPaint's pencil tool.

The Method

Find a photograph or drawing you want to trace. The first time you try this technique, use an original no larger than the size of the MacPaint window. If the original is too large or too small, you can use a photocopy machine with reduction and enlargement features to produce a copy that *will* fit within a MacPaint window. Tape a piece of acetate on the picture and trace the important outlines with a narrow-tipped permanent marker. Open MacPaint and tape the acetate tracing on the Macintosh screen within the MacPaint window, using masking tape or drafting tape. Use the pencil tool to trace the outlines from the acetate on the Mac's screen.

Figure 8-1. The MacPaint Outline

Now you can close some of the areas of your outline with *FatBits*, if necessary, so that you can fill them with patterns.

Chapter 8

Figure 8-2. The First Stage of Filling

Continue to enhance the drawing.

Figure 8-3. Added Enhancements

Chapter 8

Add some final details and a frame to complete it.

Figure 8-4. The Finished Drawing

Large Pictures

It's possible to trace the outlines of originals as large as 8 × 10 inches. First, trace the large original on the acetate. Open MacPaint and click the hand tool twice to enter *Show Page*. Move the MacPaint window frame to the top left corner and click *OK*.

Tape the top left part of your acetate tracing on the screen. When you have traced as much of the acetate outline as appears in the MacPaint window, use the hand tool to move the MacPaint drawing to the left. Reorient the acetate, making sure to register the acetate with the outline you've already drawn on the screen, and tape it back down. Now you can trace more of the drawing. Continue moving the MacPaint document page and reorienting the acetate until the entire 8 × 10 inch picture is traced.

Chapter 8

Figure 8-5. Start at the Top Left of the MacPaint Document

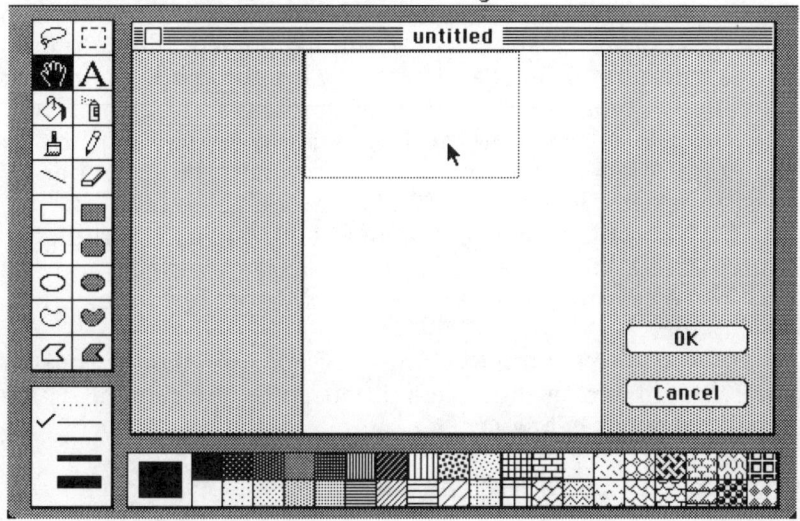

Using Camera Images

You can use large transparencies made from photographic originals such as slides or negatives for more complex images. Have your slide or negative made into a black-and-white transparency, tape the transparency to the screen, and trace it with MacPaint. This technique can be used for originals which contain a great deal of detail—those that would be difficult to trace on acetate by hand.

Using Digitizer Pads

A digitizer pad is a touch-sensitive device you write on with a special electronic pen. By simply tracing an original, it can appear in the MacPaint window. The Macintosh's screen is mapped out on the pad so that no matter where you put the pen, the relative distance of that point from other elements of the original is maintained.

Digitizer pads are much better for drawing and tracing than the mouse. The pad is easier to use because it's more like using paper and pencil. We're much more comfortable using a penlike instrument held between our fingers than rolling a box on our desk. Unfortunately, a digitizer pad is much more expensive than a mouse.

Chapter 8

Using Cameras

Imagine pointing a camera at an object and having its image appear within seconds on the Mac's screen. The camera can be used with live subjects or flat originals. The image that the camera puts on the screen can be stretched or shrunk, copied, filled, or enhanced with any of MacPaint's tools. This automatic optical process entirely eliminates the need for drawing and tracing. This tool can make it very easy for those without artistic skills to produce product labels, package designs, portraits, or any other form of visual design. Several such tools are available now.

The MicronEye. For only about $400, you can start digitizing pictures with a kit that includes a camera, an interface, and software. The MicronEye is available from Micron Technology, Inc., of Boise, Idaho.

The software for the MicronEye offers a number of commands for enhancing the image produced by the camera. Three of its menus appear below.

Figure 8-6. Menus of the MicronEye

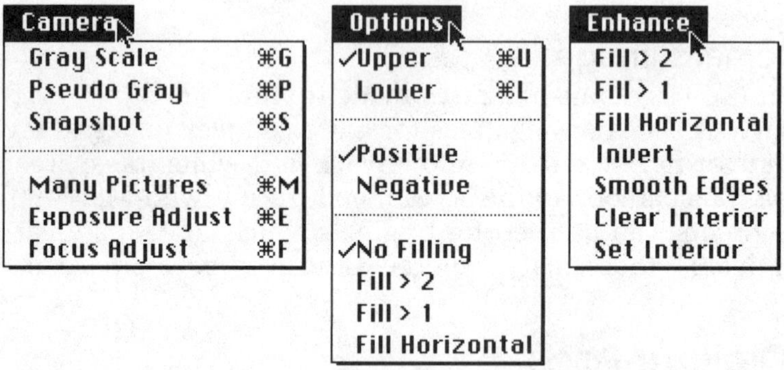

Camera		Options		Enhance
Gray Scale	⌘G	✓Upper	⌘U	Fill > 2
Pseudo Gray	⌘P	Lower	⌘L	Fill > 1
Snapshot	⌘S			Fill Horizontal
		✓Positive		Invert
Many Pictures	⌘M	Negative		Smooth Edges
Exposure Adjust	⌘E			Clear Interior
Focus Adjust	⌘F	✓No Filling		Set Interior
		Fill > 2		
		Fill > 1		
		Fill Horizontal		

The *Gray Scale* and *Pseudo Gray* features allow you to simulate continuous tones. This overcomes the camera's tendency to reproduce images of high contrast.

You can smooth the edges of your drawing, fill in white pixels with black to get richer results, and even turn your picture into a negative.

A typical screen with MicronEye looks similar to Figure 8-7.

Chapter 8

Figure 8-7. A MicronEye Screen

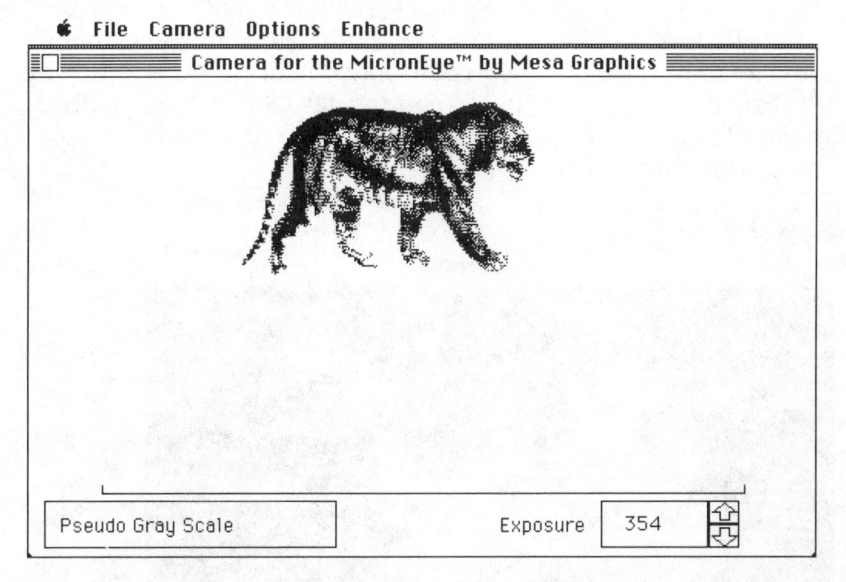

Unfortunately, several compromises have been made in the design of this digitizer. First, the size of the image that can be scanned is only about 1-3/4 inches high by 6-3/4 inches wide. This is only a fraction of the Macintosh's window size. To make larger pictures, the subject must be scanned in parts and the parts spliced together. This is a tedious process because getting just one satisfactory image with the MicronEye can take more than 20 minutes. It takes a lot of patience to fiddle with the focus and exposure adjustments until you get a good result. Another problem is the difficulty in aiming the camera at your subject. There's no way to aim the camera without having it scan to produce a picture. This wastes time. Yet another problem is that the camera sometimes has to be more than ten feet from your original to get the whole image into the scan area, even if the original is less than half the size of an 8-1/2-by-11-inch piece of paper. This distance makes it even more difficult to aim the camera.

The MicronEye digitizer has poor resolving power—the pictures it produces are coarse. The enhancement commands in the menus help compensate for the shortcomings of the camera's output, but it's difficult to improve the poor quality of the image.

Chapter 8

The scanned picture can be printed out or saved as a MacPaint document. You can use MacPaint to enhance the image, but in the time it takes to improve the image with the camera software and MacPaint, you could have made an acetate tracing.

However, with patience, good images can be made with this system. Here are two portrait samples, each of which was spliced and greatly enhanced.

Figure 8-8. Portraits

Jim Alley

242

Chapter 8

Jim Alley

MacVision. Koala Technologies of Santa Clara, California, has developed digitizing hardware and software for the Macintosh. The cost of the package is $300. You must use your own video camera or videocassette recorder to serve as an input device for MacVision.

The most striking aspect of MacVision is its speed and ease of use. You aim the camera, focus, adjust the exposure, and in five seconds, MacVision has completed its scan and an image is on the screen.

Bill Atkinson, author of MacPaint, produced the software for MacVision. The design of the software is elegant and simple. MacVision adds Camera as an option in the familiar Apple menu. Camera, then, is a desktop accessory, like the Scrapbook and Alarm Clock. You don't have to exit MacPaint to use it. When Camera is chosen, a MacVision window opens and you can start the scan.

Chapter 8

Figure 8-9. Koala Technologies' MacVision

MacVision™ by Koala Technologies is a software and digitizing hardware peripheral (camera not included) which permits any video image to be easily input, saved, edited, and printed using the Apple Macintosh personal computer.

The image can be copied into the Clipboard and pasted into MacPaint for immediate enhancement, or even into another application, such as MacWrite.

MacVision offers good resolution—320 × 240 pixels. MacVision's software digitizes images at eight bits per pixel. This makes the digitized image clear and precise. With the Camera menu (at the far right of the window) you can even repeat the scan.

Chapter 8

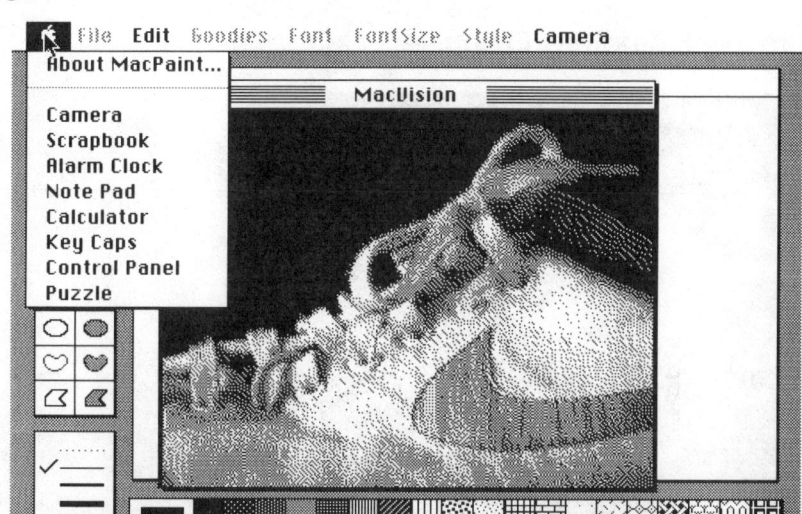

Figure 8-10. The MacVision Window

Figure 8-11. The Camera Menu

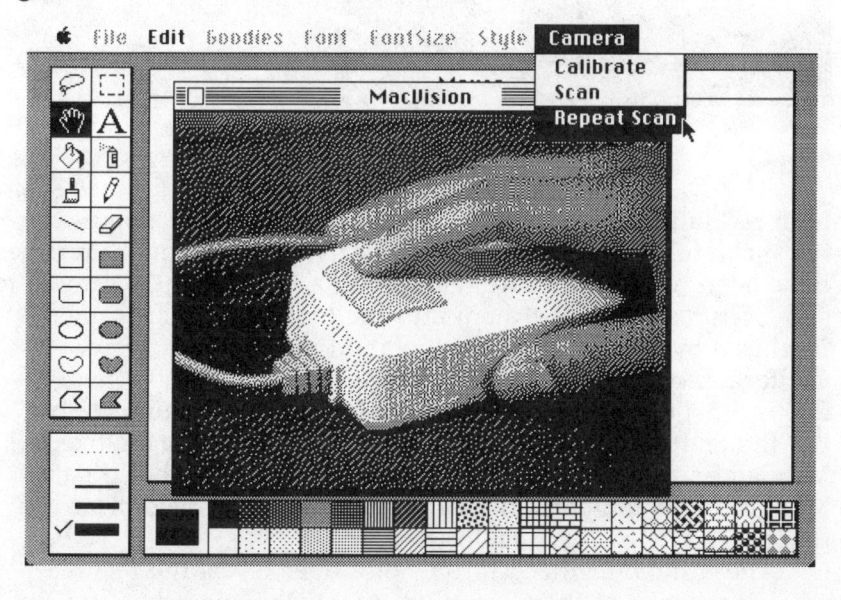

Chapter 8

Here's another example of a MacVision-produced image.

Figure 8-12. Another Example

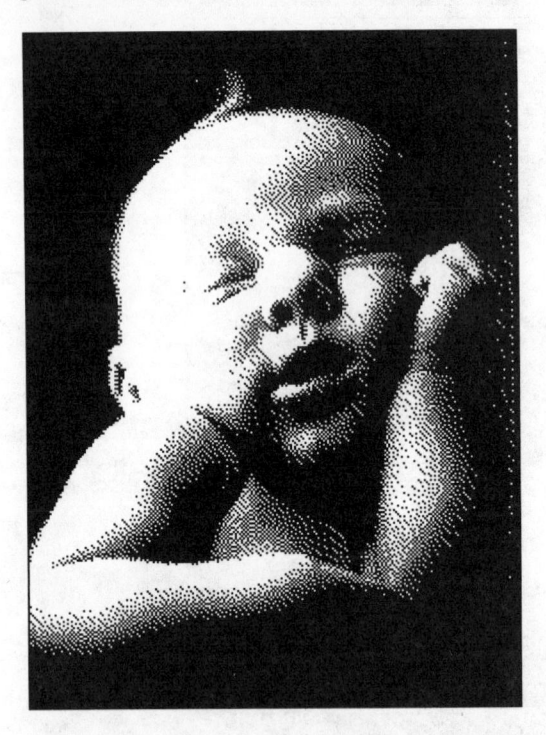

The Datacopy 610 camera. Because the Macintosh has such a high resolution for its bitmapped display, standard cameras cannot make full use of the computer's capabilities. Some companies have been writing software that allows a Datacopy 610 camera to scan pictures and insert them into the Macintosh. This camera, produced by the Datacopy Corporation of Mountain View, California, costs almost $8,000. However, with a resolution of 2000 × 3000 pixels, it provides the highest resolution possible. But the real advantage of this camera is its ability to digitize full MacPaint-size images, all the way up to 8 × 10 inches. Koala's MacVision, in comparison, can only produce digitized pictures that are 3-1/2 × 4-1/2 inches.

These three digitized images of a tiger reveal the relative resolving power of the MicronEye, MacVision, and the Datacopy 610 digitizers.

Chapter 8

Figure 8-13. Digitizer Comparison

The Micron Eye™

Koala Technologies's Mac Vision™

Apple's Digitizer

Chapter 8

The MacVision and Datacopy images are very close in quality. The software that Bill Atkinson created for the Koala product makes up for the low resolution of standard video cameras.

Here are a few more samples of digitized pictures produced with the Macintosh.

Figure 8-14. More Digitized Images

248

Chapter 8

For those who want to get an image which can be used in MacPaint or MacWrite documents quickly and accurately, a digitizing camera is a wonderful tool. With one, your Macintosh will truly be able to see the world.

249

Chapter 9
Organizing Files and Disks

Chapter 9
Organizing Files and Disks

By now you've probably created a number of pictures with MacPaint and MacDraw. These programs are so easy to use that in a short time you'll fill your disks with documents. In this chapter you'll learn how to organize these documents on specially prepared disks. By following the steps outlined here, you'll be able to find documents quickly and easily. You'll also learn how to maximize the space on your disks to avoid the alarming *Disk Full* alert. A discussion of how to copy both individual files and entire disks will help you maintain backups of all your programs. This will insure copies in case originals are lost or damaged.

What *Is* a File?

A *file* is simply a collection of information stored on a diskette. Programs, pictures, and even business letters are files. MacPaint, MacDraw, and MacWrite are application programs stored on disks as *program files*. Picture or text documents produced by these programs are *data files*. To help you remember which type a particular file is, the Macintosh displays them as icons on the desktop. Application program icons are in the shape of a square turned diagonally.

In addition to the application program icons, you'll also see icons representing documents produced by each program. Each type of document looks different. That is, all MacPaint documents are shown as pages with a paint brush, all MacWrite documents are shown as a page of text, and so on. To summarize, then, files can be either programs or documents.

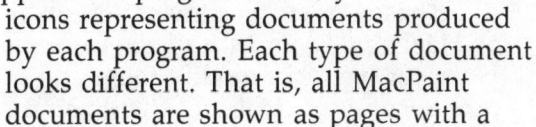

Files can also contain information the computer needs to take care of its operations. These *system files* are usually found in the System folder of a disk. To see some system files, double-click a disk icon, then double-click on the System folder to open it.

Chapter 9

Figure 9-1. An Open System Folder

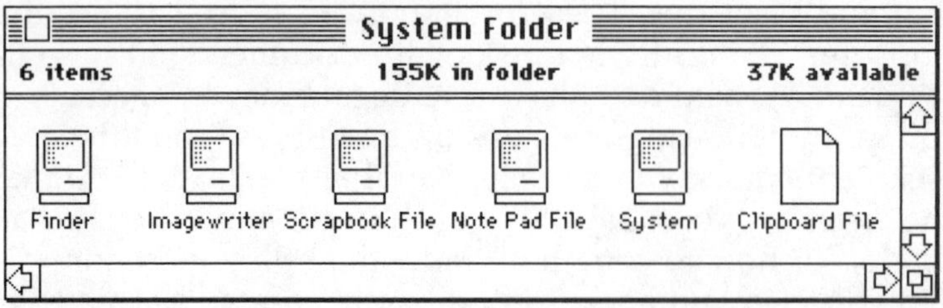

```
┌─────────────════ System Folder ════─────────────┐
│ 6 items            155K in folder      37K available │
│                                                      │
│   [ ]      [ ]      [ ]      [ ]      [ ]      [ ]   │
│  Finder Imagewriter Scrapbook File Note Pad File System Clipboard File │
└──────────────────────────────────────────────────────┘
```

System files are usually represented by icons that look like tiny Macintoshes, but there are exceptions. You can see from Figure 9-1 that the Clipboard file is shown as a page with a folded corner. Don't worry—the icon may look different from disk to disk, but the filename will always be accurate.

A file can also be a "snapshot" of a screen or window stored on disk as a MacPaint file. Remember that a screen snapshot can be recorded on disk when you press Command-Shift-3. Up to ten snapshots can be stored on a disk. The first is labeled Screen 0, the second, Screen 1, and so on up to Screen 9. If you want to create more than ten, rename the existing ones or move them to another disk.

These screen files are stored on your MacPaint working disk as MacPaint documents. They can be opened only by MacPaint. However, you can modify them and even use parts in other picture documents. Many of the illustrations in this book were created with this feature of the Macintosh.

To summarize again, a file may be a program, a document, system information, or a screen snapshot.

The Start-up Disk

The first disk you insert in the drive after you turn the computer on is called the *start-up disk*. In order to start the Macintosh, the start-up disk must contain the System and Finder files, software that provides some aspects of the computer's intelligence and personality. The System and Finder files provide, among other things, the desktop metaphor, the ability to find and maintain files on disks, and the data required to operate the Scrapbook, Clipboard, Notepad, and Imagewriter.

The Macintosh was designed to let you know when you're doing something wrong. If the start-up disk doesn't contain System and Finder files, the computer's smile disappears (it finds its brain power missing), and it spits the disk out. Turn the power off and on again before you insert a valid start-up disk.

Ejecting Disks

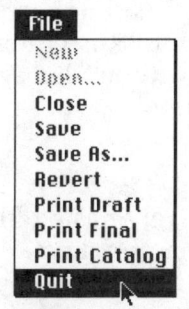

There are three ways to eject a diskette. If an application window is open, first exit the application by choosing *Quit* from the *File* menu.

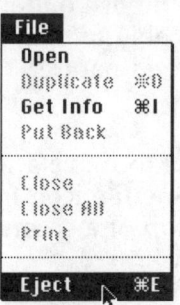

This closes the application window and returns you to the desktop. Select *Eject* from the *File* menu (or press Command-E).

The drive will spin for a moment to update the disk with the changes you made. When the update is complete, the disk ejects.

If you're using an external drive, the selected disk (the one with the black icon) is the one that's ejected when you choose *Eject* from the *File* menu. To eject both disks, Shift-click on the unselected disk icon, making it black, too, and choose *Eject*.

You can also eject disks without quitting an application. This, however, doesn't update the desktop changes. Press Command-Shift-1 to eject the disk in the internal drive and Command-Shift-2 to eject the disk in the external drive. (Remember, to properly update the desktop, quit the application before ejecting.)

If the computer locks up and doesn't allow you to enter any commands with the mouse or the keyboard, two additional means of ejecting diskettes are available. These should be used only when no other way works. Turn off the power, hold down the mouse button, and turn the power on while still pressing the

Chapter 9

mouse button. This results in the loss of the programs and data in RAM; the application program and any work you'd done up to that point (without saving to disk) is lost.

A second way to eject, without the mouse or keyboard, is to push the end of a straightened paper clip into the small hole on the right side of the drive opening. Remember, the disk isn't updated if you do this. But the disk *will* be ejected, without damaging either the computer or the diskette.

File Manipulation

Transferring, copying, renaming, protecting, and even erasing files on your diskettes is far easier on the Macintosh than on most other personal computers. Usually, it's only a matter of dragging an icon from place to place, perhaps pressing the mouse button once or twice. With just a little practice, you'll be able to manipulate files with such ease that it will be almost second nature.

Transferring Files

Whether you have one drive or two, it's very easy to move a file from one disk to another. You do it by dragging the file icon from the source disk window and putting it either on top of a second disk icon or in the open window of the second disk.

Transferring files with one drive. To transfer a file with a one-drive Macintosh system, first open the window of the disk which contains the file you want to transfer. Eject the disk. Insert the destination disk—the one you want to move the file to. If you inserted a blank disk, you'll see a dialog box offering two choices: either to initialize the disk, preparing it for information, or to eject the disk in favor of another.

Figure 9-2. Initialization Dialog Box

```
┌─────────────────────────────────────┐
│  ⌹  This disk is unreadable:        │
│      Do you want to initialize it?  │
│   ( Eject )          ( Initialize ) │
└─────────────────────────────────────┘
```

Choose *Initialize*. After the disk is initialized, another dialog box asks you to type in a disk name. You can enter any name under 27 characters. Don't use colons in the name. You'll now see

Chapter 9

the icons of both disks on the desktop. Double-click this second disk's icon.

If the disk you inserted was *not* a blank disk, all you need to do is open it by double-clicking its icon.

Figure 9-3. Open Windows of Two Disks

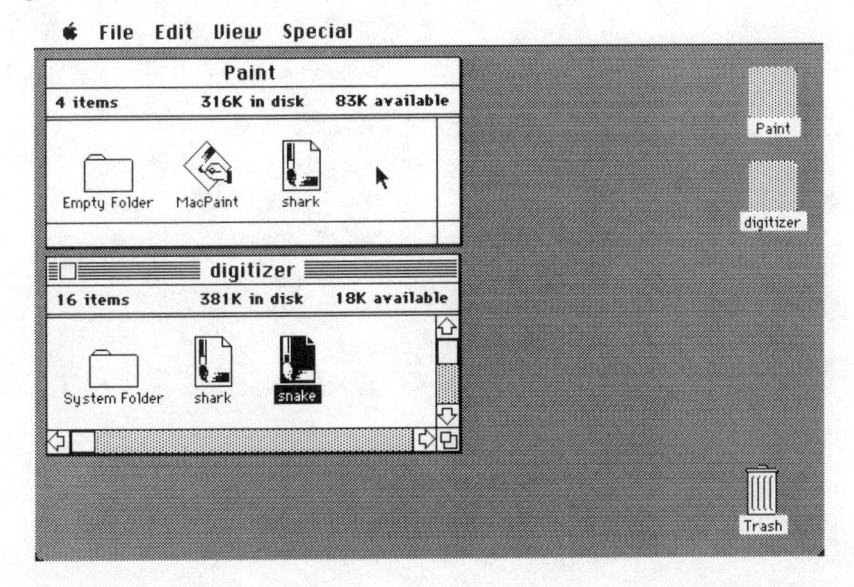

If the file you want to transfer is hidden by the window of the second disk, move the pointer to the window of the hidden disk and click. This puts that window on the top of the desktop. Or you can drag the window of the second disk so that the first's window is uncovered. Now drag the icon of the file you want to transfer from the source disk to the open window of the destination disk. In the next example, the file Shark is being dragged to the disk named Digitizer.

257

Chapter 9

Figure 9-4. Dragged Icon

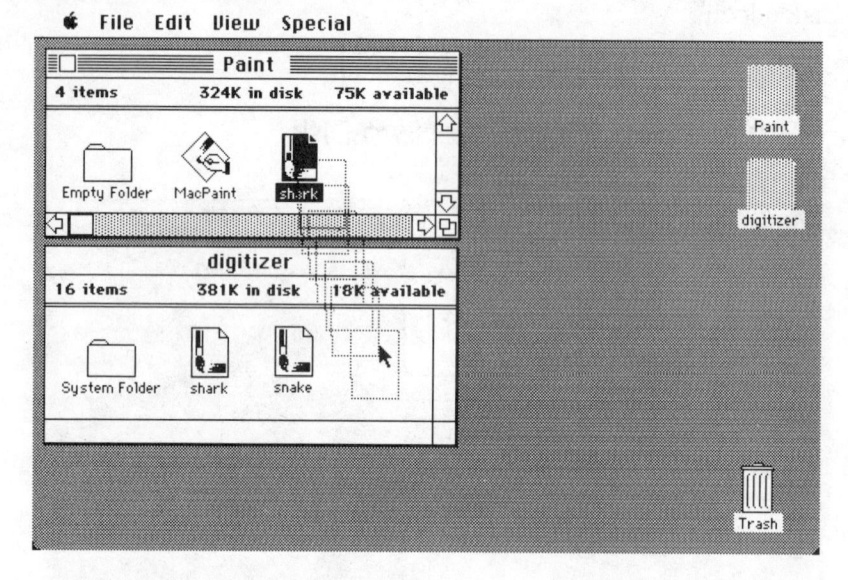

If a file with the same name already exists on the destination disk, an alert box appears and offers you the option of either replacing the contents of the existing file with the file to be transferred, or of canceling the transfer process entirely.

Figure 9-5. Replace Alert Box

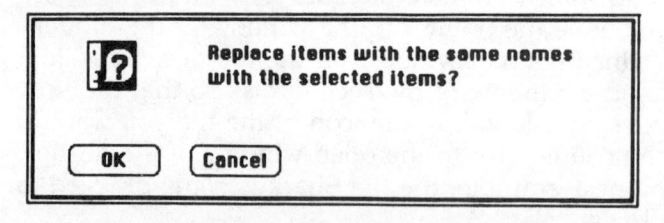

After a few disk swaps, your file is copied to the destination disk.

This process makes a copy of the file on the second disk. Keep in mind that the original file is still on the source disk. To free up space on the source disk, you must throw the original file in the trash can and then empty it by using *Empty Trash* from the *Special* menu. If you throw the file in the trash can and don't empty it, the file is not erased from the disk. You can still retrieve it by opening the trash can window and moving the icon of the

Chapter 9

file back to the source disk, or even to another disk. Starting an application program and ejecting a disk automatically empties the Trash and thus permanently erases the file.

Transferring files with two drives. File transfer is much easier with two drives. Put the source disk in one drive and the destination disk in the other. Open the window of the source disk and drag the file icon either to the icon of the second disk or to the open window of the second disk.

As with transferring with only one drive, remember that this process copies the file to the second diskette—the original is still on the source disk. Put the file in the Trash and empty it to free up space on the source disk.

Transferring several files at once. Transferring several files at once can also be done with the Macintosh. Select the files you want to transfer either by Shift-clicking their icons or by dragging the pointer arrow to surround them with the selection rectangle. Drag one of the icons to the window of the destination disk.

Figure 9-6. Drag Files to Destination Disk

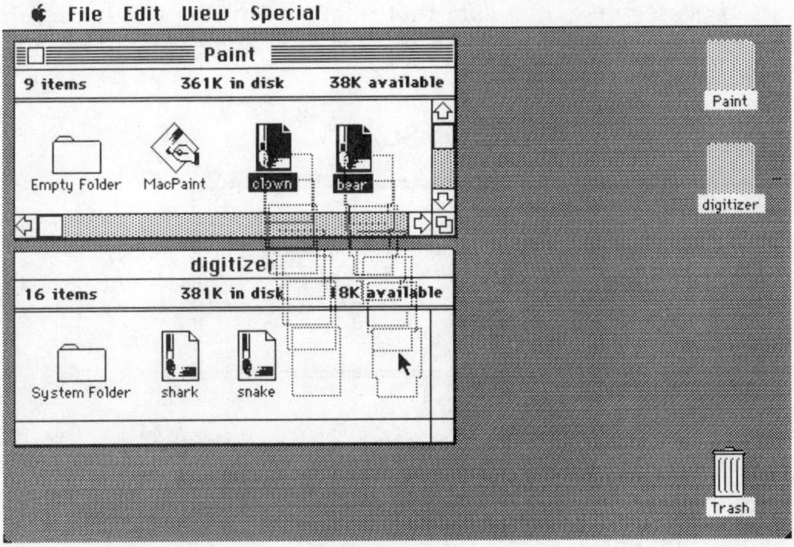

Another way of transferring several files is to drag the icon of a folder which contains those files to the window of your destination disk. All the files inside the folder will be copied to the second diskette.

259

Chapter 9

Copying Disks

You should always keep backups of all your disks. Otherwise, if data or programs are lost accidentally, you won't have something to fall back to. Some commercially available disks are copy-protected—you won't be able to make copies of them. The manual that comes with the protected software should provide instructions on how to order or create a backup disk.

Copying application disks. Copying application disks is as easy as dragging the icon of the disk you want to copy and dropping it on the icon of the disk you want to copy it to. Before you can do this, however, you must first have the icons of both source and destination disks on your desktop. Insert the application disk you want to copy. Its icon appears on the desktop. Eject this disk and insert a blank disk (you'll be asked to initialize it) or a disk that contains data you no longer need.

When icons for both disks are on the desktop, drag the icon of the disk to be copied onto the icon of the destination disk. A dialog box will ask if you want to replace the contents of the destination disk with the contents of the source disk. Because the copy process erases *any data* that might be on the destination disk, the Macintosh is giving you a chance to change your mind and cancel the process.

Figure 9-7. Replace Dialog Box

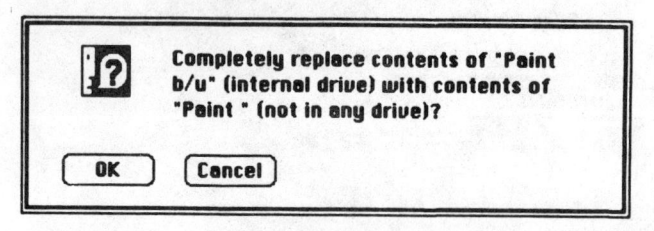

```
┌─────────────────────────────────────────────┐
│  ┌─┐   Completely replace contents of "Paint │
│  │?│   b/u" (internal drive) with contents of│
│  └─┘   "Paint " (not in any drive)?          │
│                                              │
│     ( OK )  ( Cancel )                       │
└─────────────────────────────────────────────┘
```

Notice that the dialog box tells you what is being copied (Paint) and what the source disk contains (Paint b/u).

You'll be prompted to make disk swaps until the copy process is completed.

The copy process is much easier with two drives, simply because you don't have to swap disks. Insert the source disk in one drive and the destination disk in the other. You'll be prompted to initialize the destination disk if necessary. Drag the icon of the program disk and drop it on top of the destination disk. As a safety feature, you'll be asked if you want to replace the contents of the destination disk with the contents of the source disk.

Copying data disks. Copying data disks (disks that contain only document files) is a bit different. You can't start the Macintosh with a data disk since it doesn't have the required Finder and System files on it. You'll learn how to prepare and copy a data disk later in this chapter.

The "Disk Copy" Utility

Apple has released a program called "Disk Copy." It copies disks on a one-drive system in only four disk swaps. This can be considerably faster than the method of dragging one disk icon on top of another.

If you don't have the "Disk Copy" program, your Apple dealer will probably have it available. Since instructions are built into the program, just follow the prompts to use it.

Renaming Disks, Files, and Folders

To rename a disk, insert it into the drive and click its icon to select it. Type a new name, and press Return or click anywhere outside the icon.

To rename a file or folder, click on its icon to select it. Type a new name and press Return or click anywhere outside the icon.

Names of disks, files, and folders can also be changed with the Macintosh's editing features. Select the icon and move the arrow to the name of the icon—the arrow turns into the I-beam cursor. The I-beam represents the insertion point for text. Click at the position where you want to insert text, and you'll see a blinking line. Type what you want to insert.

Figure 9-8. Inserting Text

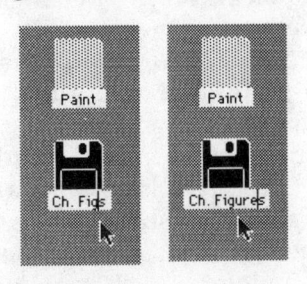

Chapter 9

To delete text, drag the I-beam cursor over a portion of it. It's highlighted to show it's selected for deletion. Press the Backspace key to actually delete it.

Figure 9-9. Select and Delete

To select an entire word for deleting, click twice on it and press Backspace.

The names you use for your files should help you identify them. Try to keep these names short, else they may overlap when displayed in a window, obscuring each other.

Figure 9-10. Long File Names

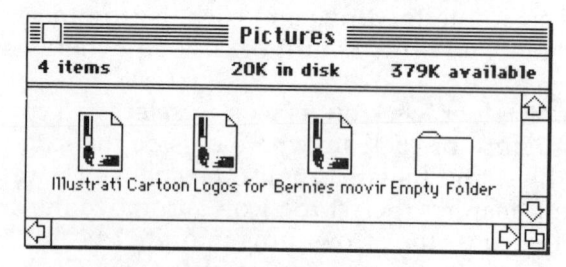

Write-Protecting Disks

You can insure that you won't accidentally alter your disks by write-protecting them. This prevents the Macintosh from changing the data on a disk. Master disks, for example, from which you make working disks, should always be stored in a write-protected form. Working disks should not be write-protected because the computer may require disk space for some of its operations.

The write-protect tab is a small plastic window at one corner of the 3-1/2-inch microfloppy diskettes. You can write-protect a disk by moving the plastic tab with a fingernail or sharp object so that the small window is open. To change it back, just move the tab so it blocks the window. Now you can alter the disk contents again.

Chapter 9

Figure 9-11. Write-Protect Window, Open and Closed

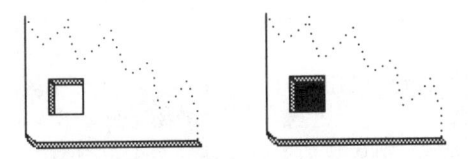

Erasing Disks and Files

To erase an entire disk, choose *Erase Disk* from the *Special* menu. This process leaves the initialization of the disk intact so that you can store new data on it.

A file or folder can be removed from a disk by dragging its icon to the trash can. When the pointer is on the Trash icon, the icon becomes black. Release the mouse button to put the selected item into the Trash. The file or folder is permanently erased when you select *Empty Trash* from the *Special* menu, run another application program, or eject your disk.

Disk Space Management

You've probably been startled by the alert box warning you that your disk is getting full. That surprise can turn into aggravation if you're confronted by this message again and again. Since programs like MacPaint use some empty disk space as a scratch pad to store information temporarily, the disk can quickly become full. Even with a two-drive system, you'll still run out of disk space because of this. If you upgrade your Macintosh to a 512K RAM machine, this won't be much of a problem. In the meantime, there are certain techniques you can use to preserve the valuable space on your disks.

Preparing Working Disks

You should prepare a working disk for each application program you use. These working disks will contain just the program itself and the System folder. Any unnecessary files will be removed to conserve disk space. Follow the procedures below to create MacPaint, MacDraw, and MacWrite working disks.

You probably have both MacPaint and MacWrite on one disk. If you also have MacPaint or MacWrite documents on this disk, temporarily transfer them to another disk (follow the instructions in "Transferring Files," an earlier section of this chapter). A bit

Chapter 9

later in this chapter you'll see exactly how to prepare data disks for storing the documents you create with the working application disks. Don't forget to delete these transferred documents from the original disk to free up space.

Make two copies of the original disk (follow the instructions in the "Copying Disks" section). Before you begin to copy disks currently in the drive, or drives, turn the computer off and on to reset it. This clears the computer's memory so that the next disk you insert will be the start-up disk; this reduces the number of swaps you must make with one drive.

Creating a MacPaint working disk. Insert one of the copies you made of MacPaint/MacWrite into the internal drive and double-click the disk icon to open its window. Delete the MacWrite application program by dragging its icon to the Trash. Select *Empty Trash* from the *Special* menu. This frees up about 55K of space on the disk.

More space can be made available by deleting some of the items from the Scrapbook file. Select Scrapbook from the Apple menu. Scroll through each item, deleting those you don't think you'll need by using *Clear* from the *Edit* menu. Put the Scrapbook away by clicking on its close box. Rename the disk Paint. This is your working MacPaint disk.

Whenever you create a screen snapshot by pressing Command-Shift-3, the data is stored on your MacPaint working disk even if you have a data disk in your external drive. Make sure you periodically remove these files to keep space open on your working disk for Macpaint's scratch pad. For best results, keep about 100K of space free on your MacPaint working disk.

You can clear even more space from your MacPaint working disk by trashing the Imagewriter file in the System folder. MacPaint doesn't use this file for printing.

Creating MacDraw and MacWrite working disks. MacDraw and MacWrite working disks can be made in the same way. First make a copy of each of the original disks. Remove documents created by MacDraw and MacWrite. Also remove application programs other than MacDraw or MacWrite. Edit the Scrapbook file to free more space. Rename the disks Draw and Write.

Setting the Start-up Program

You can cut down on the steps needed to access a program by setting it as the start-up program for its particular working disk. After doing this, the program's window automatically opens,

Chapter 9

bypassing the desktop, whenever you put the disk into the drive.

To set the start-up program, first select the application icon. For example, after opening the MacPaint working disk's icon, click on the MacPaint application icon. Now choose *Set Startup* from the *Special* menu. A dialog box asks if you're sure you want this program as the start-up. If you click, *OK* each time you turn the power on and insert this disk, MacPaint will open without showing the desktop.

Don't confuse the start-up disk with the start-up program. The first disk you insert after you turn the Mac on is the start-up disk. As the name suggests, it starts the Macintosh. When you set an application program as the start-up program, it just means it will automatically run without having to select the program from the desktop.

Removing Fonts

You can clear even more space on your working disks by removing some of the fonts from the System file. You probably won't need all the decorative fonts the Macintosh provides. You may want to remove a font which resembles another or one you don't think you'll need very often. Once this is done, their names no longer appear in the *Fonts* menu of that diskette.

The "Font Mover" program makes it easy to remove or add fonts to your working disks. If you don't have the "Font Mover" program, your Apple dealer will probably provide you with one at no charge. (It was part of an upgrade available in the summer of 1984.) This program is very easy to use. Don't worry about making mistakes—with "Font Mover" you can even move fonts back to a disk that's missing them.

First of all, transfer "Font Mover" to the working disk you want to take fonts from. Double-click the "Font Mover" icon to open it. Its window will display the names of the fonts in the System file of the disk you're working on.

265

Chapter 9

Figure 9-12. "Font Mover" Window

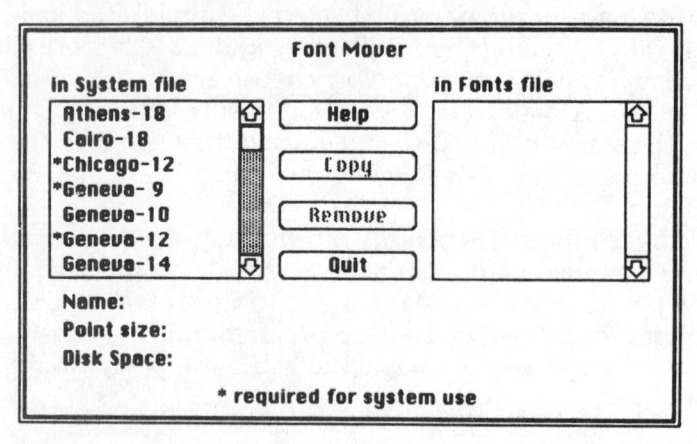

```
                         Font Mover
    in System file                    in Fonts file
    Athens-18    ⇧      ┌─────────┐                    ⇧
    Cairo-18            │  Help   │
    *Chicago-12         └─────────┘
    *Geneva- 9          ┌─────────┐
    Geneva-10           │  Copy   │
    *Geneva-12          └─────────┘
    Geneva-14    ⇩      ┌─────────┐                    ⇩
                        │ Remove  │
    Name:               └─────────┘
    Point size:         ┌─────────┐
    Disk Space:         │  Quit   │
                        └─────────┘
              * required for system use
```

Use the scroll bars of the System font window to locate a font you want to remove. When you select a font by clicking it, a sample of text is shown. The decorative fonts Athens, London, and Venice are the ones you'll probably want to remove. Click on *Athens* to select it and Shift-click on the names of any other fonts you want to remove. Click the *Remove* button. In a moment, the names of these fonts will disappear. They're no longer in the System file of your working disk. Note that "Font Mover" will not let you remove fonts marked with an asterisk (*). The Macintosh needs these for its system operations.

      If you want to store the fonts you removed so that you can move them back later, click *Copy* instead of *Remove*. This copies the selected fonts into a Fonts file.

Now click *Remove* to take that font out of the System file. You can move the Fonts file to another disk to store it. Later, you can move some of these fonts back into the System file of the disk of your choice with "Font Mover."

It's best to keep all available sizes of some of the more commonly used fonts (New York and Geneva, for instance). When you print in high-quality mode with MacWrite, the Imagewriter routine uses a font twice the size of what you entered your text in, and then reduces it by half. This process makes the letters look clearer. For example, you might have the New York font in 12-point and 24-point sizes. When you choose high-quality print mode from MacWrite, 12-point text is printed as a reduced 24-point New York font to provide high-quality output. The dots that

Chapter 9

make up the characters are merged to provide solid characters. If the 24-point font is not in the System file, you won't have the high-quality option for 12-point type and your output won't look as clear.

After you've removed the unwanted fonts, throw "Font Mover" into the Trash (only if you have another copy of it somewhere, though). If you removed the fonts to a Fonts file, move it to another disk. Don't forget to put the Fonts file into the Trash once it's been copied to another disk, and then empty the Trash.

If you want to restore one of the fonts you removed, you can do so by first moving "Font Mover" and the Fonts file back onto the working disk. Open "Font Mover" and select the fonts you want to move from the Fonts file to the System file.

You may have noticed that the menu of font sizes in applications like MacPaint displays some sizes in an outlined form.

Font sizes *not* outlined are pseudofonts—they aren't in the System file of the disk. These pseudofonts are created by the Macintosh from the outlined ones in the System file. Since the computer creates these fonts by scaling up or down from an actual font, pseudofonts don't look as good as stored fonts.

Apple has released a Cairo font made up of pictures rather than letters or numbers. When you press the l (lowercase L) key, for instance, you'll see a picture of a truck; press c to get a frog. You can get this font from your Apple dealer. It can be useful in MacPaint applications, so you should move the Cairo font to your MacPaint working disk by using "Font Mover."

Data Disks

Data disks contain just the documents you create with your working disks. The advantage of using a data disk is that all 400K of disk space is available for documents. For best results, you should not mix documents from more than one application on the same data disk. Keep all MacPaint documents, for example, on a MacPaint data disk. As you create more and more documents, you'll probably want to establish several data disks, by category, for each application's working disk. You might end up with three data disks for MacWrite, for instance: one for personal letters, one for business letters, and one for advertising flyers.

Chapter 9

Preparing data disks. It's easy to create a data disk. Insert one of your working disks into the drive as the start-up disk and then eject it. Put a blank disk into the drive and initialize it. Give the disk a name. Your data disk is now ready. Data disks should not have the System folder on them. This way, all the disk's space is available for documents.

Move all documents in your preselected category to this data disk. If it's a data disk for advertising flyers, for example, move all your advertising flyer documents to this disk.

To create a data disk with a two-drive Macintosh system, put the working disk in the internal drive and the blank disk in the external drive. You'll be prompted to initialize the blank disk. Give it a name like Letters or Reports. Your disk is now ready to receive files.

It takes a while to become accustomed to using separate program and data disks, but once you're familiar with the process of loading and saving documents with data disks, you'll find it easy to keep track of your files. You probably won't see the *Disk Full* alert box because your program disks won't be used for storing documents.

Managing Documents with One Drive

Now that you've established both working and data disks, you can use the latter to store the picture and text documents you create. This section will show you how to choose which data disk to save documents on and how to choose which data disk to load documents from.

Let's use MacPaint as an example. After you've created a picture, select *Save* from the *File* menu. The *Save* dialog box will appear.

Figure 9-13. *Save* Dialog Box for One Drive

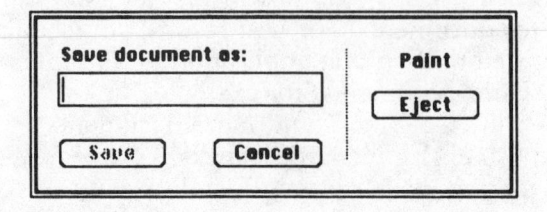

```
Save document as:           Paint
[                    ]      [ Eject ]
[ Save ]  [ Cancel ]
```

This dialog box allows you to name your document and select the disk you want to save it on. The name of your working disk,

Chapter 9

which contains the MacPaint application program, is shown above the *Eject* button. Click on *Eject* and insert your MacPaint data disk. The name of the data disk now appears above the *Eject* button. Type in a name for your document and click *Save*. Several disk swaps later your picture is saved to the data disk. The *Eject* button of this *Save* dialog box lets you replace the disk in the drive with the disk you want to save documents on.

After you've saved documents on several different data disks, how do you get the application disk out of the drive and get the data disk of your choice in? Use the *Close/Open* method. Let's use MacPaint again as an example. First, start MacPaint. When the MacPaint window is open, choose *Close* from the *File* menu. The MacPaint window disappears. Choose *Open* from the *File* menu. You'll see the following directory dialog box.

Figure 9-14. Directory Dialog Box of a Working Disk

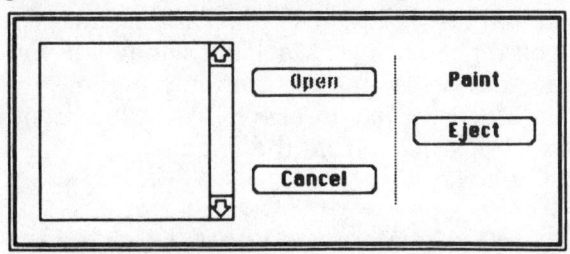

On the right side of the dialog box is the name of the disk, usually your MacPaint working disk. On the left is an alphabetically ordered list of all documents created by the MacPaint application program currently saved on the working disk. If your working disk doesn't have any MacPaint files on it, no file names will appear, just as shown in Figure 9-14.

To view the directory of a data disk, click *Eject* and insert a MacPaint data disk. Now you'll see the directory of this data disk.

Figure 9-15. Directory Dialog Box of a Data Disk

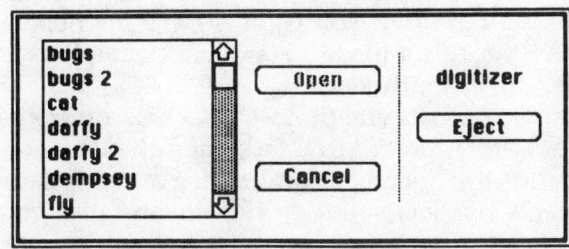

269

Chapter 9

Use the scroll bars to find the name of the document you want to load into MacPaint. To quickly find the name of the file, press the key which corresponds to its first letter. The first file name that starts with that letter will appear, already selected, at the top of the directory window. This can speed your search through data disks with numerous files. If you don't find the document you want on this data disk, click *Eject* and try another. When you find your document, click twice on its name to open it (or select it by clicking once on the name and click *Open* to open it). Opening this file will require some disk swaps.

The *Close/Open* method gives you the power to view the contents of any disk.

Managing Documents with Two Drives

With two disk drives, it's easier to manage both working and data disks. Insert your working disk into the internal drive and your data disk into the external drive. Let's use MacPaint again. When you insert the disk, you'll get an open MacPaint window if you had previously set the start-up as this application program.

After you create a MacPaint picture, save it as a document on a MacPaint data disk. Choose *Save* from the *File* menu. You'll now see the *Save* dialog box.

Figure 9-16. *Save* **Dialog Box for Two Drives**

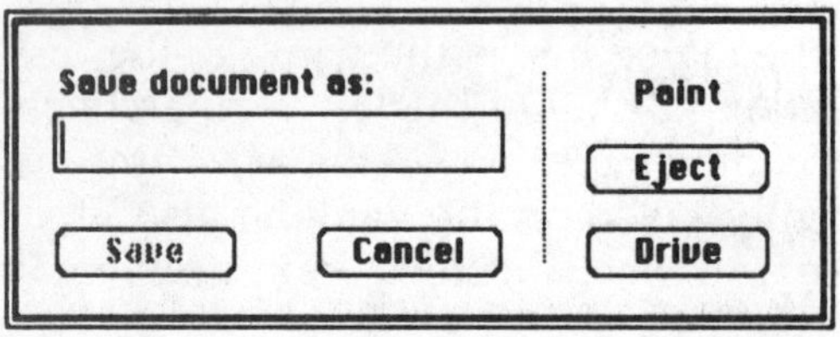

```
┌─────────────────────────────────────────────┐
│  Save document as:            Paint         │
│  ┌─────────────────────┐    ( Eject )       │
│  │                     │                    │
│  └─────────────────────┘                    │
│  ( Save )   ( Cancel )      ( Drive )       │
└─────────────────────────────────────────────┘
```

The name of the working disk appears on the right side, above the *Eject* button. To save the document on a data disk in the external drive, click *Drive*. Now you'll see the name of the data disk above the *Eject* button. If you want to save the document on this data disk, type in a filename and click *Save* (or type the filename and press the Return key).

If you want to save your document on a data disk other than the one in the external drive, press *Eject* and insert the desired disk. Type in a name for the document and click *Save* (or press Return). The *Save* dialog box lets you save files on any disk you wish. Try to use descriptive names for your documents. This will help you to remember what each document contains, as well as help locate it.

Finding documents to load into various applications is also quite simple with two drives. When an application window is open, use the *Close/Open* method to locate documents. Choose *Close* from the *File* menu and then *Open*. You'll see the directory of the working disk. To view the directory of your data disk in the external drive, just click *Drive*.

Figure 9-17. Directory Dialog Box—Two Drives

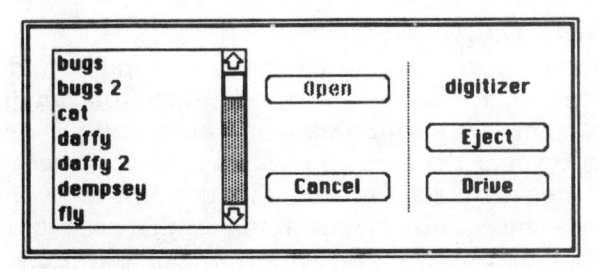

```
bugs
bugs 2          Open        digitizer
cat
daffy                       Eject
daffy 2
dempsey        Cancel        Drive
fly
```

The MacPaint document names are listed in alphabetical order. To open one, click twice on its name. This dialog box is very powerful. It allows you to choose which drive you want to access with the *Drive* button and which disk you want with the *Eject* button.

Copying Data Disks

It's imperative to store backup copies of data disks to insure against accidental loss. To copy a data disk with a one-drive system, insert a start-up disk that contains the Finder and System files (a disk with an application program such as MacPaint or MacWrite will have these files on it). Quit the application, if necessary, to get to the desktop. Now you must place the icons of both destination and source disks on the desktop. Eject the start-up disk and insert the data disk you want to copy.

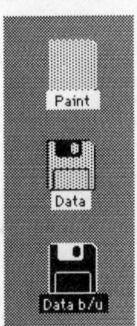

To copy, you next need to eject the data disk, then insert a blank disk. Initialize and name this as you come across the prompts. Now the icons of both disks appear below the icon of the start-up disk.

Chapter 9

Drag the icon of the disk you want to copy onto the icon of the new disk.

After a few disk swaps, your copy is complete.

This process is similar with a two-drive system, just simpler. Put the start-up disk into the internal drive and the disk you want to copy into the external drive. Now eject the disk you want to copy from the external drive. Put your blank disk into the external drive and follow the prompts.

Creating Printed Disk Directories

When you start filling disks with your creations, you might find it difficult to remember where all those documents are. You can always find the document you want by inserting disks and viewing their contents. But it would be more efficient to have a printed record. You can create such a list for each data disk and store it in a binder for easy reference. The Macintosh makes this easy to do. Start the Mac (with a start-up disk) and insert one of your data disks.

Create a folder to put your documents in by clicking on the *Empty Folder* icon and choose *Duplicate* from the *Edit* menu. This gives you a copy of the Empty folder. Select all the files you want to include in the directory printout and drag them to the copy of the Empty folder. Rename the folder.

Figure 9-18. Move Your Documents into a Folder

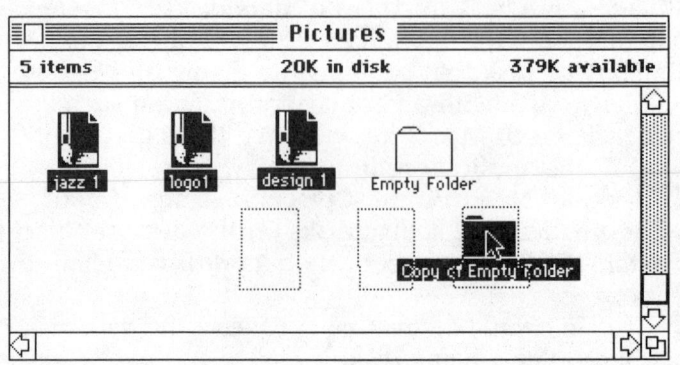

Chapter 9

Open the folder and choose *By Name* from the *View* menu. All your documents now appear in the folder window alphabetically by name. You can add more names to the list by dragging more files to the renamed folder.

Figure 9-19. Documents by Name

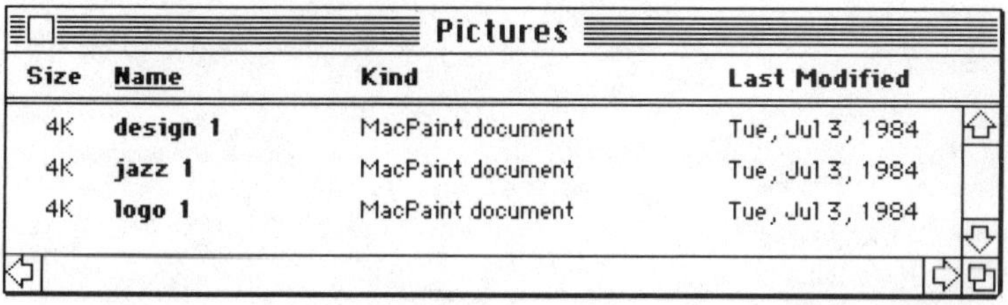

Size	Name	Kind	Last Modified
4K	design 1	MacPaint document	Tue, Jul 3, 1984
4K	jazz 1	MacPaint document	Tue, Jul 3, 1984
4K	logo 1	MacPaint document	Tue, Jul 3, 1984

You can print this window by pressing Command-Shift-4. If you repeat this process for all your data disks, you'll have a record of all your documents. Now you won't have to search by trial and error.

Files and Disks

This chapter has shown you how to manage both your files and your disks. Practice these techniques—managing files and disks should not be taken casually. To create and manage your visual creations easily and efficiently, you should follow these techniques. They'll save you time, and most important, aggravation later on.

Chapter 10
A Mac Gallery

Chapter 10

A Mac Gallery

Many artists are using the Macintosh's graphics features to help them generate visual ideas. Why are artists turning to a machine to extend their creative process? One clue is that many of these people are also photographic artists. Perhaps they see a relationship between working with the Macintosh and working with a camera.

Photography, as well as other forms of mechanically derived art (such as xerography and video art), is created through a unique combination of art and technology. It's as if the functions relegated to the left and right sides of the brain—the logical and the intuitive—become fused in the process of using these media. In a similar way, art and technology become combined with the Macintosh. The best software writers can be considered the artistic geniuses of the computer age. We must credit them for the sensitivity and forethought they've expressed in creating such delightful tools as MacPaint and MacDraw.

The rooms in the building where the Macintosh was born are named after the masters of fine art—Matisse, Picasso, Rembrandt, and da Vinci, to name a few. A keen artistic and adventurous spirit continues to permeate the development of the Macintosh and its software.

Now it's time for you to meet some artists who have used their Macs professionally to develop their visual experiments.

Jim Alley

Jim Alley is a nationally exhibited artist with a Master of Fine Arts degree in painting from Texas Christian University in Fort Worth, Texas. He currently teaches painting and drawing at Interlochen Arts Academy, Interlochen, Michigan. To date, Alley has used the Macintosh mainly for portraits, though he also has a fascination with World War I airplanes.

To create his portraits, Alley first traces a photograph of his subject on acetate, then traces the acetate outline with MacPaint's pencil tool. (This technique is described in Chapter 8.) Sometimes he creates multiple portraits, à la Warhol.

Chapter 10

Jim Alley

Jim Alley

Chapter 10

Jim Alley

Chapter 10

Jim Alley

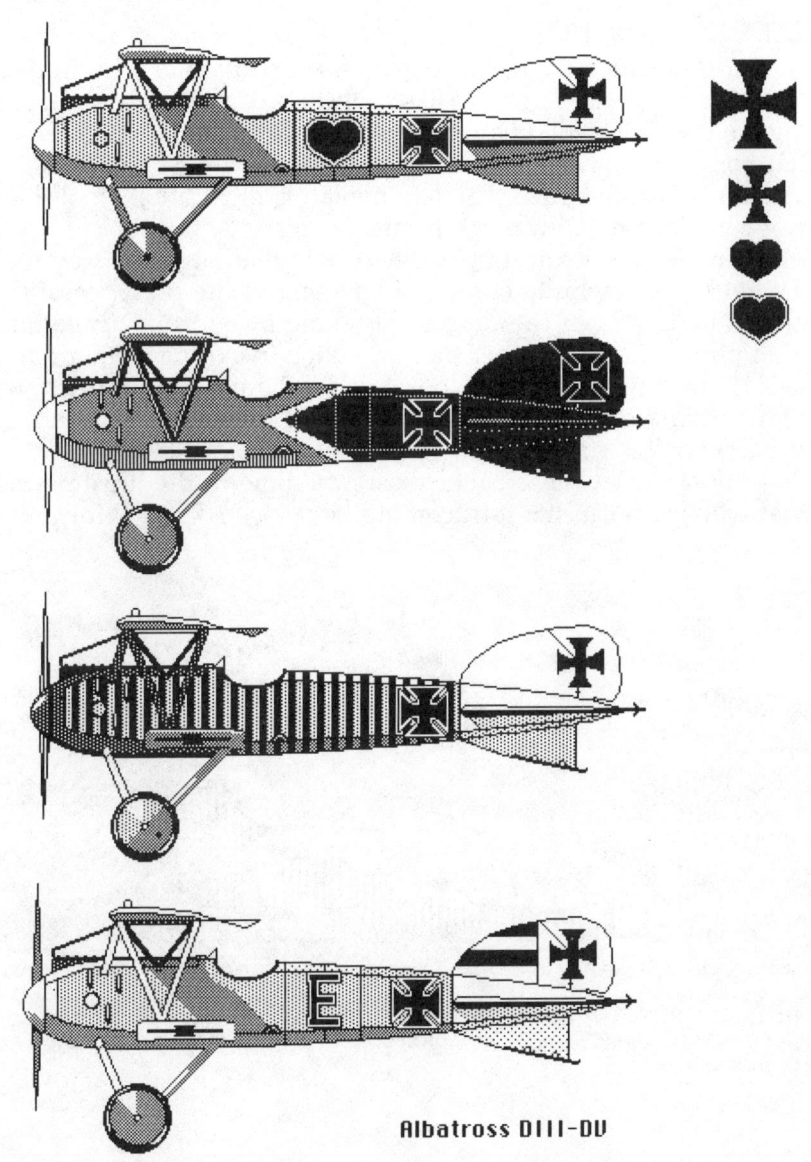

Chapter 10

Albatross DIII-DV

Jim Alley

281

Chapter 10

Daniel Pinkwater

Daniel Pinkwater is a mischievous, fun-loving man who finds release for his Peter Pan fantasies in the art of writing and illustrating children's books. His works include *Devil in the Drain* (Dutton) and *Ducks!* (Little, Brown).

Pinkwater uses MacPaint to make his illustrations look like woodcuts or linoleum block prints. He starts with a black MacPaint window and brushes with white to work his way to daylight. This technique imparts a feeling of the presence of the artist's hand and of the process of taking away from a medium with physical depth rather than applying ink or paint to a flat surface. Pinkwater's drawings look less mechanical and more hand-drawn than Jim Alley's. Thus, the role of the computer is not as apparent in his drawings.

These Pinkwater creations are just some of the illustrations that will appear in his forthcoming book, *Jolly Roger* (Morrow).

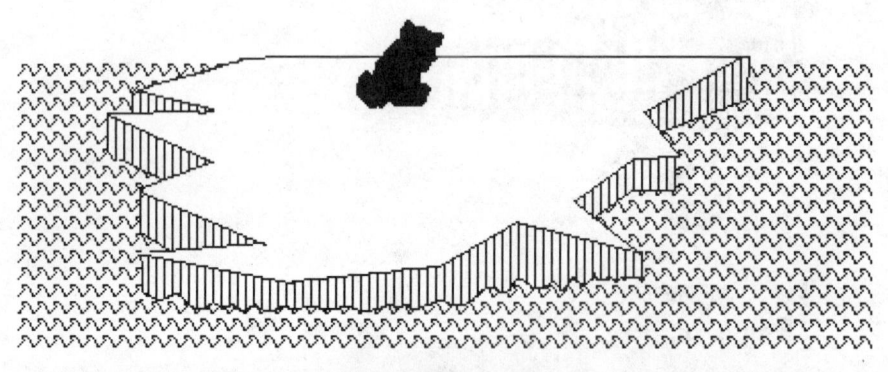

From JOLLY ROGER by Daniel Pinkwater. Copyright by Daniel Pinkwater. By permission of Lothrup, Lee, & Shepard Books (A Division of William Morrow & Company).

Chapter 10

From JOLLY ROGER by Daniel Pinkwater. Copyright by Daniel Pinkwater. By permission of Lothrup, Lee, & Shepard Books (A Division of William Morrow & Company).

From JOLLY ROGER by Daniel Pinkwater. Copyright by Daniel Pinkwater. By permission of Lothrup, Lee, & Shepard Books (A Division of William Morrow & Company).

Chapter 10

From JOLLY ROGER by Daniel Pinkwater. Copyright by Daniel Pinkwater. By permission of Lothrup, Lee, & Shepard Books (A Division of William Morrow & Company).

From JOLLY ROGER by Daniel Pinkwater. Copyright by Daniel Pinkwater. By permission of Lothrup, Lee, & Shepard Books (A Division of William Morrow & Company).

Chapter 10

Robert Fichter

Robert Fichter is an incessant doodler. Lunch with him is a banquet of napkins covered with doodles, sketches, and captions. Any smooth surface that can record a pencil mark is a potential home for a drawing. It's no surprise that the Mac's infinite supply of blank pages and drawing tools appeal to such an artist.

Fichter is a professor of art at Florida State University in Tallahassee, where he teaches painting and photography. His involvement in art has been primarily with machine-associated processes, such as xerography, photography, and printmaking. He has an international reputation and his works populate numerous private and public collections. Fichter deals with every aspect of his life as art, and every bit of his art is alive with his spirit.

Fichter's Macintosh drawings have led to the development of large paintings. For example, his experiments with MacPaint's Brush Mirrors tool led to the creation of 12 large works. Fichter also plans to produce a coloring book of Macintosh art. His pencil tool drawings are ideal for this application.

The look of Mac's lines reminds Fichter of the lines produced in etchings. The stepped, diagonal lines that you see on Mac's screen have a similarity to the broken lines that can be produced with the etching process. What some see as a coarse, imperfect line, Fichter sees as a wonderful aesthetic detail that he can exploit.

The Mac is the doodler's dream come true. Fichter can generate images quickly, and he can cut and paste items into the Scrapbook for use in other documents. Fichter's photographic art deals with collage and the arrangement of a variety of objects in front of the camera. He then works on the photographs with drawing tools. The Macintosh makes it easy for him to incorporate "found" images such as clip art into his drawings. The next logical step for him is to work with Koala Technologies' MacVision.

Chapter 10

Robert Fichter

Chapter 10

Robert Fichter

Chapter 10

Robert Fichter

Chapter 10

Ms Bones at Aurther Murrays

Grown ladies taught to Dance

after Dodd

Robert Fichter

Chapter 10

Robert Fichter

Chapter 10

Paul Rutkovsky

Paul Rutkovsky is an assistant professor of art at Florida State University in Tallahassee, where he teaches painting, drawing, and design. Rutkovsky has a lot to say, but he'd rather show you his ideas with pictures than with words. His satiric visual comments are often political and social in nature. He likes to comment on a society that sometimes forgets to take its eyes from the television set. So Rutkovsky generates his satiric comments with the Macintosh. There's an interesting irony in satire about television created on a computer screen.

Rutkovsky uses the Macintosh to publish two tabloids: *Get* and *Doo Daa Florida*. The computer makes it possible for him to produce camera-ready graphics mixed with text quickly and easily. He also uses the Macintosh as a sketchbook for the development of his visual ideas.

Chapter 10

COOKING WITH GET

TELEVISION LOAF

2 TO 3 CITY SERVINGS

TV LOAF RECIPE

INGREDIENTS:
One 21" Sony Trinitron
$2,500.00 in cash
Transportation
Shopping Mall

DIRECTIONS:
Mix together slowly for one business day – Monday
Wait three business days – Tuesday, Wednesday, Thursday
Eat on Friday

Paul Rutkovsky

Chapter 10

GET #1

EATING WHEELS

Paul Rutkovsky

Chapter 10

TV IN US

Paul Rutkovsky

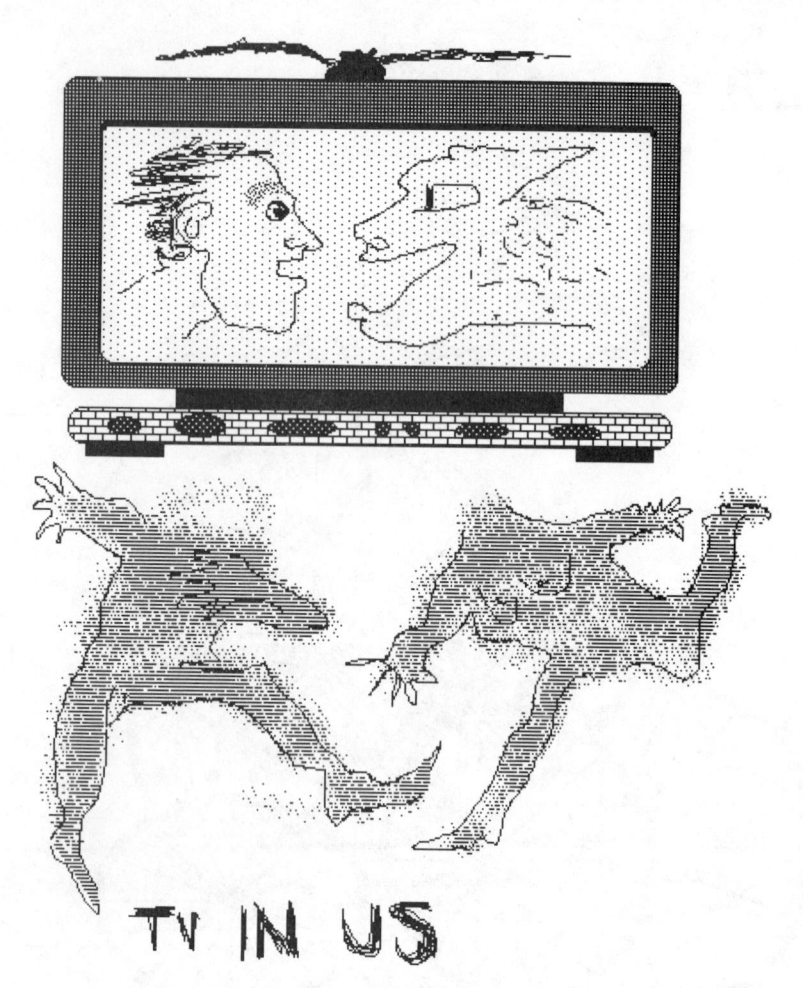

Chapter 10

Richard Bloch

Richard Bloch uses a Macintosh for his graphic design business, but sometimes he takes time to relax and draw fun art with the Mac. His skyscrapers demonstrate a technique that you may want to use in your designs.

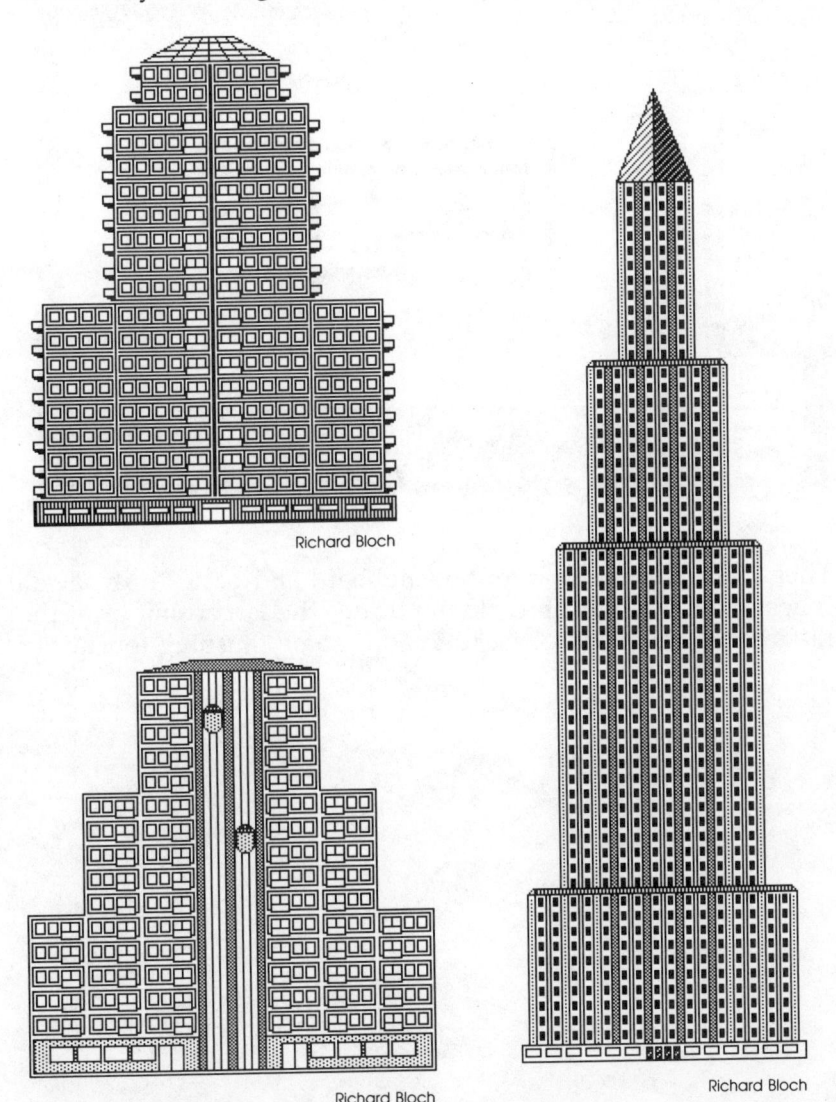

Richard Bloch

Richard Bloch

Richard Bloch

Chapter 10

The first step in creating such repeating forms is to design a single unit of the building. Bloch uses *FatBits* to design the unit.

Fatbits

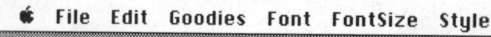

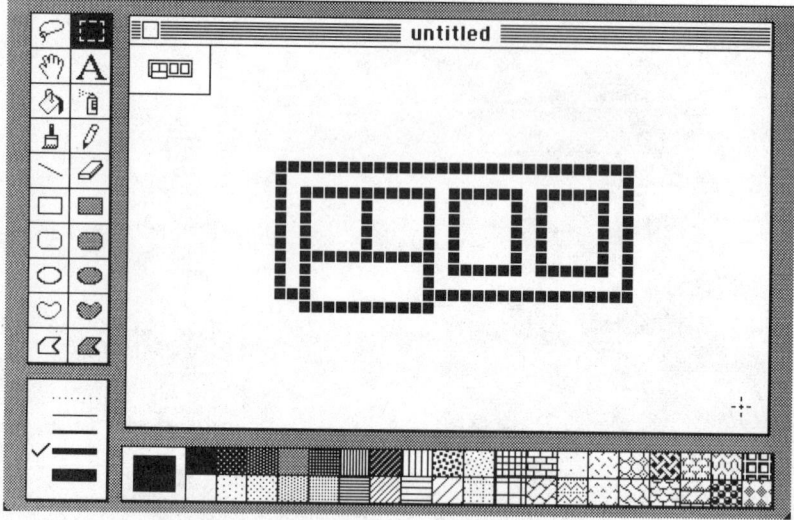

Then he puts the unit into the Clipboard and pastes it in several times to get a larger unit. He duplicates the larger unit until the main structure is complete, then adds some finishing touches.

Chapter 10

Duplicate

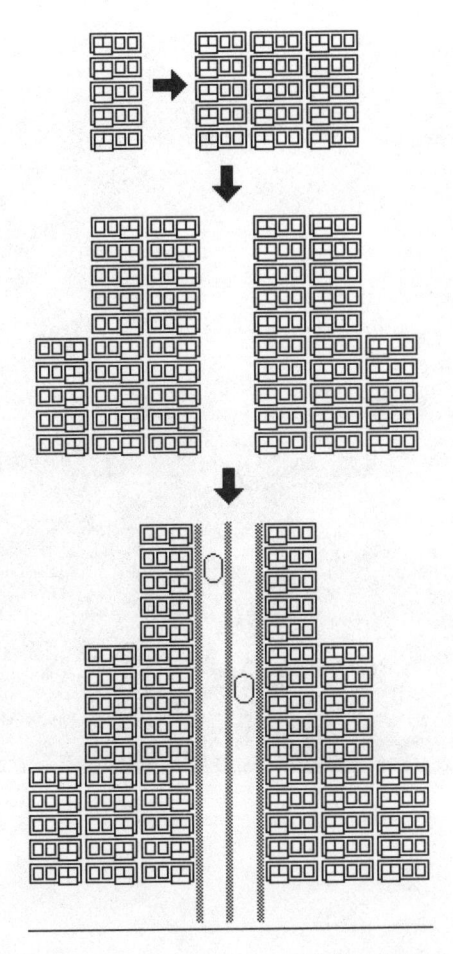

Richard Bloch

Chapter 10

Here's another sample of Bloch's work:

Richard Bloch

Chapter 10

Bill Jonas

Bill Jonas is a graphic artist and vice president of Artworks Unlimited, Inc., of Jupiter, Florida. He studied at the Art Institute of Chicago. Many examples of his work were presented in Chapter 6 to illustrate the application of the Macintosh's graphic arts' powers. When he takes time off from designing signs and wall murals, he has fantasies about sign painting that go something like this:

Bill Jonas, Artworks, Inc.

Chapter 10

Your Gallery?

This gallery of Macintosh art demonstrates the diversity of work that can be created with your computer. As the capabilities of the Macintosh are more fully explored, even more artists will turn to the Mac to generate their visual ideas. Perhaps you'll use it in just the same way.

Appendix A
Products for the Macintosh

As a Macintosh owner, you're very lucky. So much excitement has been generated by the revolutionary design of the Macintosh that many hardware and software developers have already created products for the Mac. The availability of such a wide variety of materials that support the Macintosh will make it a truly powerful productivity tool for general users and visual artists alike.

The items described here, of course, do not comprise a comprehensive list of all available Macintosh products. Instead, they are those I believe to be of most interest to Macintosh owners who want to use their computer to design and create visual effects.

Graphics Aids

Mac the Knife. A fine line of products for the artist. Volumes of clip art for the general artist as well as a disk containing additional fonts are valuable additions to everyone's Macintosh system.

Miles Computing
7136 Haskell Avenue, Suite 212
Van Nuys, CA 91406
(818) 994-7901

ClickArt Personal Graphics, ClickArt Letters, and ClickArt Publications. A collection of clip art for general users, artists, and those involved in the publishing business.

T/Maker Company
2115 Landings Drive
Mountain View, CA 94043
(415) 962-0195

Animation Toolkit 1. A realtime animation package that can help you create animated films. You can view your film clip in slow motion and even perform dissolves.

Ann Arbor Softworks, Inc.
308-1/2 South State Street
Ann Arbor, MI 48104
(313) 996-3838

da Vinci. Three disks (Buildings, Landscapes, and Interiors) of excellent clip art. With these tools you can easily design a building, its grounds, and its interior finishings. Designed to be used with MacPaint.

Appendix A

Hayden Software
600 Suffolk Street
Lowell, MA 01854
(617) 937-0200

Filevision. A visual data base for the Macintosh. By combining an object-oriented graphics editor that resembles MacDraw with a data base program, this package lets you organize large groups of data with graphic annotations. This will help you create a file of data with visual details.

Telos Software Products
3420 Ocean Park Boulevard
Santa Monica, CA 90405
(213) 450-2424

Printer Supplies

Sharp Color Ribbon Cartridges. Now you can explore color with the Mac. This unique product allows you to blend your own ink colors for Imagewriter ribbons. Since the cartridges are self-inking, the life of the ribbons will be extended by almost 300 percent.

Sharp Color
400 North High Street, Box 175
Columbus, OH 43215
(614) 221-0502

Iron-on transfer ribbons. With iron-on ribbons, you can create a picture with the Macintosh, print it out, and transfer it to a T-shirt with an iron.

Distributed by:
Express Computer Supplies
2215-R Market Street, #292
San Francisco, CA 94114
(415) 864-3026

Hard Disk Drives

Davong's Mac Disk. Choices of 5, 10, 15, 21, 32, and 40 megabyte hard disk drives.

Davong Systems, Inc.
217 Humboldt Court
Sunnyvale, CA 94089
(408) 734-4900

Appendix A

Tecmar's MacDrive. Choices of 5 and 10 megabyte hard disk drives. The 5 megabyte drive has a removable cartridge.

Tecmar, Inc.
6225 Cochran Road
Solon, OH 44139-3377
(216) 349-0600

Corvus. Choice of 5, 11, 16, and 45 megabyte capacities that can be partitioned into volumes.

Corvus Systems, Inc.
2100 Corvus Drive
San Jose CA 95124
(408) 559-7000

HyperDrive. A ten-megabyte hard disk drive that fits inside the Macintosh's case. It can be partitioned into 32 volumes. Upgrade to 512K Macintosh also available.

General Computer Co.
215 First Street
Cambridge MA 02142
(617) 492-5500

Digitizers

MicronEye. A camera, interface, and software that allow you to create digitized pictures in the form of MacPaint documents.

Micron Technology, Inc.
Vision Systems Group
2805 East Columbia Road
Boise, ID 83706
(208) 383-4147

MacVision. An interface board and software that allow you to enter digitized images into the Macintosh from either a video camera or a videocassette recorder. A terrific artist's tool.

Koala Technologies Corporation
3100 Patrick Henry Drive
Santa Clara, CA 95052-8100
(408) 986-8866

Datacopy 610 camera. A high-resolution camera which lets you input digitized images into the computer. Software not included.

Appendix A

Datacopy Corporation
1215 Terra Bella Avenue
Mountain View, CA 94043
(415) 965-7900

Magic: Macintosh Graphics Input Controller. A device that allows you to capture images with a video camera quickly and easily. Offers a variety of special features.

New Image Technology
10300 Greenbelt Road, Suite 104
Seabrook MD 20706
(301) 464-3100

ThunderScan. A high-resolution digitizer which reads pictures from the Imagewriter printer.

Thunderware, Inc.
19G Orinda Way
Orinda CA 94563
(415) 254-6581

Typesetting Services

ReadySetGo. Typeset MacWrite or MacPaint documents directly from disk files with the best quality.

Manhattan Graphics
163 Varick Street
New York, NY 10013
(212) 924-2778

Screens. This process makes distortion-free prints of Macintosh files quickly and inexpensively. Prints are available in high resolution (724 pixels per inch) or laser (300 pixels per inch).

GEORGE Graphics
650 Second Street
San Francisco, CA 94107
(415) 397-2400

Input Device

MacTablet. A digitizer pad with stylus for the Macintosh.

Summagraphics Corporation
777 State Street Extension
Fairfield CT 06430
(203) 384-1344

Appendix B
Cairo Font

Lowercase Pictures

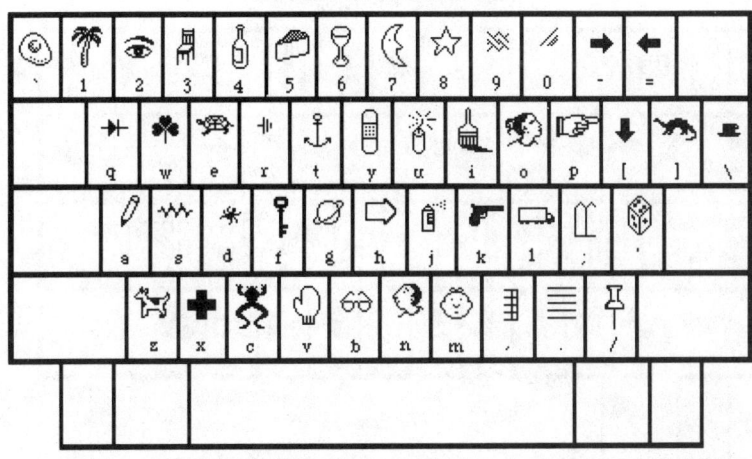

Uppercase Pictures

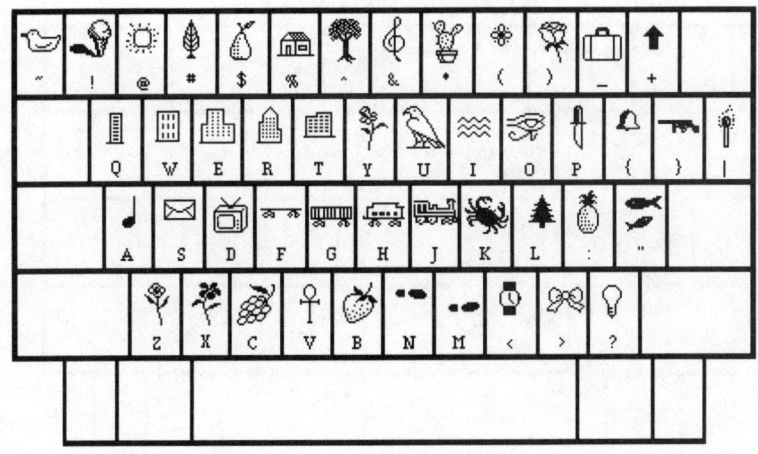

Appendix C
Fallingwater Font

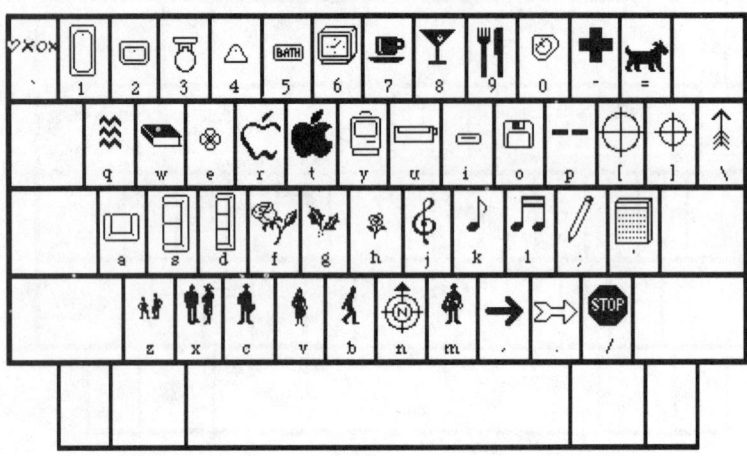

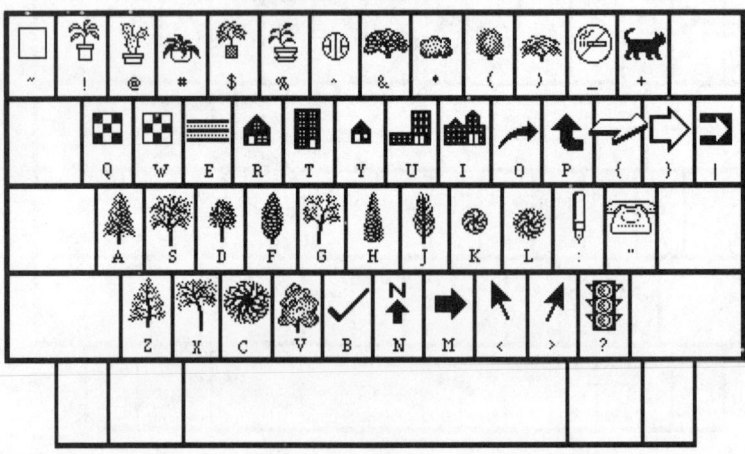

Index

A

advertising
  flyer 177–81
  layouts 175–77
  text with MacWrite 40–44
alert box 258, 268
Align Objects 52, 182
Align to Grid 52, 124, 182
Alley, Jim 277–81
alphabetic keys 10
announcements 172–74
  format for 173
Apple II 6
application disks
  copying 260–61
  preparing 263–64
application icons 20
applications software 19
architectural design 196–201
arcs 51
arrows
  MacDraw 139–41
  MacPaint 183–84

B

Backspace key 42
  to clear selection 79, 130
bas-relief 103
"before and after" designs 202–3
bitmapped screen 50, 52
Bloch, Richard 208, 295–98
book illustrations 210–12
borders
  complex 118–19
  corners 118–19
  custom 113–14
  examples 117
  repeating 113–14
  with direction 115–16
Bring to Back 133–35
Bring to Front 133–34
brush shapes, custom 91
business cards 167–70
business graphics
  charts 182–84
  graphs 184–87
  maps 188–89
By name 273

C

Cairo font 267
camera-ready art 211–12
cameras 240–49
Caps Lock key 10–11
caption text 151–53
  changing style of 152–53

carrying case 5, 16
centering
  pasted item in MacWrite 65, 67
  text in MacWrite 41, 43
charts 184–87
circles
  concentric (MacPaint) 105–6
  introduction 61–63
  MacDraw 36
  MacPaint 25
Clear 62, 79, 151
Clipboard 61–74
  for moving data between applications 65–69
  for moving data within a document 107
  for moving large pictures 70–74
  vs. Scrapbook 63
close/open method
  one drive 269–70
  two drives 270–71
color display 7
columns of text 43–45
Command-click to enter *FatBits* 89
Command key
  function 13–14
  to select MacDraw tools 146
Command-Shift to stretch or shrink in proportions 56
computer system 4
concentric circles (MacPaint) 105–6
constrain shapes
  MacDraw 129–30
  MacPaint 100
Copy 61–63, 101
copying disks
  application disks 260–61
  data disks 261, 271–72
copying printouts 230
Corvus hard disk drive 303
cover design 207–9
custom borders (MacPaint) 113–14
custom brush shapes (MacPaint) 91
custom eraser shapes (MacPaint) 90
custom grid (MacDraw) 125–26
custom lettering (MacPaint) 108–12
custom patterns (MacPaint) 96–102
  creating a file of 100–102
custom repeating shapes (MacPaint) 90–91
Custom Rulers 30–31, 34–35, 55, 124–26
Cut 61–63, 79

D

Datacopy 610 camera 246
data disks

307

copying 261, 271–72
preparing 268
viewing directory 269–70
data files 253
delete text (MacWrite) 42
design
  architectural 196–201
  engineering 195–96
  interior 201–3
  landscape 203–4
  printing and publishing 205–7
  product 190–95
desktop 221, 253
digitizer pads 239
digitizers. *See* video digitizers
"Disk Copy" program 261
disk directory
  one drive 269–70
  two drives 270–71
disk drive 4, 8–9
  capacity 9
  external 4, 15
  hard 15, 302–3
diskettes. *See* disks
Disk Full alert box 26, 253
disks
  application,
    changing 270–71
  data 271–72
  ejecting 255–56
  erasing 263
  renaming 261–62
  space management 263–64
  write-protecting 262–63
documents. *See* files
double-click 78
draft print mode 224–25
drawing size 214
drawing tools (MacPaint) 21
drop shadow 25–27
Duplicate 187, 272
duplicating forms
  MacDraw 32–33, 36, 131
  MacPaint 25–26

E

editing (MacWrite) 42
ejecting disks 255–56
Empty Trash 258, 263
engineering design 195–96
Enlarge 55, 158
Enter key 14
Erase 263
eraser shapes, custom (MacPaint) 90

erasing
  disks 263
  files 263
  in MacDraw 159–60
  in MacPaint 90
  in MacWrite 42
exploded views 212
external drive 4, 15

F

Fallingwater font 307
FatBits
  for control 49–50, 106, 110–11, 168
  getting in and out of 81
  moving around in 81
Fichter, Robert 213–14, 285–90
files
  application 253
  data 253
  defined 253
  managing with one drive 268–70
  managing with two drives 270–71
  manipulating 256–63
  program 253
  renaming 261–62
  system 253–54
  transferring with one drive 256–57
  transferring with two drives 259
Fill
  MacDraw 139, 152
  MacPaint 26, 92, 96–97
  None 153–54, 187
filled oval tool (MacPaint) 25
filled rectangle tool (MacPaint) 22
Flip (MacPaint) 183
Flip Horizontal (MacDraw) 38
floor plans 202–3
flow charts 186
folders 261–62
"Font Mover" program 265–67
fonts
  Cairo 305
  Fallingwater 307
  file 266
  for high-resolution printing 266–67
  MacPaint 27
  menu (MacWrite) 42
  moving 265–67
  pseudofonts 267
  removing 266
  Style (MacPaint) 27
  types 109
FontSize 27, 176
  outlined fonts 176
freehand tool (MacDraw) 50

308

G

graphic arts
  advertising flyers 177–81
  advertising layouts 175–77
  announcements 172–74
  business cards 167–70
  logos 166–67
  post cards 174–75
graphics aids 301–2
graphics, combined with text 6–7
graphs 182–84
Grid (MacPaint)
  advanced uses 83–87
  even patterns with 84–85
  lining up shapes with 25, 83–84, 182
  matching patterns with 84
  moving shapes with 84
  stretch or shrink patterned forms with 86
  tidy patterns with 23
  vs. MacDraw's *Align to Grid* 52
  with text 172
Grid, custom (MacDraw) 125–26
grouping
  altering size 143
  Group 37, 51–52, 142–44, 146, 197
  stretching grouped shapes 143

H

handles 32, 35, 48, 65, 133
hand tool 25
hard disk drives 15, 302–3
hardware 4–16
Hide Rulers 44
high-resolution printing 219, 224
horizontal layouts 157–58
HyperDrive 303

I

icons 20
illustrating
  books 207–12
  manuals 210–12
Imagewriter printer
  adjusting 221
  characteristics 219
  introduction 14–15
  paper jams, avoiding 221
  screen size vs printed size 220–21
input devices
  cameras 240–49
  digitizer pads 239
  keyboard 10–14
  mouse 9–10
insertion point 42–44, 65

Insert Ruler (MacWrite) 43–44
interior design 201–3
Invert 23–24, 92–93, 102
invoices, illustrated 194–95
isometric drawings 199–200

J

Jonas, Bill 190–94, 209, 299
justification 41, 43

K

keyboard 5, 10–14
kilobyte 8

L

landscape design 203–4
large drawings 156–58
  finding objects in 158
  zooming in and out of 158
lasso tool 23, 26, 63
layering (MacDraw) 133–38
letterheads 170–72
lettering, custom (MacPaint) 108–12
Lines (MacDraw) 140
line spacing (MacWrite) 41
line thickness
  MacDraw 140
  MacPaint 114
Lock 144, 146, 197
lock up 255–56
logos
  design 22–27
  samples 166–67

M

MacDraw
  complete elements 126–38
  difference from MacPaint 28, 45–57
  features 20, 28
  Fill 139–41
  interactions with MacPaint and MacWrite 29
  introduction 28–39
  layering 133–39
  Lines 139–41
  masking 158–61
  menus 46
  organizing objects in 51–52
  pasting into MacPaint 68–70
  pasting into MacWrite 66–67
  Pen 139–41
  perspective drawings 145–51
  roll of film 156–58
  scale drawings 28–29, 55–56
  size of drawings 52–55

taping items down 144–45
taping items together 142–44
text in 151–56
tips and advanced techniques 123–61
working disk 264
Macintosh computer
  ease of use 3–4
  hardware 4–16
  128K 8
  512K 8
MacPaint
  bas-relief 103
  borders and frames 113–19
  brush shapes 91–92
  clearing document 103
  concentric circles 105–6
  difference from MacPaint 28, 45–57
  eraser shapes 90
  features 20
  fill and refill 96–97
  Grid 83–87
  introduction 21–27
  lettering, custom 108–12
  menus 46
  ornaments 119–20
  page 82–83
  pasting into MacWrite 65–66
  patterns 97–102
  repeating shapes 90–91
  shading 106–8
  shadowed text 104–5
  shortcuts 77–81
  text entry 172
  text in reverse 92–93
  Trace Edges 87–90
  transparency 93–96
  versions 20–21, 221, 224
  working from black 91–92
  work space 82–83
MacTablet 304
MacVision 243–46, 303
MacWrite
  features 40
  introduction 40–44
  working disk 264
magazine layout 207
Magic video digitizer 303
maps 188–89
margins (MacWrite) 41, 43
marquee tool 47, 63, 71
  double-click 71
masking (MacDraw)
  to enhance 160
  to erase 159–60
  to repair 160–61
MC68000 chip 6

microfloppy disk drive 4, 8–9
MicronEye 240–43, 303
microprocessor chip 6
modems 4, 15–16
monitor 4, 6
monochrome display 7
mouse
  button 10
  care 10
  cleaning 9
  surface 10

N

naming disks 268–69
negative image 24
newsletters 205–6
newspaper layout 205–6
None 145
numeric keypad 16
numeric keys 10

O

one-point perspective drawings 145–48
opacity (MacPaint) 94
optional hardware 14–16
Option key 12
  for current pattern 80
  for patterned borders 89
  to move around in *FatBits* 81
organizational chart 187–88
organizing objects 51–52
ornaments (MacPaint) 119–120
oval tool (MacDraw) 36
overlapping forms 49

P

page layouts 205–7
Page Setup 157
paper
  cut 227–28
  fanfold 227
  problems with 228–29
  quality 227–29
paragraph indentation 41
paragraph text
  changing shape of 156
  changing style of 154–56
  word-wrap 153–54
Paste 62, 101, 169
Paste in Back 137–38
Paste in Front 137–38
Patterns (MacPaint) 21, 23
  changing 96–97
  creating a file of 100–102
  custom 96–102

310

picking up 97–98
picking up combined patterns 98–99
picking up random patterns 99–100
Pen 141
pencil tool 50
perspective
　architectural 200–201
　horizon line 145, 148
　lines 146, 148
　shadows 151
　vanishing point 145, 148
photographic reductions of drawings 211
photographing output 215–16
Pinkwater, Daniel 282–84
pixels 6, 21, 47
polygon
　automatically filled 78–79
　tool (MacDraw) 34–35, 130–32
portability 5
ports 4
post cards 174–75
　format for 175
Print 221
Print Catalog 223–24
Print Draft 222, 230
printer
　laser 230
　ribbons 226
　supplies 302
Print Final 222, 230
printing
　catalogs 223–24
　disk directories 272–73
　from applications 222
　from desktop 221
　in color 230–31
　introduction 4
　modes for 224–25
　paper quality 227–29
　problems with 225
　quality of 224–31
　screen dumps 222
　window dumps 223
printing and publishing 205–12
product design 190–95
products for Macintosh 301–4
program
　files 253
　updates 21
　versions 20–21, 222, 224
project development
　slides 215–16
　story boards 214
　visual diary 213–14

Q

Quit 77–78, 255

R

RAM. See Random Access Memory
Random Access Memory (RAM) 8, 61, 63
Read Only Memory (ROM) 7–8
rectangle tool
　MacDraw 32
　MacPaint 24
Reduce 54, 158
Reduce to Fit
　editing in 54–55
　roll of film 156–58
　story boards 214
　view large drawings 54
renaming
　disks 261
　files or folders 261–62
repeating circles 114
repeating shapes, custom (MacPaint) 90–91
　circles 114
Reshape Arc 51
Reshape Polygon 147
resolution
　of monitor 6
　of printer 6, 219
Return key 14
ribbons 226
ROM. See Read Only Memory
rotate 183
rulers
　adjust rulers (MacDraw) 34
　adjust rulers (MacWrite) 41–43
　custom (MacDraw) 12, 30–31, 34–35, 55, 124–26
　default values (MacDraw) 123–24
Rutkovsky, Paul 291–94

S

Save As 27, 39
saving
　on a different disk 268–69
　with one drive 268–69
　with two drives 270–71
scale drawings 29–39, 55–56
Scrapbook
　for clip art 183–85, 197, 203
　for moving data within applications 70
　for moving large documents 70–74
　vs. Clipboard 63
screen dumps 169–170, 254
scrolling 35, 67, 266, 270
Select All 37
Send to Back 48, 134–35
separating forms 47–48
Set Startup 77, 264–65
shadowed text 104–5

311

Shift-click 42, 53
Shift key
  for multiple selection 42, 51, 150, 159, 255
  to constrain 25
  with Option and Command keys 86–87
  with Option key 12–13
Short Cuts 81
Show Clipboard 62, 66
Show Page 53–54, 102–3
  to clear MacPaint document 102–3
  vs. *Reduce to Fit* 54–55
Show Rulers 30
Show Size 32, 55–56, 168
shrinking
  MacDraw 48, 56
  MacPaint 56, 179
size
  changing 56–57, 143–44
  of drawings 52–54
slides of drawings 215–16
snapshot of screen 254
special keys 10
spray-can tool 50
standard print mode 224
start-up disk 254–55, 265
story boards 214
stretching
  MacDraw 34, 56, 143
  MacPaint 57, 86–87
structural design 195–96
system
  files 253–54
  fonts 266

T

Tab key 44
text
  caption text 151–53
  characteristics of (MacWrite) 42
  editing (MacDraw) 151–52, 154
  in MacPaint 27
  in reverse (MacPaint) 92–93
  paragraph text 153–56
  with graphics 6–7
Tilde key 79, 106
Trace Edges 87–90
tracing pictures
  transparencies 236–37
  with mouse 235

transferring data
  between documents of one application 70–74
  introduction to 61
  from MacDraw to MacPaint 68–70
  from MacDraw to MacWrite 66–67
  from MacPaint to MacWrite 65–66
transferring files
  pictures 61
  with one drive 256–57
  with two drives 259
transparency
  by leaking 93–94
  of forms 96
  of painted forms 95
  of shadows 95
  of shapes (MacDraw) 128
Turn Grid Off 146
two-point perspective 148–50
typesetting services 303–4

U

Undo
  MacDraw 33, 50
  MacPaint 79–80
Ungroup 144
Unlock 145, 148

V

vanishing point 145, 148
vertical layouts 157
video digitizers
  comparison 247–48
  Datacopy 610, 246, 303
  MacVision 243–46, 303
  manufacturers 303–4
  MicronEye 240–43
  ThunderScan 304
video screen 6
visual diary 213–14

W

windows 21, 53
working disks 263–64
write-protecting disks 262–63

Z

zero point 31–32
zooming 158, 214

312